Modern Python Standard Library Cookbook

Over 100 recipes to fully leverage the features of the standard library in Python

Alessandro Molina

BIRMINGHAM - MUMBAI

Modern Python Standard Library Cookbook

Commissioning Editor: Aaron Lazar
Acquisition Editor: Chaitanya Nair
Content Development Editor: Rohit Singh
Technical Editor: Romy Dias
Copy Editor: Safis Editing
Project Coordinator: Vaidehi Sawant
Proofreader: Safis Editing
Indexer: Mariammal Chettiyar
Graphics: Jason Monteiro
Production Coordinator: Deepika Naik

First published: August 2018

Production reference: 1300818

Published by Packt Publishing Ltd.
Livery Place
35 Livery Street
Birmingham
B3 2PB, UK.

ISBN 978-1-78883-082-9

www.packtpub.com

`mapt.io`

Mapt is an online digital library that gives you full access to over 5,000 books and videos, as well as industry leading tools to help you plan your personal development and advance your career. For more information, please visit our website.

Why subscribe?

- Spend less time learning and more time coding with practical eBooks and videos from over 4,000 industry professionals

- Improve your learning with Skill Plans built especially for you

- Get a free eBook or video every month

- Mapt is fully searchable

- Copy and paste, print, and bookmark content

PacktPub.com

Did you know that Packt offers eBook versions of every book published, with PDF and ePub files available? You can upgrade to the eBook version at `www.PacktPub.com` and as a print book customer, you are entitled to a discount on the eBook copy. Get in touch with us at `service@packtpub.com` for more details.

At `www.PacktPub.com`, you can also read a collection of free technical articles, sign up for a range of free newsletters, and receive exclusive discounts and offers on Packt books and eBooks.

Contributors

About the author

Alessandro Molina has been a Python developer since 2001, and has always been interested in Python as a web development platform. He has worked as a CTO and a team leader of Python teams for the past 10 years and is currently the core developer of the TurboGears2 web framework and maintainer of Beaker Caching/Session framework. He authored the DEPOT file storage framework and the DukPy JavaScript interpreter for Python and has collaborated with various Python projects related to web development, such as FormEncode, ToscaWidgets, and the Ming MongoDB ORM.

To Stefania for constantly supporting me through the late nights and pushing me to write one paragraph when I felt like slacking, without her continuous support I would have never finished this book.

To the Python community, for being such a great and positive environment where discussions can flourish within respect for each other and to all Python conferences organizers for giving us a great chance to discuss our ideas with other great developers in front of a cold beer.

About the reviewer

Simone Marzola is a software engineer and technical lead with 10 years of experience. He is passionate about Python and machine learning, which lead him to be an active contributor in open source communities such as Mozilla Services and Pylons Project, and involved in European conferences as a speaker. Simone has been a lecturer on the Big Dive data science and machine learning course. He is currently a CTO and Scrum Master at Oval Money.

Packt is searching for authors like you

If you're interested in becoming an author for Packt, please visit authors.packtpub.com and apply today. We have worked with thousands of developers and tech professionals, just like you, to help them share their insight with the global tech community. You can make a general application, apply for a specific hot topic that we are recruiting an author for, or submit your own idea.

Table of Contents

Preface

Python is a very powerful and widespread language, with a fully-featured standard library. It's said to come with *batteries included*, which means that most of what you will have to do will be available in the standard library.

Such a big set of functions might make developers feel lost, and it's not always clear which of the available tools are the best for solving a specific task. For many of these tasks, external libraries will also be available that you can install to solve the same problem. So, you might not only find yourself wondering which class or function to use from all the features provided by the standard library, but you will also wonder when it's best to switch to an external library to achieve your goals.

This book tries to provide a general overview of the tools available in the Python standard library to solve many common tasks and recipes to leverage those tools to achieve specific results. For cases where the solution based on the standard library might get too complex or limited, it will also try to suggest tools out of the standard library that can help you do the next step.

Who this book is for

This book is well suited for developers who want to write expressive, highly responsive, manageable, scalable, and resilient code in Python. Prior programming knowledge of Python is expected.

What this book covers

Chapter 1, *Containers and Data Structures,* covers less obvious cases of data structures and containers provided by the standard library. While more basic containers such as `list` and `dict` are taken for granted, the chapter will dive into less common containers and more advanced usages of the built-in containers.

Chapter 2, *Text Management,* covers text manipulation, string comparison, matching, and the most common needs when formatting output for text-based software.

Chapter 3, *Command Line,* covers how to write terminal/shell based software, parsing arguments, writing interactive shells, and implement logging.

Chapter 4, *Filesystem and Directories*, covers how to work with directories and files, traverse filesystems and work with multiple encoding types related to filesystems and filenames.

Chapter 5, *Date and Time*, covers how to parse dates and times, format them, and apply math over dates to compute past and future dates.

Chapter 6, *Read/Write Data*, covers how to read and write data in common file formats, such as CSV, XML, and ZIP, and how to properly manage encoding text files.

Chapter 7, *Algorithms*, covers some of the most common algorithms for sorting, searching, and zipping, and common operations that you might have to apply on any kind of sets of data.

Chapter 8, *Cryptography*, covers security-related functions that are provided by the standard library or that can be implemented with the hashing functions available in the standard library.

Chapter 9, *Concurrency*, covers the various concurrency models provided by the standard library, such as threads, processes, and coroutines, with a specific focus on the orchestration of those executors.

Chapter 10, *Networking*, covers features provided by the standard library to implement networking-based applications, how to read from some common protocols, such as FTP and IMAP, and how to implement general-purpose TCP/IP applications.

Chapter 11, *Web Development*, covers how to implement HTTP-based applications, simple HTTP servers, and fully-featured web applications. It will also cover how to interact with third-party software through HTTP.

Chapter 12, *Multimedia*, covers basic operations on detecting file types, checking images, and generating sounds.

Chapter 13, *Graphical User Interfaces*, covers the most common building blocks of UI-based applications that can be combined to create simple applications for desktop environments.

Chapter 14, *Development Tools*, covers tools provided by the standard library to help developers in their everyday work, such as writing tests and debugging software.

To get the most out of this book

Readers are expected to already have prior knowledge of Python and program
Developers that come from other languages or that are intermediate with Pyth
the most out of this book.

This book takes for granted that readers have a working installation of Python 3.5+, and
most of the recipes show examples for Unix-based systems (such as macOS or Linux) but
are expected to work on Windows system too. Windows users can rely on the Windows
subsystem for Linux to perfectly reproduce the examples.

Download the example code files

You can download the example code files for this book from your account at
`www.packtpub.com`. If you purchased this book elsewhere, you can visit
`www.packtpub.com/support` and register to have the files emailed directly to you.

You can download the code files by following these steps:

1. Log in or register at `www.packtpub.com`.
2. Select the **SUPPORT** tab.
3. Click on **Code Downloads & Errata**.
4. Enter the name of the book in the **Search** box and follow the onscreen
   instructions.

Once the file is downloaded, please make sure that you unzip or extract the folder using the
latest version of:

- WinRAR/7-Zip for Windows
- Zipeg/iZip/UnRarX for Mac
- 7-Zip/PeaZip for Linux

The code bundle for the book is also hosted on GitHub at `https://github.com/`
`PacktPublishing/Modern-Python-Standard-Library-Cookbook`. We also have other code
bundles from our rich catalog of books and videos available at `https://github.com/`
`PacktPublishing/`. Check them out!

ace

Conventions used

There are a number of text conventions used throughout this book.

`CodeInText`: Indicates code words in text, database table names, folder names, filenames, file extensions, pathnames, dummy URLs, user input, and Twitter handles. Here is an example: "We can also get rid of the last `.get` call by combining `ChainMap` with `defaultdict`."

A block of code is set as follows:

```
for word in 'hello world this is a very nice day'.split():
    if word in counts:
        counts[word] += 1
```

When we wish to draw your attention to a particular part of a code block, the relevant lines or items are set in bold:

```
class Bunch(dict):
    def __init__(self, **kwds):
        super().__init__(**kwds)
        self.__dict__ = self
```

Any command-line input or output is written as follows:

```
>>> print(population['japan'])
127
```

Bold: Indicates a new term, an important word, or words that you see onscreen. For example, words in menus or dialog boxes appear in the text like this. Here is an example: "If a **continuous integration** system is involved"

Warnings or important notes appear like this.

Tips and tricks appear like this.

Sections

In this book, you will find several headings that appear frequently (*Getting ready,How to do it..., How it works..., There's more...,* and *Seealso*).

To give clear instructions on how to complete a recipe, use these sections as follows:

Getting ready

This section tells you what to expect in the recipe and describes how to set up any software or any preliminary settings required for the recipe.

How to do it...

This section contains the steps required to follow the recipe.

How it works...

This section usually consists of a detailed explanation of what happened in the previous section.

There's more...

This section consists of additional information about the recipe in order to make you more knowledgeable about the recipe.

See also

This section provides helpful links to other useful information for the recipe.

Get in touch

Feedback from our readers is always welcome.

General feedback: Email feedback@packtpub.com and mention the book title in the subject of your message. If you have questions about any aspect of this book, please email us at questions@packtpub.com.

Errata: Although we have taken every care to ensure the accuracy of our content, mistakes do happen. If you have found a mistake in this book, we would be grateful if you would report this to us. Please visit www.packtpub.com/submit-errata, selecting your book, clicking on the Errata Submission Form link, and entering the details.

Piracy: If you come across any illegal copies of our works in any form on the internet, we would be grateful if you would provide us with the location address or website name. Please contact us at copyright@packtpub.com with a link to the material.

If you are interested in becoming an author: If there is a topic that you have expertise in and you are interested in either writing or contributing to a book, please visit authors.packtpub.com.

Reviews

Please leave a review. Once you have read and used this book, why not leave a review on the site that you purchased it from? Potential readers can then see and use your unbiased opinion to make purchase decisions, we at Packt can understand what you think about our products, and our authors can see your feedback on their book. Thank you!

For more information about Packt, please visit packtpub.com.

Containers and Data Structures

1

In this chapter, we will cover the following recipes:

- Counting frequencies—count occurrences of any hashable value
- Dictionary with fallback—have a fallback value for any missing key
- Unpacking multiple—keyword arguments—how to use ** more than once
- Ordered dictionaries—maintaining order of keys in a dictionary
- MultiDict—dictionary with multiple values per key
- Prioritizing entries—efficiently get the top of sorted entries
- Bunch—dictionaries that behave like objects
- Enumerations—handle a known set of states

Introduction

Python has a very easy and flexible set of built-in containers. As a Python developer, there is little you can't achieve with a `dict` or a `list`. The convenience of Python dictionaries and lists is such that developers often forget that those have limits. Like any data structure, they are optimized and designed for specific use cases and might be inefficient in some conditions, or even unable to handle them.

Ever tried to put a key in a dictionary twice? Well you can't, because Python dictionaries are designed as hash tables with unique keys, but the *MultiDict* recipe will show you how to do that. Ever tried to grab the lowest/highest values out of a list without traversing it whole? The list itself can't, but in the *Prioritized entries* recipe, we will see how to achieve that.

The limits of standard Python containers are well known to Python experts. For that reason, the standard library has grown over the years to overcome those limits, and frequently there are patterns so common that their name is widely recognized, even though they are not formally defined.

Counting frequencies

A very common need in many kinds of programs is to count the occurrences of a value or of an event, which means counting frequency. Be it the need to count words in text, count likes on a blog post, or track scores for players of a video game, in the end counting frequency means counting how many we have of a specific value.

The most obvious solution for such a need would be to keep around counters for the things we need to count. If there are two, three, or four, maybe we can just track them in some dedicated variables, but if there are hundreds, it's certainly not feasible to keep around such a large amount of variables and we will quickly end up with a solution based on a container to collect all those counters.

How to do it...

Here are the steps for this recipe:

1. Suppose we want to track the frequency of words in text; the standard library comes to our rescue and provides us with a very good way to track counts and frequencies, which is through the dedicated `collections.Counter` object.

2. The `collections.Counter` object not only keeps track of frequencies, but provides some dedicated methods to retrieve the most common entries, entries that appear at last once and quickly count any iterable.

3. Any iterable you provide to the `Counter` is "counted" for its frequency of values:

```
>>> txt = "This is a vast world you can't traverse world in a day"
>>>
>>> from collections import Counter
>>> counts = Counter(txt.split())
```

4. The result would be exactly what we expect, a dictionary with the frequencies of the words in our phrase:

```
Counter({'a': 2, 'world': 2, "can't": 1, 'day': 1, 'traverse': 1,
         'is': 1, 'vast': 1, 'in': 1, 'you': 1, 'This': 1})
```

5. Then, we can easily query for the most frequent words:

```
>>> counts.most_common(2)
[('world', 2), ('a', 2)]
```

6. Get the frequency of a specific word:

```
>>> counts['world']
2
```

Or, get back the total number of occurrences:

```
>>> sum(counts.values())
12
```

7. And we can even apply some set operations on counters, such as joining them, subtracting them, or checking for intersections:

```
>>> Counter(["hello", "world"]) + Counter(["hello", "you"])
Counter({'hello': 2, 'you': 1, 'world': 1})
>>> Counter(["hello", "world"]) & Counter(["hello", "you"])
Counter({'hello': 1})
```

How it works...

Our counting code relies on the fact that `Counter` is just a special kind of dictionary, and that dictionaries can be built by providing an iterable. Each entry in the iterable will be added to the dictionary.

In the case of a counter, adding an element means incrementing its count; for every "word" in our list, we add that word multiple times (one every time it appears in the list), so its value in the `Counter` continues to get incremented every time the word is encountered.

There's more...

Relying on `Counter` is actually not the only way to track frequencies; we already know that `Counter` is a special kind of dictionary, so reproducing the `Counter` behavior should be quite straightforward.

Probably every one of us came up with a dictionary in this form:

```
counts = dict(hello=0, world=0, nice=0, day=0)
```

Whenever we face a new occurrence of `hello`, `world`, `nice`, or `day`, we increment the associated value in the dictionary and call it a day:

```
for word in 'hello world this is a very nice day'.split():
    if word in counts:
        counts[word] += 1
```

By relying on `dict.get`, we can also easily adapt it to count any word, not just those we could foresee:

```
for word in 'hello world this is a very nice day'.split():
    counts[word] = counts.get(word, 0) + 1
```

But the standard library actually provides a very flexible tool that we can use to improve this code even further, `collections.defaultdict`.

`defaultdict` is a plain dictionary that won't throw `KeyError` for any missing value, but will call a function we can provide to generate the missing value.

So, something such as `defaultdict(int)` will create a dictionary that provides 0 for any key that it doesn't have, which is very convenient for our counting purpose:

```
from collections import defaultdict

counts = defaultdict(int)
for word in 'hello world this is a very nice day'.split():
    counts[word] += 1
```

The result will be exactly what we expect:

```
defaultdict(<class 'int'>, {'day': 1, 'is': 1, 'a': 1, 'very': 1, 'world':
1, 'this': 1, 'nice': 1, 'hello': 1})
```

As for each word, the first time we face it, we will call `int` to get the starting value and then add 1 to it. As `int` gives 0 when called without any argument, that achieves what we want.

While this roughly solves our problem, it's far from being a complete solution for counting—we track frequencies, but on everything else, we are on our own. What if we want to know the most frequent entry in our bag of words?

The convenience of `Counter` is based on the set of additional features specialized for counting that it provides; it's not just a dictionary with a default numeric value, it's a class specialized in keeping track of frequencies and providing convenient ways to access them.

Dictionary with fallback

When working with configuration values, it's common to look them up in multiple places—maybe we load them from a configuration file—but we can override them with an environment variable or a command-line option, and in case the option is not provided, we can have a default value.

This can easily lead to long chains of `if` statements like these:

```
value = command_line_options.get('optname')
if value is None:
    value = os.environ.get('optname')
if value is None:
    value = config_file_options.get('optname')
if value is None:
    value = 'default-value'
```

This is annoying, and while for a single value it might be just annoying, it will tend to grow into a huge, confusing list of conditions as more options get added.

Command-line options are a very frequent use case, but the problem is related to chained scopes resolution. Variables in Python are resolved by looking at `locals()`; if they are not found, the interpreter looks at `globals()`, and if they are not yet found, it looks for built-ins.

How to do it...

For this step, you need to go through the following steps:

1. The alternative for chaining default values of `dict.get`, instead of using multiple `if` instances, probably wouldn't improve much the code and if we want to add one additional scope, we would have to add it in every single place where we are looking up the values.

2. `collections.ChainMap` is a very convenient solution to this problem; we can provide a list of mapping containers and it will look for a key through them all.

3. Our previous example involving multiple different `if` instances can be converted to something like this:

```
import os
from collections import ChainMap

options = ChainMap(command_line_options, os.environ,
config_file_options)
value = options.get('optname', 'default-value')
```

4. We can also get rid of the last `.get` call by combining `ChainMap` with `defaultdict`. In this case, we can use `defaultdict` to provide a default value for every key:

```
import os
from collections import ChainMap, defaultdict

options = ChainMap(command_line_options, os.environ,
config_file_options,
                   defaultdict(lambda: 'default-value'))
value = options['optname']
value2 = options['other-option']
```

5. Print `value` and `value2` will result in the following:

```
optvalue
default-value
```

`optname` will be retrieved from the `command_line_options` containing it, while `other-option` will end up being resolved by `defaultdict`.

How it works...

The `ChainMap` class receives multiple dictionaries as arguments; whenever a key is requested to `ChainMap`, it's actually going through the provided dictionaries one by one to check whether the key is available in any of them. Once the key is found, it is returned, as if it was a key owned by `ChainMap` itself.

The default value for options that are not provided is implemented by having `defaultdict` as the last dictionary provided to `ChainMap`. Whenever a key is not found in any of the previous dictionaries, it gets looked up in `defaultdict`, which uses the provided factory function to return a default value for all keys.

There's more...

Another great feature of ChainMap is that it allows updating too, but instead of updating the dictionary where it found the key, it always updates the first dictionary. The result is the same, as on next lookup of that key, we would have the first dictionary override any other value for that key (as it's the first place where the key is checked). The advantage is that if we provide an empty dictionary as the first mapping provided to ChainMap, we can change those values without touching the original container:

```
>>> population=dict(italy=60, japan=127, uk=65)
>>> changes = dict()
>>> editablepop = ChainMap(changes, population)

>>> print(editablepop['japan'])
127
>>> editablepop['japan'] += 1
>>> print(editablepop['japan'])
128
```

But even though we changed the population of Japan to 128 million, the original population didn't change:

```
>>> print(population['japan'])
127
```

And we can even use changes to find out which values were changed and which values were not:

```
>>> print(changes.keys())
dict_keys(['japan'])
>>> print(population.keys() - changes.keys())
{'italy', 'uk'}
```

It's important to know, by the way, that if the object contained in the dictionary is mutable and we directly mutate it, there is little ChainMap can do to avoid mutating the original object. So if, instead of numbers, we store lists in the dictionaries, we will be mutating the original dictionary whenever we append values to the dictionary:

```
>>> citizens = dict(torino=['Alessandro'], amsterdam=['Bert'],
raleigh=['Joseph'])
>>> changes = dict()
>>> editablecits = ChainMap(changes, citizens)
>>> editablecits['torino'].append('Simone')
>>> print(editablecits['torino']) ['Alessandro', 'Simone']
>>> print(changes)
{}
```

```
>>> print(citizens)
{'amsterdam': ['Bert'],
 'torino': ['Alessandro', 'Simone'],
 'raleigh': ['Joseph']}
```

Unpacking multiple keyword arguments

Frequently, you ended up in a situation where you had to provide arguments to a function from a dictionary. If you've ever faced that need, you probably also ended up in a case where you had to take the arguments from multiple dictionaries.

Generally, Python functions accept arguments from a dictionary through unpacking (the ** syntax), but so far, it hasn't been possible to use unpacking twice in the same call, nor was there an easy way to merge two dictionaries.

How to do it...

The steps for this recipe are:

1. Given a function, f, we want to pass the arguments from two dictionaries, d1 and d2 as follows:

    ```
    >>> def f(a, b, c, d):
    ...     print (a, b, c, d)
    ...
    >>> d1 = dict(a=5, b=6)
    >>> d2 = dict(b=7, c=8, d=9)
    ```

2. `collections.ChainMap` can help us achieve what we want; it can cope with duplicated entries and works with any Python version:

    ```
    >>> f(**ChainMap(d1, d2))
    5 6 8 9
    ```

3. In Python 3.5 and newer versions, you can also create a new dictionary by combining multiple dictionaries through the literal syntax, and then pass the resulting dictionary as the argument of the function:

    ```
    >>> f(**{**d1, **d2})
    5 7 8 9
    ```

4. In this case, the duplicated entries are accepted too, but are handled in reverse order of priority to `ChainMap` (so right to left). Notice how b has a value of 7, instead of the 6 it had with `ChainMap`, due to the reversed order of priorities.

This syntax might be harder to read due to the amount of unpacking operators involved, and with `ChainMap` it is probably more explicit what's happening for a reader.

How it works...

As we already know from the previous recipe, `ChainMap` looks up keys in all the provided dictionaries, so it's like the sum of all the dictionaries. The unpacking operator (**) works by inviting all keys to the container and then providing an argument for each key.

As `ChainMap` has keys resulting from the sum of all the provided dictionaries keys, it will provide the keys contained in all the dictionaries to the unpacking operator, thus allowing us to provide keyword arguments from multiple dictionaries.

There's more...

Since Python 3.5 through PEP 448, it's now possible to unpack multiple mappings to provide keyword arguments:

```
>>> def f(a, b, c, d):
...     print (a, b, c, d)
...
>>> d1 = dict(a=5, b=6)
>>> d2 = dict(c=7, d=8)
>>> f(**d1, **d2)
5 6 7 8
```

This solution is very convenient, but has two limits:

- It's only available in Python 3.5+
- It chokes on duplicated arguments

If you don't know where the mappings/dictionaries you are unpacking come from, it's easy to end up with the issue of duplicated arguments:

```
>>> d1 = dict(a=5, b=6)
>>> d2 = dict(b=7, c=8, d=9)
>>> f(**d1, **d2)
Traceback (most recent call last):
```

```
File "<stdin>", line 1, in <module>
TypeError: f() got multiple values for keyword argument 'b'
```

In the previous example, the b key is declared in both d1 and d2, and that causes the function to complain that it received duplicate arguments.

Ordered dictionaries

One of the most surprising aspects of Python dictionaries for new users is that their order is unpredictable and can change from environment to environment. So, the order of keys you expected on your system might be totally different on your friend's computer.

This frequently causes unexpected failures during tests; if a continuous integration system is involved, the ordering of dictionary keys on the system running the tests can be different from the ordering on your system, which might lead to random failures.

Suppose you have a snippet of code that generates an HTML tag with some attributes:

```
>>> attrs = dict(style="background-color:red", id="header")
>>> '<span {}>'.format(' '.join('%s="%s"' % a for a in attrs.items()))
'<span id="header" style="background-color:red">'
```

It might surprise you that on some systems you end up with this:

```
'<span id="header" style="background-color:red">'
```

While on others, the result might be this:

```
'<span style="background-color:red" id="header">'
```

So, if you expect to be able to compare the resulting string to check whether your function did the right thing when generating this tag, you might be disappointed.

How to do it...

Keys ordering is a very convenient feature and in some cases, it's actually necessary, so the Python standard library comes to help and provides the collections.OrderedDict container.

In the case of `collections.OrderedDict`, the keys are always in the order they were inserted in:

```
>>> attrs = OrderedDict([('id', 'header'), ('style', 'background-
color:red')])
>>> '<span {}>'.format(' '.join('%s="%s"' % a for a in attrs.items()))
'<span id="header" style="background-color:red">'
```

How it works...

`OrderedDict` stores both a mapping of the keys to their values and a list of keys that is used to preserve the order of them.

So whenever your look for a key, the lookup goes through the mapping, but whenever you want to list the keys or iterate over the container, you go through the list of keys to ensure they are processed in the order they were inserted in.

The main problem when using `OrderedDict` is that Python on versions before 3.6 didn't guarantee any specific order of keyword arguments:

```
>>> attrs = OrderedDict(id="header", style="background-color:red")
```

This would have again introduced a totally random order of keys even though `OrderedDict` was used. Not because `OrderedDict` didn't preserve the order of those keys, but because it would have received them in a random order.

Thanks to PEP 468, the order of arguments is now guaranteed in Python 3.6 and newer versions (the order of dictionaries is still not, remember; so far it's just by chance that they are ordered). So if you are using Python 3.6 or newer, our previous example would work as expected, but if you are on older versions of Python, you would end up with a random order.

Thankfully, this is an issue that is easily solved. Like standard dictionaries, `OrderedDict` supports any iterable as the source of its content. As long as the iterable provides a key and a value, it can be used to build `OrderedDict`.

So by providing the keys and values in a tuple, we can provide them at construction time and preserve the order in any Python version:

```
>>> OrderedDict((('id', 'header'), ('style', 'background-color:red')))
OrderedDict([('id', 'header'), ('style', 'background-color:red')])
```

There's more...

Python 3.6 introduced a guarantee of preserving the order of dictionary keys as a side effect of some changes to dictionaries, but it was considered an internal implementation detail and not a language guarantee. Since Python 3.7, it became an official feature of the language so it's actually safe to rely on dictionary ordering if you are using Python 3.6 or newer.

MultiDict

If you have ever need to provide a reverse mapping, you have probably discovered that Python lacks a way to store more than a value for each key in a dictionary. This is a very common need, and most languages provide some form of multimap container.

Python tends to prefer having a single way of doing things, and as storing multiple values for the key means just storing a list of values for a key, it doesn't provide a specialized container.

The issue with storing a list of values is that to be able to append to values to our dictionary, the list must already exist.

How to do it...

Proceed with the following steps for this recipe:

1. As we already know, defaultdict will create a default value by calling the provided callable for every missing key. We can provide the list constructor as a callable:

```
>>> from collections import defaultdict
>>> rd = defaultdict(list)
```

2. So, we insert keys into our multimap by using rd[k].append(v) instead of the usual rd[k] = v:

```
>>> for name, num in [('ichi', 1), ('one', 1), ('uno', 1), ('un',
1)]:
...     rd[num].append(name)
...
>>> rd
defaultdict(<class 'list'>, {1: ['ichi', 'one', 'uno', 'un']})
```

How it works...

MultiDict works by storing a list for each key. Whenever a key is accessed, the list containing all the values for that key is retrieved.

In the case of missing keys, an empty list will be provided so that values can be added for that key.

This works because every time defaultdict faces a missing key, it will insert it with a value generated by calling list. And calling list will actually provide an empty list. So, doing rd[v] will always provide a list, empty or not, depending on whether v was an already existing key or not. Once we have our list, adding a new value is just a matter of appending it.

There's more...

Dictionaries in Python are associative containers where keys are unique. A key can appear a single time and has exactly one value.

If we want to support multiple values per key, we can actually solve the need by saving list as the value of our key. This list can then contain all the values we want to keep around for that key:

```
>>> rd = {1: ['one', 'uno', 'un', 'ichi'],
...       2: ['two', 'due', 'deux', 'ni'],
...       3: ['three', 'tre', 'trois', 'san']}
>>> rd[2]
['two', 'due', 'deux', 'ni']
```

If we want to add a new translation to 2 (Spanish, for example), we would just have to append the entry:

```
>>> rd[2].append('dos')
>>> rd[2]
['two', 'due', 'deux', 'ni', 'dos']
```

The problem arises when we want to introduce a new key:

```
>>> rd[4].append('four')
Traceback (most recent call last):
    File "<stdin>", line 1, in <module>
KeyError: 4
```

For key 4, no list exists, so there is nowhere we can append it. So, our snippet to automatically reverse the mapping can't be easily adapted to handle multiple values, as it would fail with key errors the first time it tries to insert a value:

```
>>> rd = {}
>>> for k,v in d.items():
...     rd[v].append(k)
Traceback (most recent call last):
    File "<stdin>", line 2, in <module>
KeyError: 1
```

Checking for every single entry, whether it's already in the dictionary or not, and acting accordingly is not very convenient. While we can rely on the `setdefault` method of dictionaries to hide that check, we can get a far more elegant solution by using `collections.defaultdict`.

Prioritizing entries

Picking the first/top entry of a set of values is a pretty frequent need; this usually means defining one value that has priority over the other and involves sorting.

But sorting can be expensive and re-sorting every time you add an entry to your values is certainly not a very convenient way to pick the first entry out of a set of values with some kind of priority.

How to do it...

Heaps are a perfect match for everything that has priorities, such as a priority queue:

```
import time
import heapq

class PriorityQueue:
    def __init__(self):
        self._q = []

    def add(self, value, priority=0):
        heapq.heappush(self._q, (priority, time.time(), value))

    def pop(self):
        return heapq.heappop(self._q)[-1]
```

Then, our `PriorityQueue` can be used to retrieve entries given a priority:

```
>>> def f1(): print('hello')
>>> def f2(): print('world')
>>>
>>> pq = PriorityQueue()
>>> pq.add(f2, priority=1)
>>> pq.add(f1, priority=0)
>>> pq.pop()()
hello
>>> pq.pop()()
world
```

How it works...

`PriorityQueue` works by storing everything in an heap. Heaps are particularly efficient at retrieving the top/first element of a sorted set without having to actually sort the whole set.

Our priority queue stores all the values in a three-element tuple: `priority`, `time.time()`, and `value`.

The first entry of our tuple is `priority` (lower is better). In the example, we recorded `f1` with a better priority than `f2`, which ensures than when we use `heap.heappop` to fetch tasks to process, we get `f1` and then `f2`, so that we end up with the `hello world` message and not `world hello`.

The second entry, `timestamp`, is used to ensure that tasks that have the same priority are processed in their insertion order. The oldest task will be served first as it will have the smallest timestamp.

Then, we have the value itself, which is the function we want call for our task.

There's more...

A very common approach to sorting is to keep a list of entries in a tuple, where the first element is `key` for which we are sorting and the second element is the value itself.

For a scoreboard, we can keep each player's name and how many points they got:

```
scores = [(123, 'Alessandro'),
          (143, 'Chris'),
          (192, 'Mark']
```

Storing those values in tuples works because comparing two tuples is performed by comparing each element of the first tuple with the element in the same index position in the other tuple:

```
>>> (10, 'B') > (10, 'A')
True
>>> (11, 'A') > (10, 'B')
True
```

It's very easy to understand what's going on if you think about strings. `'BB' > 'BB'` is the same as `('B', 'B') > ('B', 'A')`; in the end, a string is just a list of characters.

We can use this property to sort our `scores` and retrieve the winner of a competition:

```
>>> scores = sorted(scores)
>>> scores[-1]
(192, 'Mark')
```

The major problem with this approach is that every time we add an entry to our list, we have to sort it again, or our scoreboard would became meaningless:

```
>>> scores.append((137, 'Rick'))
>>> scores[-1]
(137, 'Rick')
>>> scores = sorted(scores)
>>> scores[-1]
(192, 'Mark')
```

This is very inconvenient because it's easy to miss re-sorting somewhere if we have multiple places appending to the list, and sorting the whole list every time can be expensive.

The Python standard library offers a data structure that is a perfect match when we're interested in finding out the winner of a competition.

In the `heapq` module, we have a fully working implementation of a heap data structure, a particular kind of tree where each parent is smaller than its children. This provides us with a tree that has a very interesting property: the root element is always the smallest one.

And being implemented on top of a list, it means that `l[0]` is always the smallest element in a `heap`:

```
>>> import heapq
>>> l = []
>>> heapq.heappush(l, (192, 'Mark'))
>>> heapq.heappush(l, (123, 'Alessandro'))
```

```
>>> heapq.heappush(l, (137, 'Rick'))
>>> heapq.heappush(l, (143, 'Chris'))
>>> l[0]
(123, 'Alessandro')
```

You might have noticed, by the way, that the heap finds the loser of our tournament, not the winner, and we were interested in finding the best player, with the highest value.

This is a minor problem we can easily solve by storing all scores as negative numbers. If we store each score as $* -1$, the head of the heap will always be the winner:

```
>>> l = []
>>> heapq.heappush(l, (-143, 'Chris'))
>>> heapq.heappush(l, (-137, 'Rick'))
>>> heapq.heappush(l, (-123, 'Alessandro'))
>>> heapq.heappush(l, (-192, 'Mark'))
>>> l[0]
(-192, 'Mark')
```

Bunch

Python is very good at shapeshifting objects. Each instance can have its own attributes and it's absolutely legal to add/remove the attributes of an object at runtime.

Once in a while, our code needs to deal with data of unknown shapes. For example, in the case of a user-submitted data, we might not know which fields the user is providing; maybe some of our users have a first name, some have a surname, and some have one or more middle name fields.

If we are not processing this data ourselves, but are just providing it to some other function, we really don't care about the shape of the data; as long as our objects have those attributes, we are fine.

A very common case is when working with protocols, if you are an HTTP server, you might want to provide to the application running behind you a `request` object. This object has a few known attributes, such as `host` and `path`, and it might have some optional attributes, such as a `query` string or a `content` type. But, it can also have any attribute the client provided, as HTTP is pretty flexible regarding headers, and our clients could have provided an `x-totally-custom-header` that we might have to expose to our code.

When representing this kind of data, Python developers often tend to look at dictionaries. In the end, Python objects themselves are built on top of dictionaries and they fit the need to map arbitrary values to names.

So, we will probably end up with something like the following:

```
>>> request = dict(host='www.example.org', path='/index.html')
```

A side effect of this approach is pretty clear once we have to pass this object around, especially to third-party code. Functions usually work with objects, and while they don't require a specific kind of object as duck-typing is the standard in Python, they will expect certain attributes to be there.

Another very common example is when writing tests, Python being a duck-typed language, it's absolutely reasonable to want to provide a fake object instead of providing a real instance of the object, especially when we need to simulate the values of some properties (as declared with @property), so we don't want or can't afford to create real instances of the object.

In such cases, using a dictionary is not viable as it will only provide access to its values through the request['path'] syntax and not through request.path, as probably expected by the functions we are providing our object to.

Also, the more we end up accessing this value, the more it's clear that the syntax using dot notation conveys the feeling of an entity that collaborates to the intent of the code, while a dictionary conveys the feeling of plain data.

As soon as we remember that Python objects can change shape at any time, we might be tempted to try creating an object instead of a dictionary. Unfortunately, we won't be able to provide the attributes at initialization time:

```
>>> request = object(host='www.example.org', path='/index.html')
Traceback (most recent call last):
    File "<stdin>", line 1, in <module>
TypeError: object() takes no parameters
```

Things don't improve much if we try to assign those attributes after the object is built:

```
>>> request = object()
>>> request.host = 'www.example.org'
Traceback (most recent call last):
    File "<stdin>", line 1, in <module>
AttributeError: 'object' object has no attribute 'host'
```

How to do it...

With a little effort, we can create a class that leverages dictionaries to contain any we want and allow access both as a dictionary and through properties:

```
>>> class Bunch(dict):
...     def __getattribute__(self, key):
...         try:
...             return self[key]
...         except KeyError:
...             raise AttributeError(key)
...
...     def __setattr__(self, key, value):
...         self[key] = value
...
>>> b = Bunch(a=5)
>>> b.a
5
>>> b['a']
5
```

How it works...

The Bunch class inherits dict, mostly as a way to provide a context where values can be stored, then most of the work is done by __getattribute__ and __setattr__. So, for any attribute that is retrieved or set on the object, they will just retrieve or set a key in self (remember we inherited from dict, so self is in fact a dictionary).

This allows the Bunch class to store and retrieve any value as an attribute of the object. The convenient feature is that it can behave both as an object and as a dict in most contexts.

For example, it is possible to find out all the values that it contains, like any other dictionary:

```
>>> b.items()
dict_items([('a', 5)])
```

It is also able to access those as attributes:

```
>>> b.c = 7
>>> b.c
7
>>> b.items()
dict_items([('a', 5), ('c', 7)])
```

There's more...

Our `bunch` implementation is not yet complete, as it will fail any test for class name (it's always named `Bunch`) and any test for inheritance, thus failing at faking other objects.

The first step is to make `Bunch` able to shapeshift not only its properties, but also its name. This can be achieved by creating a new class dynamically every time we create `Bunch`. The class will inherit from `Bunch` and will do nothing apart from providing a new name:

```
>>> class BunchBase(dict):
...     def __getattribute__(self, key):
...         try:
...             return self[key]
...         except KeyError:
...             raise AttributeError(key)
...
...     def __setattr__(self, key, value):
...         self[key] = value
...
>>> def Bunch(_classname="Bunch", **attrs):
...     return type(_classname, (BunchBase, ), {})(**attrs)
>>>
```

The `Bunch` function moved from being the class itself to being a factory that will create objects that all act as `Bunch`, but can have different classes. Each `Bunch` will be a subclass of `BunchBase`, where the `_classname` name can be provided when `Bunch` is created:

```
>>> b = Bunch("Request", path="/index.html", host="www.example.org")
>>> print(b)
{'path': '/index.html', 'host': 'www.example.org'}
>>> print(b.path)
/index.html
>>> print(b.host)
www.example.org
```

This will allow us to create as many kinds of `Bunch` objects as we want, and each will have its own custom type:

```
>>> print(b.__class__)
<class '__main__.Request'>
```

The next step is to make our `Bunch` actually look like any other type that it has to impersonate. That is needed for the case where we want to use `Bunch` in place of another object. As `Bunch` can have any kind of attribute, it can take the place of any kind of object, but to be able to, it has to pass type checks for custom types.

We need to go back to our `Bunch` factory and make the `Bunch` objects not only have a custom class name, but also appear to be inherited from a custom parent.

To better understand what's going on, we will declare an example `Person` type; this type will be the one our `Bunch` objects will try to fake:

```
class Person(object):
    def __init__(name, surname):
        self.name = name
        self.surname = surname

    @property
    def fullname(self):
        return '{} {}'.format(self.name, self.surname)
```

Specifically, we are going to print `Hello Your Name` through a custom `print` function that only works for `Person`:

```
def hello(p):
    if not isinstance(p, Person):
        raise ValueError("Sorry, can only greet people")
    print("Hello {}".format(p.fullname))
```

We want to change our `Bunch` factory to accept the class and create a new type out of it:

```
def Bunch(_classname="Bunch", _parent=None, **attrs):
    parents = (_parent, ) if parent else tuple()
    return type(_classname, (BunchBase, ) + parents, {})(**attrs)
```

Now, our `Bunch` objects will appear as instances of a class named what we wanted, and will always appear as a subclass of _parent:

```
>>> p = Bunch("Person", Person, fullname='Alessandro Molina')
>>> hello(p)
Hello Alessandro Molina
```

`Bunch` can be a very convenient pattern; in both its complete and simplified versions, it is widely used in many frameworks with various implementations that all achieve pretty much the same result.

The showcased implementation is interesting because it gives us a clear idea of what's going on. There are ways to implement `Bunch` that are very smart, but might make it hard to guess what's going on and customize it.

Another possible way to implement the `Bunch` pattern is by patching the __dict__ class, which contains all the attributes of the class:

```
class Bunch(dict):
    def __init__(self, **kwds):
        super().__init__(**kwds)
        self.__dict__ = self
```

In this form, whenever `Bunch` is created, it will populate its values as a `dict` (by calling `super().__init__`, which is the `dict` initialization) and then, once all the attributes provided are stored in `dict`, it swaps the __dict__ object, which is the dictionary that contains all object attributes, with `self`. This makes the `dict` that was just populated with all the values also the `dict` that contains all the attributes of the object.

Our previous implementation worked by replacing the way we looked for attributes, while this implementation replaces the place where we look for attributes.

Enumerations

Enumeration is a common way to store values that can only represent a few states. Each symbolic name is bound to a specific value, usually numeric, that represents the states the enumeration can have.

Enumerations are very common in other programming languages, but until recently, Python didn't have any explicit support for enumerations.

How to do it...

Typically, enumerations are implemented by mapping symbolic names to numeric values; this is allowed in Python through `enum.IntEnum`:

```
>>> from enum import IntEnum
>>>
>>> class RequestType(IntEnum):
...     POST = 1
...     GET = 2
>>>
>>> request_type = RequestType.POST
>>> print(request_type)
RequestType.POST
```

How it works...

`IntEnum` is an integer, apart from the fact that all possible values are created when the class is defined. `IntEnum` inherits from `int`, so its values are real integers.

During the `RequestType` definition, all the possible values for `enum` are declared within the class body and the values are verified against duplicates by the metaclass.

Also, `enum` provides support for a special value, `auto`, which means *just put in a value, I don't care.* As you usually only care whether it's `POST` or `GET`, you usually don't care whether `POST` is 1 or 2.

Last but not least, enumerations cannot be subclassed if they define at least one possible value.

There's more...

`IntEnum` values behave like `int` in most cases, which is usually convenient, but they can cause problems if the developer doesn't pay attention to the type.

For example, a function might unexpectedly perform the wrong thing if another enumeration or an integer value is provided, instead of the proper enumeration value:

```
>>> def do_request(kind):
...     if kind == RequestType.POST:
...         print('POST')
...     else:
...         print('OTHER')
```

As an example, invoking `do_request` with `RequestType.POST` or 1 will do exactly the same thing:

```
>>> do_request(RequestType.POST)
POST
>>> do_request(1)
POST
```

When we want to avoid treating our enumerations as numbers, we can use `enum.Enum`, which provides enumerated values that are not considered plain numbers:

```
>>> from enum import Enum
>>>
>>> class RequestType(Enum):
...        POST = 1
...        GET = 2
>>>
>>> do_request(RequestType.POST)
POST
>>> do_request(1)
OTHER
```

So generally, if you need a simple set of enumerated values or possible states that rely on `enum`, `Enum` is safer, but if you need a set of numeric values that rely on `enum`, `IntEnum` will ensure that they behave like numbers.

Text Management 2

In this chapter, we will cover the following recipes:

- Pattern matching—regular expressions are not the only way to parse patterns; Python provides easier and just as powerful tools to parse patterns
- Text similarity—detecting how two similar strings in a performing way can be hard but Python has some easy-to-use built-in tools
- Text suggestion—Python looks for the most similar one to suggest to the user the right spelling
- Templating—when generating text, templating is the easiest way to define the rules
- Splitting strings preserving spaces—splitting on empty spaces can be easy, but gets harder when you want to preserve some spaces
- Cleanup text—removes any punctuation or odd character from text
- Normalizing text—when working with international text, it's often convenient to avoid having to cope with special characters and misspelling of words
- Aligning text—when outputting text, properly aligning it greatly increases readability

Introduction

Python was born for system engineering and a very frequent need when working with shell scripts and shell-based software is to create and parse text. That's why Python has very powerful tools to handle text.

Pattern matching

When looking for patterns in text, regular expressions are frequently the most common way to attach those kind of problems. They are very flexible and powerful, and even though they cannot express all kinds of grammar they frequently can handle most common cases.

The power of regular expressions comes out of the wide set of symbols and expressions they can generate. The problem is that for developers that are not used to regular expressions, they can look just like plain noise, and even people who have experience with them will frequently have to think a bit before understanding an expression like the following one:

```
"^(*d{3})*( |-)*d{3}( |-)*d{4}$"
```

This expression actually tries to detect phone numbers.

For most common cases, developers need to look for very simple patterns: for example, file extensions (does it end with .txt?), separated text, and so on.

How to do it...

The fnmatch module provides a simplified pattern-matching language with a very quick and easy-to-understand syntax for most developers.

Very few characters have a special meaning:

- * means any text
- ? means any character
- [...] means the contained characters within square brackets
- [!...] means everything apart from the characters contained within the square brackets

You will probably recognize this syntax from your system shell, so it's easy to see how *.txt means *every name that has a .txt extension*:

```
>>> fnmatch.fnmatch('hello.txt', '*.txt')
True
>>> fnmatch.fnmatch('hello.zip', '*.txt')
False
```

There's more...

Practically, `fnmatch` can be used to recognize pieces of text separated by some ki㼿
constant value.

For example, if I have a pattern that defines the `type`, `name`, and `value` of a variable
separated by `:`, we can recognize it through `fnmatch` and then declare the described
variable:

```
>>> def declare(decl):
...     if not fnmatch.fnmatch(decl, '*:*:*'):
...         return False
...     t, n, v = decl.split(':', 2)
...     globals()[n] = getattr(__builtins__, t)(v)
...     return True
...
>>> declare('int:somenum:3')
True
>>> somenum
3
>>> declare('bool:somebool:True')
True
>>> somebool
True
>>> declare('int:a')
False
```

Where `fnmatch` obviously shines is with filenames. If you have a list of files, it's easy to
extract only those that match a specific pattern:

```
>>> os.listdir()
['.git', '.gitignore', '.vscode', 'algorithms.rst', 'concurrency.rst',
 'conf.py', 'crypto.rst', 'datastructures.rst', 'datetimes.rst',
 'devtools.rst', 'filesdirs.rst', 'gui.rst', 'index.rst', 'io.rst',
 'make.bat', 'Makefile', 'multimedia.rst', 'networking.rst',
 'requirements.txt', 'terminal.rst', 'text.rst', 'venv', 'web.rst']
>>> fnmatch.filter(os.listdir(), '*.git*')
['.git', '.gitignore']
```

While very convenient, `fnmatch` is surely limited, but one of the best things a tool can do
when it reaches its limits is to provide compatibility with an alternative tool that can
overcome them.

For example, if I wanted to find all files that contained the word `git` or `vs`, I couldn't do
that in a single `fnmatch` pattern. I have to declare two different patterns and then join the
results. But, if I could use a regular expression, that is absolutely possible.

`fnmatch.translate` bridges between `fnmatch` patterns and regular expressions, providing the regular expression that describes an `fnmatch` pattern, so that it can be extended how you wish.

For example, we could create a regular expression that matches both patterns:

```
>>> reg = '({})|({})'.format(fnmatch.translate('*.git*'),
                             fnmatch.translate('*vs*'))
>>> reg
'(.*\.git.*\Z(?ms))|(.*vs.*\Z(?ms))'
>>> import re
>>> [s for s in os.listdir() if re.match(reg, s)]
['.git', '.gitignore', '.vscode']
```

The real advantage of `fnmatch` is that it is an easy and safe enough language that you can expose to your users. Suppose you are writing an email client and you want to provide a search feature, how could you let your users search for Smith as a name or surname if you have emails from Jane Smith and Smith Lincoln?

Well with `fnmatch` that's easy because you can just expose it to your users and let them write `*Smith` or `Smith*`, depending on whether they are looking for someone named Smith or with Smith as a surname:

```
>>> senders = ['Jane Smith', 'Smith Lincoln']
>>> fnmatch.filter(senders, 'Smith*')
['Smith Lincoln']
>>> fnmatch.filter(senders, '*Smith')
['Jane Smith']
```

Text similarity

In many cases, when working with text, we might have to recognize text that is similar to other text, even when the two are not equal. This is a very common case in record linkage, finding duplicate entries, or for typing errors correction.

Finding similarity across text is not a straightforward task. If you try to go your own way, you will quickly realize that it gets complex and slow pretty soon.

The Python library provides tools to detect differences between two sequences in the `difflib` module. Since text itself is a sequence (a sequence of characters), we can apply the provided functions to detect similarities in strings.

How to do it...

Perform the following steps for this recipe:

1. Given a string, we want to compare:

```
>>> s = 'Today the weather is nice'
```

2. Furthermore, we want to compare a set of strings to the first string:

```
>>> s2 = 'Today the weater is nice'
>>> s3 = 'Yesterday the weather was nice'
>>> s4 = 'Today my dog ate steak'
```

3. We can use `difflib.SequenceMatcher` to compute the similitude (from 0 to 1) between the strings:

```
>>> import difflib
>>> difflib.SequenceMatcher(None, s, s2, False).ratio()
0.9795918367346939
>>> difflib.SequenceMatcher(None, s, s3, False).ratio()
0.8
>>> difflib.SequenceMatcher(None, s, s4, False).ratio()
0.46808510638297873
```

So `SequenceMatcher` was able to detect that s and s2 are very similar (98%), and apart from a typo in `weather`, they are in fact the same exact phrase. Then it stated that `Today the weather is nice` is 80% similar to `Yesterday the weather was nice` and finally that `Today the weather is nice` and `Today my dog ate steak` have very little in common.

There's more...

The `SequenceMatcher` provides support for marking some values as *junk*. You might expect this to mean that those values are ignored, but in fact that's not what happens.

Computing ratios with and without junk will return the same value in most cases:

```
>>> a = 'aaaaaaaaaaaaaXaaaaaaaaaa'
>>> b = 'X'
>>> difflib.SequenceMatcher(lambda c: c=='a', a, b, False).ratio()
0.08
>>> difflib.SequenceMatcher(None, a, b, False).ratio()
0.08
```

The a results were not ignored even though we provided an `isjunk` function that reports all a results as junk (the first argument to `SequenceMatcher`).

You can see by using `.get_matching_blocks()` that in both cases the only parts of the string that match are the X in position 13 and 0 for a and b:

```
>>> difflib.SequenceMatcher(None, a, b, False).get_matching_blocks()
[Match(a=13, b=0, size=1), Match(a=24, b=1, size=0)]
>>> difflib.SequenceMatcher(lambda c: c=='a', a, b,
False).get_matching_blocks()
[Match(a=13, b=0, size=1), Match(a=24, b=1, size=0)]
```

If you want to ignore some characters when computing the difference, you will have to strip them before running the `SequenceMatcher`, maybe using a translation map that discards them all:

```
>>> discardmap = str.maketrans({"a": None})
>>> difflib.SequenceMatcher(None, a.translate(discardmap),
b.translate(discardmap), False).ratio()
1.0
```

Text suggestion

In our previous recipe, we saw how `difflib` can compute the similitude between two strings. This means that we can compute the similitude between two words and suggest corrections to our users.

If the set of *correct* words is known (which usually is for any language), we can first check if the word is in this set and, if not, we can look for the most similar one to suggest to the user the right spelling.

How to do it...

The steps to follow this recipe are:

1. First of all we need the set of valid words. To avoid bringing in the whole English dictionary, we will just sample some words:

```
dictionary = {'ability', 'able', 'about', 'above', 'accept',
              'according',
              'account', 'across', 'act', 'action', 'activity',
              'actually',
              'add', 'address', 'administration', 'admit', 'adult',
```

```
'affect',
'after', 'again', 'against', 'age', 'agency',
'agent', 'ago',
'agree', 'agreement', 'ahead', 'air', 'all', 'allow',
'almost',
'alone', 'along', 'already', 'also', 'although',
'always',
'American', 'among', 'amount', 'analysis', 'and',
'animal',
'another', 'answer', 'any', 'anyone', 'anything',
'appear',
'apply', 'approach', 'area', 'argue',
'arm', 'around', 'arrive',
'art', 'article', 'artist', 'as', 'ask', 'assume',
'at', 'attack',
'attention', 'attorney', 'audience', 'author',
'authority',
'available', 'avoid', 'away', 'baby', 'back', 'bad',
'bag',
'ball', 'bank', 'bar', 'base', 'be', 'beat',
'beautiful',
'because', 'become'}
```

2. Then we can make a function that for any provided phrase looks for the words in our dictionary and, if they are not there, provides the most similar candidate through difflib:

```python
import difflib

def suggest(phrase):
    changes = 0
    words = phrase.split()
    for idx, w in enumerate(words):
        if w not in dictionary:
            changes += 1
            matches = difflib.get_close_matches(w, dictionary)
            if matches:
                words[idx] = matches[0]
    return changes, ' '.join(words)
```

3. Our `suggest` function will be able to detect misspellings and suggest a corrected phrase:

```
>>> suggest('assume ani answer')
(1, 'assume any answer')
>>> suggest('anoter agrement ahead')
(2, 'another agreement ahead')
```

The first returned argument is the number of wrong words detected and the second is the string with the most reasonable corrections.

4. If our phrase has no errors, we will just get back 0 with the original phrase:

```
>>> suggest('beautiful art')
(0, 'beautiful art')
```

Templating

A very frequent need when showing text to users is to generate it dynamically depending on the state of the software.

Typically, this leads to code like this:

```
name = 'Alessandro'
messages = ['Message 1', 'Message 2']

txt = 'Hello %s, You have %s message' % (name, len(messages))
if len(messages) > 1:
    txt += 's'
txt += ':n'
for msg in messages:
    txt += msg + 'n'
print(txt)
```

This makes it very hard to foresee the upcoming structure of the message and it's also very hard to maintain in the long term. To generate text, it's usually more convenient to reverse the approach and instead of putting text in code, we shall put code in text. That's exactly what template engines do and, while the standard library has very complete solutions for formatting, it lacks a template engine out of the box, but it can easily be extended to make one.

How to do it...

The steps for this recipe are:

1. The `string.Formatter` object allows you to extend its syntax, so we can specialize it to support injecting code into the expressions that it's going to accept:

```
import string

class TemplateFormatter(string.Formatter):
    def get_field(self, field_name, args, kwargs):
        if field_name.startswith("$"):
            code = field_name[1:]
            val = eval(code, {}, dict(kwargs))
            return val, field_name
        else:
            return super(TemplateFormatter,
self).get_field(field_name, args, kwargs)
```

2. Our `TemplateFormatter` can then be used to generate text similar to our example in a much cleaner way:

```
messages = ['Message 1', 'Message 2']

tmpl = TemplateFormatter()
txt = tmpl.format("Hello {name}, "
                  "You have {$len(messages)} message{$len(messages)
and 's'}:n{$'\n'.join(messages)}",
                  name='Alessandro', messages=messages)
print(txt)
```

The result should be:

```
Hello Alessandro, You have 2 messages:
Message 1
Message 2
```

How it works...

The `string.Formatter` supports the same language that the `str.format` method supports. Practically, it parses expressions contained with `{}` according to what Python calls *format string syntax*. Everything outside of `{}` is preserved as is, while anything within `{}` is parsed for the `field_name!conversion:format_spec` specification. So, as our `field_name` doesn't contain `!` or `:`, it can be anything else.

The `field_name` extracted is then provided to `Formatter.get_field` to look up the value of that field in the provided arguments of the `format` method.

So, for example, take an expression like:

```
string.Formatter().format("Hello {name}", name='Alessandro')
```

This leads to:

```
Hello Alessandro
```

Because the `{name}` is identified as a block to parse, the name is looked up in `.format` arguments and the rest is preserved as is.

This is very convenient and can solve most string formatting needs, but it lacks the power of a real template engine like loops and conditionals.

What we did is extended `Formatter` not only to resolve variables specified in `field_name`, but also to evaluate Python expressions.

As we know that all `field_name` resolutions go through `Formatter.get_field`, overriding that method in our own custom class would allow us to change what happens whenever a `field_name` like `{name}` is evaluated:

```
class TemplateFormatter(string.Formatter):
    def get_field(self, field_name, args, kwargs):
```

To distinguish plain variables from expressions, we used the `$` symbol. As a Python variable could never start with `$`, there was no risk that we would collide with an argument provided to format (as `str.format($something=5` is actually a syntax error in Python). So, a `field_name` like `{$something}` would not mean looking up the value of `'$something`, but to evaluate the `something` expression:

```
if field_name.startswith("$"):
    code = field_name[1:]
    val = eval(code, {}, dict(kwargs))
```

The `eval` function runs any code written in a string and restricts execution to an expression (expressions in Python always lead to a value, differently from statements which don't), so we also had syntax checking that would prevent template users from writing `if something: x='hi'`, which wouldn't provide any value to display in the text resulting from rendering the template.

Then, as we want users to be able to look up any variable that was referenced by the expressions they provided (like `{$len(messages)}`), we provide `kwargs` as the `locals` variables to `eval`, so that any expression referring to a variable would properly resolve. We also provide an empty global context `{}`, so that we don't inadvertently touch any global variable of our software.

The final part left is just returning the result of the expression execution provided by `eval` as the result of the `field_name` resolution:

```
return val, field_name
```

The really interesting part is that as all the processing happens in the `get_field` phase. Conversion and format specification are still supported as they are applied over the value returned by `get_field`.

This allows us to write something like:

```
{$3/2.0:.2f}
```

We get back `1.50` as the output instead of `1.5`. This is because we evaluate `3/2.0` as first thing in our specialized `TemplateFormatter.get_field` method and then the parser goes on applying the formatter specification (`.2f`) to the resulting value.

There's more...

Our simple template engine is convenient, but limited to cases where we can express the code generating our text as a set of expressions and static text.

The problem is that more advanced templates are not always possible to represent. We are restricted to plain expressions, so practically anything that cannot be represented in a `lambda` cannot be executed by our template engine.

While some would argue that very complex software can be written by combining multiple `lambda`, most people would recognize that statements lead to far more readable code.

For that reason, if you need to process very complex text, you should go to a full-featured template engine and look for something such as Jinja, Kajiki, or Mako as a solution to your problem. Especially for generating HTML, solutions such as Kajiki, which is also able to validate your HTML, are very convenient and can go much further than our `TemplateFormatter`.

Splitting strings and preserving spaces

Usually when splitting strings on spaces, developers will tend to rely on `str.split`, which is able to serve that purpose pretty well. But when the need to *split some spaces and preserve others* arises, things quickly become harder and implementing a custom solution can require investing time in proper escaping.

How to do it...

Just rely on `shlex.split` instead of `str.split`:

```
>>> import shlex
>>>
>>> text = 'I was sleeping at the "Windsdale Hotel"'
>>> print(shlex.split(text))
['I', 'was', 'sleeping', 'at', 'the', 'Windsdale Hotel']
```

How it works...

`shlex` is a module originally created to parse Unix shell code. For that reason, it supports preserving phrases through quotes. Typically, in Unix command lines, words separated by spaces are provided as arguments to the called command, but if you want to provide multiple words as a single argument, you can use quotes to group them.

That's exactly what `shlex` reproduces, providing us with a reliable way to drive the splitting. We just need to wrap everything we want to preserve in double or single quotes.

Cleanup text

When analyzing user-provided text, we are frequently interested only in meaningful words; punctuation, spaces, and conjunctions might easily get in our way. Suppose you want to count word frequencies in a book, you don't want to end up with "world" and "world" being counted as two different words.

How to do it...

You have to perform the following steps:

1. Supply the text you want to clean up:

```
txt = """And he looked over at the alarm clock,
ticking on the chest of drawers. "God in Heaven!" he thought.
It was half past six and the hands were quietly moving forwards,
it was even later than half past, more like quarter to seven.
Had the alarm clock not rung? He could see from the bed that it
had been set for four o'clock as it should have been; it certainly
must have rung.
Yes, but was it possible to quietly sleep through that furniture-
rattling noise?
True, he had not slept peacefully, but probably all the more deeply
because of that."""
```

2. We can rely on `string.punctuation` to know which characters we want to discard and make a translation table to discard them all:

```
>>> import string
>>> trans = str.maketrans('', '', string.punctuation)
>>> txt = txt.lower().translate(trans)
```

The result will be a cleaned-up version of our text:

```
"""and he looked over at the alarm clock
ticking on the chest of drawers god in heaven he thought
it was half past six and the hands were quietly moving forwards
it was even later than half past more like quarter to seven
had the alarm clock not rung he could see from the bed that it
had been set for four oclock as it should have been it certainly must have
rung
yes but was it possible to quietly sleep through that furniturerattling
noise
true he had not slept peacefully but probably all the more deeply because
of that"""
```

How it works...

The core of this recipe is the usage of translation tables. Translation tables are mappings that link a character to its replacement. A translation table like {'c': 'A'} means that any 'c' must be replaced with an 'A'.

str.maketrans is the function used to build translation tables. Each character in the first argument will be mapped to the character in the same position in the second argument. Then all characters in the last argument will be mapped to None:

```
>>> str.maketrans('a', 'b', 'c')
{97: 98, 99: None}
```

The 97, 98, and 99 are the Unicode values for 'a', 'b', and 'c':

```
>>> print(ord('a'), ord('b'), ord('c'))
97 98 99
```

Then our mapping can be passed to str.translate to apply it on the target string. The interesting part is that any character that is mapped to None will be just removed:

```
>>> 'ciao'.translate(str.maketrans('a', 'b', 'c'))
'ibo'
```

In our previous example, we provided as str.maketrans the third argument string.punctuation.

string.punctuation is a string that contains the most common punctuation characters:

```
>>> string.punctuation
'!"#$%&\'()*+,-./:;<=>?@[\\]^_`{|}~'
```

By doing so, we built a transaction map that mapped each punctuation character to None and didn't specify any other mapping:

```
>>> str.maketrans('', '', string.punctuation)
{64: None, 124: None, 125: None, 91: None, 92: None, 93: None,
 94: None, 95: None, 96: None, 33: None, 34: None, 35: None,
 36: None, 37: None, 38: None, 39: None, 40: None, 41: None,
 42: None, 43: None, 44: None, 45: None, 46: None, 47: None,
 123: None, 126: None, 58: None, 59: None, 60: None, 61: None,
 62: None, 63: None}
```

This, once applied with `str.translate`, made it so that punctuation characters were all discarded, preserving all the other characters as they were:

```
>>> 'This, is. A test!'.translate(str.maketrans('', '',
string.punctuation))
'This is A test'
```

Normalizing text

In many cases, a single word can be written in multiple ways. For example, users who wrote "Über" and "Uber" probably meant the same word. If you were implementing a feature like tagging for a blog, you certainly don't want to end up with two different tags for the two words.

So, before saving your tags, you might want to normalize them to plain ASCII characters so that they end up all being considered as the same tag.

How to do it...

What we need is a translation map that converts all accented characters to their plain representation:

```
import unicodedata, sys

class unaccented_map(dict):
    def __missing__(self, key):
        ch = self.get(key)
        if ch is not None:
            return ch
        de = unicodedata.decomposition(chr(key))
        if de:
            try:
```

```
                    ch = int(de.split(None, 1)[0], 16)
            except (IndexError, ValueError):
                ch = key
        else:
            ch = key
        self[key] = ch
        return ch


unaccented_map = unaccented_map()
```

Then we can apply it to any word to normalize it:

```
>>> 'Über'.translate(unaccented_map) Uber >>>
'garçon'.translate(unaccented_map) garcon
```

How it works...

We already know as explained in the *Cleanup text* recipe how `str.translate` works: each character is looked up in a translation table and it's substituted with the replacement specified in the table.

So, what we need is a translation table that maps "Ü" to "U" and "ç" to "c", and so on.

But how can we know all these mappings? One interesting property of these characters is that they can be considered plain characters with an added symbol. Much like à can be considered an a with an accent.

Unicode equivalence knows this and provides multiple ways to write what's considered the same character. What we are really interested in is decomposed form, which means to write a character as multiple separated symbols that define it. For example, é would be decomposed to `0065` and `0301`, which are the code points for e and the accent.

Python provides a way to know the decomposed version of a character through the `unicodedata.decompostion` function:

```
>>> import unicodedata
>>> unicodedata.decomposition('é')
'0065 0301'
```

The first code point is the one of the base character, while the second is the added symbol. So to normalize our è, we would pick the first code point `0065` and throw away the symbol:

```
>>> unicodedata.decomposition('é').split()[0]
'0065'
```

Now we can't use the code point by itself, but we want the character it represents. Luckily, the `chr` function provides a way to get a character from the integer representation of its code point.

The `unicodedata.decomposition` function provided the code points as strings representing hexadecimal numbers, so first we need to convert them to integers:

```
>>> int('0065', 16)
101
```

Then we can apply `chr` to know the actual character:

```
>>> chr(101)
'e'
```

Now we know how to decompose these characters and get the base characters to which we want to normalize them all, but how can we build a translation map for all of them?

The answer is we don't. Building the translation map beforehand for all characters wouldn't be very convenient, so we can use a feature provided by dictionaries to build the translation for a character dynamically when it's needed.

Translation maps are dictionaries and whenever a dictionary needs to look up a key that it doesn't know, it can rely on the `__missing__` method to generate a value for that key. So our `__missing__` method has to do what we just did and use `unicodedata.decomposition` to grab the normalized version of a character whenever `str.translate` tries to look it up in our translation map.

Once we have computed the translation for the requested character, we just store it in the dictionary itself, so the next time it will be asked for, we won't have to compute it again.

So, the `unaccented_map` of our recipe is just a dictionary providing a `__missing__` method that relies on `unicodedata.decompostion` to retrieve the normalized version of each provided character.

If it is unable to find a denormalized version of the character, it will just return the original version once so that the string doesn't get corrupted.

Aligning text

When printing tabular data, it's usually very important to ensure that the text is properly aligned to a fixed length, no longer and no shorter than the space we reserved for our table cell.

If the text is too short, the next column might start too early; if it's too long, it might start too late. This leads to results like this:

```
col1 | col2-1
col1-2 | col2-2
```

Or this:

```
col1-000001 | col2-1
col1-2 | col2-2
```

Both of these are really hard to read and are far from showing a proper table.

Given a fixed column width (20 characters), we want our text to always be of that exact length so that it won't result in a misaligned table.

How to do it...

Here are the steps for this recipe:

1. The `textwrap` module once combined with the features of the `str` object can help us achieve the expected result. First we need the content of the columns we want to print:

```
cols = ['hello world',
        'this is a long text, maybe longer than expected, surely
long enough',
        'one more column']
```

2. Then we need to fix the size of a column:

```
COLSIZE = 20
```

3. Once those are ready, we can actually implement our indentation function:

```
import textwrap, itertools

def maketable(cols):
    return 'n'.join(map(' | '.join, itertools.zip_longest(*[
        [s.ljust(COLSIZE) for s in textwrap.wrap(col, COLSIZE)] for
col in cols
    ], fillvalue=' '*COLSIZE)))
```

4. Then we can properly print any table:

```
>>> print(maketable(cols))
hello world          | this is a long text, | one more column
                     | maybe longer than    |
                     | expected, surely     |
                     | long enough          |
```

How it works...

There are three problems we have to solve to implement our `maketable` function:

- Lengthen text shorter than 20 characters
- Split text longer than 20 characters on multiple lines
- Fill missing lines in columns with fewer lines

If we decompose our `maketable` function, the first thing it does is to split text longer than 20 characters into multiple lines:

```
[textwrap.wrap(col, COLSIZE) for col in cols]
```

That applied to each column leads us to having a list of columns, each containing a list of rows:

```
[['hello world'],
 ['this is a long text,', 'maybe longer than', 'expected, surely', 'long
enough'],
 ['one more column']]
```

Then we need to ensure that each row shorter than 20 characters is extended to be exactly 20 characters, so that our table retains shape, and that's achieved by applying the `ljust` method to each row:

```
[[s.ljust(COLSIZE) for s in textwrap.wrap(col, COLSIZE)] for col in cols]
```

Combining `ljust` with `textwrap` leads to the result we were looking for: a list of columns containing rows of 20 characters each:

```
[['hello world          '],
 ['this is a long text,', 'maybe longer than   ', 'expected, surely    ',
'long enough          '],
 ['one more column      ']]
```

Now we need to find a way to flip rows and columns, as when printing we need to print by row due to the `print` function printing one row at a time. Also, we need to ensure that each column has the same amount of rows, as we need to print all the rows when printing by row.

Both these needs can be solved by the `itertools.zip_longest` function, which will generate a new list by interleaving the values contained in each one of the provided lists until the longest list is exhausted. As `zip_longest` goes on until the longest iterable is exhausted, it supports a `fillvalue` argument that can be used to specify a value used to fill values for shorter lists:

```
list(itertools.zip_longest(*[
    [s.ljust(COLSIZE) for s in textwrap.wrap(col, COLSIZE)] for col in cols
], fillvalue=' '*COLSIZE))
```

The result will be a list of rows, each containing a column, with empty columns for rows that didn't have a value for them:

```
[('hello world          ', 'this is a long text,', 'one more column      '),
 ('                      ', 'maybe longer than   ', '                     '),
 ('                      ', 'expected, surely    ', '                     '),
 ('                      ', 'long enough         ', '                     ')]
```

The tabular form of the text is now clearly visible. The last two steps in our function involve adding a | separator between the columns and merging the columns in a single string through ' | '.join:

```
map(' | '.join, itertools.zip_longest(*[
    [s.ljust(COLSIZE) for s in textwrap.wrap(col, COLSIZE)] for col in cols
], fillvalue=' '*COLSIZE))
```

This will result in a list of strings containing the text of all three columns:

```
['hello world          | this is a long text, | one more column      ',
 '                      | maybe longer than    |                      ',
 '                      | expected, surely     |                      ',
 '                      | long enough           |                     ']
```

Finally, the rows can be printed. For the purpose of returning a single string, our function applies one last step and joins all the lines in a single string separated by newline characters by applying a final `'n'.join()`, which leads to returning a single string containing the whole text ready for printing:

```
'''hello world        | this is a long text, | one more column
                       | maybe longer than    |
                       | expected, surely     |
                       | long enough          |                    '''
```

3
Command Line

In this chapter, we will cover following recipes:

- Basic logging—logging allows you to keep track of what the software is doing, and it's usually unrelated to its output
- Logging to file—when logging is frequent, it is necessary to store the logs on a disk
- Logging to Syslog—if your system has a Syslog daemon, you might want to log in to Syslog instead of using a standalone file
- Parsing arguments—when writing with command-line tools, you need parsing options for practically any tool
- Interactive shells—sometimes options are not enough and you need a form of Read-Eval-Print Loop to drive your tool
- Sizing terminal text—to align the displayed output properly, we need to know the terminal window size
- Running system commands—how to integrate other third-party commands in your software
- Progress bar—how to show a progress bar in your text tool
- Message boxes—how to display an OK/cancel message box in a text tool
- Input box—how to ask for input in a text tool

Introduction

When writing a new tool, one of the first needs that arises is making it able to interact with the surrounding environment—to display results, track errors, and receive inputs.

Users are accustomed to certain standard ways a command-line tool interacts with them and with the system, and following this standard might be time-consuming and hard if done from scratch.

That's why the standard library in Python provides tools to achieve the most common needs in implementing software that is able to interact through a shell and through text.

In this chapter, we will see how to implement some forms of logging, so that our program can keep a log file; we will see how to implement both options-based and interactive software, and then we will see how to implement more advanced graphical output based on text.

Basic logging

One of the first requirements of a console software is for it to log what it does, that is, what's happened, and any warnings or errors. Especially when we are talking about long-term software or daemons running in the background.

Sadly, if you've ever tried to use the Python `logging` module, you've probably noticed that you can't get any output apart from errors.

That's because the default enabled level is WARNING, so that only warnings and worse are tracked. Little tweaks are needed to make logging generally available.

How to do it...

For this recipe, the steps are as follows:

1. The `logging` module allows us to easily set up the logging configuration through the `basicConfig` method:

    ```
    >>> import logging, sys
    >>>
    >>> logging.basicConfig(level=logging.INFO, stream=sys.stderr,
    ...                     format='%(asctime)s %(name)s %(levelname)s:
    %(message)s')
    >>> log = logging.getLogger(__name__)
    ```

2. Now that our `logger` is properly configured, we can try using it:

    ```
    >>> def dosum(a, b, count=1):
    ...     log.info('Starting sum')
    ...     if a == b == 0:
    ...         log.warning('Will be just 0 for any count')
    ...     res = (a + b) * count
    ...     log.info('(%s + %s) * %s = %s' % (a, b, count, res))
    ```

```
...         print(res)
...
>>> dosum(5, 3)
2018-02-11 22:07:59,870 __main__ INFO: Starting sum
2018-02-11 22:07:59,870 __main__ INFO: (5 + 3) * 1 = 8
8
>>> dosum(5, 3, count=2)
2018-02-11 22:07:59,870 __main__ INFO: Starting sum
2018-02-11 22:07:59,870 __main__ INFO: (5 + 3) * 2 = 16
16
>>> dosum(0, 1, count=5)
2018-02-11 22:07:59,870 __main__ INFO: Starting sum
2018-02-11 22:07:59,870 __main__ INFO: (0 + 1) * 5 = 5
5
>>> dosum(0, 0)
2018-02-11 22:08:00,621 __main__ INFO: Starting sum
2018-02-11 22:08:00,621 __main__ WARNING: Will be just 0 for any
count
2018-02-11 22:08:00,621 __main__ INFO: (0 + 0) * 1 = 0
0
```

How it works...

logging.basicConfig configures the root logger (the main logger, Python will use if no specific configuration for the used logger is found) to write anything at the INFO level or greater. This will allow us to show everything apart from the debugging messages. The format argument specifies how our logging messages should be formatted; in this case, we added the date and time, the name of the logger, the level at which we are logging, and the message itself. Finally, the stream argument tells the logger to write its output to the standard error.

Once we have the root logger configured, any logging we pick that doesn't have a specific configuration will just end up using the root logger one.

So the next line, logging.getLogger(__name__), gets a logger named similar to the Python module that it's executing. If you saved your code to a file, the logger will be named something such as dosum (given your file is named dosum.py); if you didn't, then the logger will be named __main__, as in the previous example.

Python loggers are created the first time they are retrieved with `logging.getLogger`, and any subsequent call to `getLogger` will just return the already existing one. While, for a very simple program, the name won't matter much, in bigger software, it's usually a good idea to grab more than one logger, so that you can distinguish from which subsystem of your software the messages are coming.

There's more...

You might be wondering why we configured `logging` to send its output to `stderr`, instead of the standard output. This allows us to separate the output of our software (which is written to `stdout` through the print statements) from the logging information. This is usually a good practice because the user of your tool might need to call the output of your tool without all the noise generated by logging messages, and doing so allows us to call our script with something such as the following:

```
$ python dosum.py 2>/dev/null
8
16
5
0
```

We'll only get back the results, without all the noise, because we redirected `stderr` to `/dev/null`, which on Unix systems leads to throwing away all that was written to `stderr`.

Logging to file

For long-running programs, logging to the screen is not a very viable option. After running the code for hours, the oldest logged messages will be lost, and even if they were still available, it wouldn't be very easy to read all the logs or search through them.

Saving logs to a file allows for unlimited length (as far as our disk allows it) and enables the usage of tools, such as `grep`, to search through them.

By default, Python logging is configured to write to screen, but it's easy to provide a way to write to any file when logging is configured.

How to do it...

To test `logging` to a file, we are going to create a short tool that computes up to the nth Fibonacci number based on the current time. If it's 3:01 P.M., we want to compute only 1 number, while if it's 3:59 P.M., we want to compute 59 numbers.

The software will provide the computed numbers as the output, but we also want to log up to which number it computed and when it was run:

```python
import logging, sys

if __name__ == '__main__':
    if len(sys.argv) < 2:
        print('Please provide logging file name as argument')
        sys.exit(1)

    logging_file = sys.argv[1]
    logging.basicConfig(level=logging.INFO, filename=logging_file,
                        format='%(asctime)s %(name)s %(levelname)s:
%(message)s')

log = logging.getLogger(__name__)

def fibo(num):
    log.info('Computing up to %sth fibonacci number', num)
    a, b = 0, 1
    for n in range(num):
        a, b = b, a+b
        print(b, '', end='')
    print(b)

if __name__ == '__main__':
    import datetime
    fibo(datetime.datetime.now().second)
```

How it works...

The code is split into three sections: initializing logging, the `fibo` function, and the `main` function of our tool. We explicitly divided code this way because the `fibo` function might be used in other modules, and in such a case, we don't want `logging` to be reconfigured; we just want to use the logging configuration that the program will provide. For that reason, the `logging.basicConfig` call is wrapped in `__name__ == '__main__'` so that `logging` is only configured when the module is called directly as a tool and not when it's imported by other modules.

When multiple `logging.basicConfig` instances are called, only the first one will be considered. If we didn't wrap our logging configuration in `if` when imported by other modules, it might end up driving the whole software logging configuration, depending on the order the modules were imported in, which is something we clearly don't want.

Differently from our previous recipe, `basicConfig` is configured with the `filename` argument instead of the `stream` argument. This means `logging.FileHandler` will be created to handle the logging messages and the messages will be appended to that file.

The central part of the code is the `fibo` function itself, and the last part is a check to see whether the code was called as a Python script or imported as a module. When imported as a module, we just want to provide the `fibo` function and avoid running it, but when executed as a script, we want to compute the Fibonacci numbers.

You might be wondering why I used two `if __name__ == '__main__'` sections; if you merge the two into one, the script will continue to work. But it's usually a good idea to ensure that `logging` is configured before trying to use it, or the result will be that we will end up using the `logging.lastResort` handler, which will just write to `stderr` until the logging is configured.

Logging to Syslog

Unix-like systems usually provide a way to gather logging messages through the `syslog` protocol, which allows us to separate the system storing the logs from the one generating them.

Especially in the context of applications distributed across multiple servers, this is very convenient; you certainly don't want to log into 20 different servers to gather all the logs of your Python application because it was running on multiple nodes. Especially for web applications, this is very common nowadays with cloud providers, so it's very convenient to be able to gather all the Python logs in a single place.

That's exactly what using `syslog` allows us to do; we will see how to send the log messages to the daemon running on our system, but it's possible to send them to any system.

Getting ready

While this recipe doesn't need a `syslog` daemon to work, you will need one to check that it's properly working or the messages won't be readable. In the case of Linux or macOS systems, this is usually configured out of the box, but in the case of a Windows system, you will need to install a Syslog server or use a cloud solution. Many exist and a quick search on Google should provide you with some cheap or even free alternatives.

How to do it...

When using a heavily customized solution for logging, it's not possible to rely on `logging.basicConfig` anymore, so we will have to manually set up the logging environment:

```python
import logging
import logging.config

# OSX logs through /var/run/syslog this should be /dev/log
# on Linux system or a tuple ('ADDRESS', PORT) to log to a remote server
SYSLOG_ADDRESS = '/var/run/syslog'

logging.config.dictConfig({
    'version': 1,
    'formatters': {
        'default': {
            'format': '%(asctime)s %(name)s: %(levelname)s %(message)s'
        },
    },
    'handlers': {
        'syslog': {
            'class': 'logging.handlers.SysLogHandler',
            'formatter': 'default',
            'address': SYSLOG_ADDRESS
        }
    },
    'root': {
        'handlers': ['syslog'],
        'level': 'INFO'
    }
})

log = logging.getLogger()
log.info('Hello Syslog!')
```

If this worked properly, your message should be recorded by Syslog and visible when running the `syslog` command on macOS or with `tail` as `/var/log/syslog` on Linux:

```
$ syslog | tail -n 2
Feb 18 17:52:43 Pulsar Google Chrome[294] <Error>: ... SOME CHROME ERROR
MESSAGE ...
Feb 18 17:53:48 Pulsar 2018-02-18 17[4294967295] <Info>: 53:48,610 INFO
root Hello Syslog!
```

 The `syslog` file path might change from distribution to distribution; if `/var/log/syslog` doesn't work, try `/var/log/messages` or refer to your distribution documentation.

There's more...

As we relied on `dictConfig`, you noticed that our configuration is a bit more complex than in previous recipes. This is because we configured the bits that are part of the logging infrastructure ourselves.

Whenever you configure logging, you write your messages with a logger. By default, the system only has one logger: the `root` logger (the one you get if you call `logging.getLogger` without providing any specific name).

The logger doesn't handle messages itself, as writing or printing log messages is something handlers are in charge of. Consequently, if you want to read the log messages you send, you need to configure a handler. In our case, we use `SysLogHandler`, which writes to Syslog.

Handler is then in charge of writing a message, but doesn't really get involved in how that message should be built/formatted. You noticed that apart your own message, when you log something, you also get the log level, logger name, timestamp, and a few details that are added by the logging system for you. Adding those details to the message is usually the formatter's work. The formatter takes all the information made available by the logger and packs them in a message that should be written by the handler.

Last but not least, your logging configuration can be very complex. You can set up some messages to go to a local file and some messages to go to Syslog and more that should be printed on screen. This would involve multiple handlers, which should know which messages they should threat and which they should ignore. Allowing this knowledge is the job of filters. Once you attach a filter to a handler, it's possible to control which messages should be saved by that handler and which should be ignored.

The Python logging system might now look very intuitive, and that's because it's a very powerful solution that can be configured in many ways, but once you understand the building blocks that are available, it's possible to combine them in very flexible ways.

Parsing arguments

When writing command-line tools, it's usually common to have it change behavior based on options provided to the executable. These options are usually available in `sys.argv` together with the executable name, but parsing them is not as easy as it might seem, especially when multiple arguments must be supported. Also, when an option is malformed, it's usually a good idea to provide a usage message to inform the user about the right way to use the tool.

How to do it...

Perform the following steps for this recipe:

1. The `argparse.ArgumentParser` object is the primary object in charge of parsing command-line options:

```
import argparse
import operator
import logging
import functools

parser = argparse.ArgumentParser(
    description='Applies an operation to one or more numbers'
)
parser.add_argument("number",
                    help="One or more numbers to perform an
operation on.",
                    nargs='+', type=int)
parser.add_argument('-o', '--operation',
                    help="The operation to perform on numbers.",
                    choices=['add', 'sub', 'mul', 'div'],
default='add')
parser.add_argument("-v", "--verbose", action="store_true",
                    help="increase output verbosity")

opts = parser.parse_args()

logging.basicConfig(level=logging.INFO if opts.verbose else
logging.WARNING)
```

```
log = logging.getLogger()

operation = getattr(operator, opts.operation)
log.info('Applying %s to %s', opts.operation, opts.number)
print(functools.reduce(operation, opts.number))
```

2. Once our command is called without any arguments, it will provide a short usage text:

```
$ python /tmp/doop.py
usage: doop.py [-h] [-o {add,sub,mul,div}] [-v] number [number ...]
doop.py: error: the following arguments are required: number
```

3. If we provide the -h option, argparse will generate a complete usage guide for us:

```
$ python /tmp/doop.py -h
usage: doop.py [-h] [-o {add,sub,mul,div}] [-v] number [number ...]

Applies an operation to one or more numbers

positional arguments:
number                  One or more numbers to perform an operation
on.

optional arguments:
-h, --help              show this help message and exit
-o {add,sub,mul,div}, --operation {add,sub,mul,div}
                        The operation to perform on numbers.
-v, --verbose           increase output verbosity
```

4. Using the command will lead to the expected result:

```
$ python /tmp/dosum.py 1 2 3 4 -o mul
24
```

How it works...

We used the ArgumentParser.add_argument method to populate the list of available options. For every argument, it's possible to also provide a help option, which will declare the help string for that argument.

Positional arguments are provided with just the name of the argument:

```
parser.add_argument("number",
                    help="One or more numbers to perform an operation on.",
                    nargs='+', type=int)
```

The `nargs` option tells `ArgumentParser` how many times we expect that argument to be specified, the + value means at least once or more than once. Then `type=int` tells us that the arguments should be converted to integers.

Once we have the numbers to which we want to apply the operation, we need to know the operation itself:

```
parser.add_argument('-o', '--operation',
                    help="The operation to perform on numbers.",
                    choices=['add', 'sub', 'mul', 'div'], default='add')
```

In this case, we specified an option (starts with a dash, -), which can be provided both as -o or --operation. We stated that the only possible values are 'add', 'sub', 'mul', or 'div' (providing a different value will result in `argparse` complaining), and that the default value, if the user didn't specify one, is `add`.

As a best practice, our command prints only the result; it was convenient to be able to ask some logging about what it was going to do. For this reason, we provided the `verbose` option, which drives the logging level we enabled for our command:

```
parser.add_argument("-v", "--verbose", action="store_true",
                    help="increase output verbosity")
```

If that option is provided, we will just store that `verbose` mode is enabled (`action="store_true"` makes it so that `True` is stored in `opts.verbose`) and we will configure the `logging` module accordingly, such that our `log.info` is only visible when `verbose` is enabled.

Finally, we can actually parse the command-line options and get the result back into the `opts` object:

```
opts = parser.parse_args()
```

Once we have the options available, we configure logging so that we can read the `verbose` option and configure it accordingly:

```
logging.basicConfig(level=logging.INFO if opts.verbose else
logging.WARNING)
```

Once options are parsed and `logging` is configured, the rest is just actually performing the expected operation on the set of provided numbers and printing the result:

```
operation = getattr(operator, opts.operation)
log.info('Applying %s to %s', opts.operation, opts.number)
print(functools.reduce(operation, opts.number))
```

There's more...

If you mix command-line options with the *Dictionary with fallback* recipe in `Chapter 1`, *Containers and Data Structures*, you can extend the behavior of your tools to not only read options from the command line, but also from environment variables, which is usually very convenient when you don't have complete control over how the command is called but you can set environment variables.

Interactive shells

Sometimes, writing a command-line tool is not enough, and you need to be able to provide some sort of interactivity. Suppose you want to write a mail client. In this case, it's not very convenient to have to call `mymail list` to see your mail, or `mymail read` to read a specific mail from your shell, and so on. Furthermore, if you want to implement stateful behaviors—such as a `mymail reply` instance that should reply to the current mail you are viewing—this might not even be possible.

Interactive programs are better in these cases, and the Python standard library provides all the tools we need to write one through the `cmd` module.

We can try to write an interactive shell for our `mymail` program; it won't read real email, but we will fake the behavior enough to showcase a fully featured shell.

How to do it...

The steps for this recipe are as follows:

1. The `cmd.Cmd` class allows us to start interactive shells and implement commands based on them:

```
EMAILS = [
    {'sender': 'author1@domain.com', 'subject': 'First email',
     'body': 'This is my first email'},
```

```
        {'sender': 'author2@domain.com', 'subject': 'Second email',
         'body': 'This is my second email'},
]

import cmd
import shlex

class MyMail(cmd.Cmd):
    intro = 'Simple interactive email client.'
    prompt = 'mymail> '

    def __init__(self, *args, **kwargs):
        super(MyMail, self).__init__(*args, **kwargs)
        self.selected_email = None

    def do_list(self, line):
        """list

        List emails currently in the Inbox"""
        for idx, email in enumerate(EMAILS):
            print('[{idx}] From: {e[sender]} -
                    {e[subject]}'.format(
                    idx=idx, e=email
            ))

    def do_read(self, emailnum):
        """read [emailnum]

        Reads emailnum nth email from those listed in the Inbox"""
        try:
            idx = int(emailnum.strip())
        except:
            print('Invalid email index {}'.format(emailnum))
            return

        try:
            email = EMAILS[idx]
        except IndexError:
            print('Email {} not found'.format(idx))
            return

        print('From: {e[sender]}\n'
              'Subject: {e[subject]}\n'
              '\n{e[body]}'.format(e=email))
        # Track the last read email as the selected one for reply.
        self.selected_email = idx

    def do_reply(self, message):
```

```
        """reply [message]

        Sends back an email to the author of the received email"""
        if self.selected_email is None:
            print('No email selected for reply.')
            return

        email = EMAILS[self.selected_email]
        print('Replied to {e[sender]} with: {message}'.format(
            e=email, message=message
        ))

    def do_send(self, arguments):
        """send [recipient] [subject] [message]

        Send a new email with [subject] to [recipient]"""
        # Split the arguments with shlex
        # so that we allow subject or message with spaces.
        args = shlex.split(arguments)
        if len(args) < 3:
            print('A recipient, a subject and a message are
                    required.')
            return

        recipient, subject, message = args[:3]
        if len(args) >= 4:
            message += ' '.join(args[3:])

        print('Sending email {} to {}: "{}"'.format(
            subject, recipient, message
        ))

    def complete_send(self, text, line, begidx, endidx):
        # Provide autocompletion of recipients for send command.
        return [e['sender'] for e in EMAILS if
e['sender'].startswith(text)]

    def do_EOF(self, line):
        return True

if __name__ == '__main__':
    MyMail().cmdloop()
```

2. Starting our script should provide a nice interactive prompt:

```
$ python /tmp/mymail.py
Simple interactive email client.
mymail> help
```

```
Documented commands (type help <topic>):
========================================
help  list  read  reply  send

Undocumented commands:
======================
EOF
```

3. As stated with documents, we should be able to read the list of emails, read a specific email, and reply to the currently open one:

```
mymail> list
[0] From: author1@domain.com - First email
[1] From: author2@domain.com - Second email
mymail> read 0
From: author1@domain.com
Subject: First email

This is my first email
mymail> reply Thanks for your message!
Replied to author1@domain.com with: Thanks for your message!
```

4. Then, we can rely on the more advanced send commands, which also provide autocompletion of recipients for our new emails:

```
mymail> help send
send [recipient] [subject] [message]

Send a new email with [subject] to [recipient]
mymail> send author
author1@domain.com  author2@domain.com
mymail> send author2@domain.com "Saw your email" "I saw your
message, thanks for sending it!"
Sending email Saw your email to author2@domain.com: "I saw your
message, thanks for sending it!"
mymail>
```

How it works...

The `cmd.Cmd` loop prints the `prompt` we provided through the `prompt` class property and awaits a command. Anything we write after `prompt` is split and the first part is looked up against the list of methods provided by our own subclass.

Whenever a command is provided, `cmd.Cmd.cmdloop` calls the associated method and then starts again.

Any method starting with do_* is a command, and the part after do_ is the command name. Any docstring of the method implementing the command is then reported in our tool's documentation if the help command is used within the interactive prompt.

The Cmd class provides no facility to parse arguments for a command, so if your command has more than a single argument, your have to split them yourself. In our case, we relied on shlex so that the user has control over how the arguments should be split. This allowed us to parse subjects and messages while providing a way to include spaces in them. Otherwise, we would have no way to know where the subject ends and the message starts.

The send command also supports autocompleting recipients, through the complete_send method. If a complete_* method is provided, it is called by Cmd when *Tab* is pressed to autocomplete command arguments. The method receives the text that needs to be completed and some details about the whole line of text and the current position of the cursor. As nothing is done to parse the arguments, the position of the cursors and the whole line of text can help in providing different autocomplete behaviors for each argument. In our case, we could only autocomplete the recipient, so there was no need to distinguish between the various arguments.

Last but not least, the do_EOF command allows a way to exit the command line when *Ctrl + D* is pressed. Otherwise, we would have to way to quit the interactive shell. That's a convention provided by Cmd, and if the do_EOF command returns True, it means that the shell can quit.

Sizing terminal text

We saw the *Aligning text* recipe in Chapter 2, *Text Management*, which showcased a possible solution to align text within a fixed space. The amount of space available was defined in a COLSIZE constant that was chosen to fit most terminals with three columns (most terminals fit 80 columns).

But what happened if the user had a terminal window smaller than 60 columns? Our alignment would have been broken badly. Also, on very big windows, while the text wouldn't be broken, it would have looked too small compared to the window.

For this reason, it's usually better to also take into consideration the size of the user terminal window whenever displaying text that should retain proper alignment properties.

How to do it...

The steps are as follows:

1. The `shutil.get_terminal_size` function can give guidance on the terminal window size and provide a fallback for cases where it's not available. We will adapt the `maketable` function from the *Aligning text* recipe of `Chapter 2`, *Text Management* to account for terminal size:

```
import shutil
import textwrap, itertools

def maketable(cols):
    term_size = shutil.get_terminal_size(fallback=(80, 24))
    colsize = (term_size.columns // len(cols)) - 3
    if colsize < 1:
        raise ValueError('Column too small')
    return '\n'.join(map(' | '.join, itertools.zip_longest(*[
        [s.ljust(colsize) for s in textwrap.wrap(col, colsize)] for
col in cols
    ], fillvalue=' '*colsize)))
```

2. Now it is possible to print any text in multiple columns and see it adapt to the size of your terminal window:

```
COLUMNS = 5
TEXT = ['Lorem ipsum dolor sit amet, consectetuer adipiscing elit.
'
        'Aenean commodo ligula eget dolor. Aenean massa. '
        'Cum sociis natoque penatibus et magnis dis parturient
montes, '
        'nascetur ridiculus mus'] * COLUMNS

print(maketable(TEXT))
```

If you try to resize you terminal window and rerun the script, you will notice that the text is now always aligned differently to ensure it fits the space available.

How it works...

Instead of relying on a constant for the size of a column, our `maketable` function now computes it by taking the terminal width (`term_size.columns`) and dividing it by the number of columns to show.

Three characters are always subtracted, because we want to account for the space consumed by the | separator.

The size of the terminal (`term_size`) is fetched through `shutil.get_terminal_size`, which will look at `stdout` to check the size of the connected terminal.

If it fails to retrieve the size or something that is not a terminal is connected as the output, then a fallback value is used. You can check the fallback value is working as expected simply by redirecting the output of your script to a file:

```
$ python myscript.py > output.txt
```

If you open `output.txt`, you should see that the fallback of 80 characters was used as a file doesn't have any specified width.

Running system commands

In some cases, especially when writing system tools, there might be work that you need to offload to another command. For example, if you have to decompress a file, in many cases, it might make sense to offload the work to `gunzip`/`zip` commands instead or trying to reproduce the same behavior in Python.

While there are many ways in Python to handle this work, they all have subtle differences that might make the life of any developer hard, so it's good to have a generally working solution that tackles the most common issues.

How to do it...

Perform the following steps:

1. Combining the `subprocess` and `shlex` modules allows us to build a solution that is reliable in most cases:

```
import shlex
import subprocess
```

```
def run(command):
    try:
        result = subprocess.check_output(shlex.split(command),
                                         stderr=subprocess.STDOUT)
        return 0, result
    except subprocess.CalledProcessError as e:
        return e.returncode, e.output
```

2. It's easy to check that it works as expected both for successful and failing commands:

```
for path in ('/', '/should_not_exist'):
    status, out = run('ls "{}"'.format(path))
    if status == 0:
        print('<Success>')
    else:
        print('<Error: {}>'.format(status))
    print(out)
```

3. On my system, this properly lists the root of the filesystem and complains for a non-existing path:

```
<Success>
Applications
Developer
Library
LibraryPreferences
Network
...

<Error: 2>
ls: cannot access /should_not_exist: No such file or directory
```

How it works...

Calling the command itself is performed by the `subprocess.check_output` function, but before we can call it, we need to properly split the command in a list containing the command itself and its arguments. Relying on `shlex` allows us to drive and distinguish how arguments should be split. To see its effect, you can try to compare `run('ls / var')` with `run('ls "/ var"')` on any Unix-like system. The first will print a lot of files, while the second will complain that the path doesn't exist. That's because, in the first case, we actually sent two different arguments to `ls` (/ and var), while in the second case, we sent a single argument ("/ var"). If we didn't use `shlex`, there would have been no way to distinguish between the two cases.

Passing the `stderr=subprocess.STDOUT` option then takes care of cases where the command fails (which we can detect because the `run` function will return a status that is not zero), allowing us to receive the failure description.

The heavy lifting of calling our command is then performed by `subprocess.check_output`, which, in fact, is a wrapper around `subprocess.Popen` that will do two things:

1. Spawn the required command with `subprocess.Popen`, configured to write the output into a pipe, so that the parent process (our own program) can read from that pipe and grab the output.
2. Spawn threads to continuously consume from the content of the pipes opened to communicate with the child process. This ensures that they never fill up, as, if they did, the command we called would just block as it would be unable to write any more output.

There's more...

One important thing to note is that our `run` function will look for an executable that can satisfy the requested command, but won't run any shell expression. So, it's not possible to send shell scripts to it. If that's required, the `shell=True` option can be passed to `subprocess.check_output`, but that's heavily discouraged because it allows the injection of shell code into our program.

Suppose you want to write a command that prints the content of a directory that the user choose; a very simple solution might be the following:

```python
import sys
if len(sys.argv) < 2:
    print('Please provide a directory')
    sys.exit(1)
_, out = run('ls {}'.format(sys.argv[1]))
print(out)
```

Now, what would happen if we allowed `shell=True` in `run` and the user provided a path such as `/var; rm -rf /`? The user might end up deleting the whole system disk, and while this is still limited by the fact that we are relying on `shlex` to split arguments, it's still not safe to go through a shell to just run a command.

Progress bar

When doing work that requires a lot of time (usually anything that requires I/O endpoints, such as disk or network), it's a good idea to let your user know that you are moving forward and how much work is left to do. Progress bars, while not precise, are a very good way to give our users an overview of how much work we have done so far and how much we have left to do.

How to do it...

The recipe steps are as follows:

1. The progress bar itself will be displayed by a decorator, so that we can apply it to any function for which we want to report progress with minimum effort:

```python
import shutil, sys

def withprogressbar(func):
    """Decorates ``func`` to display a progress bar while running.

    The decorated function can yield values from 0 to 100 to
    display the progress.
    """
    def _func_with_progress(*args, **kwargs):
        max_width, _ = shutil.get_terminal_size()

        gen = func(*args, **kwargs)
        while True:
            try:
                progress = next(gen)
            except StopIteration as exc:
                sys.stdout.write('\n')
                return exc.value
            else:
                # Build the displayed message so we can compute
                # how much space is left for the progress bar
                #   itself.
                message = '[%s] {}%%'.format(progress)
                # Add 3 characters to cope for the %s and %%
                bar_width = max_width - len(message) + 3

                filled = int(round(bar_width / 100.0 * progress))
                spaceleft = bar_width - filled
                bar = '=' * filled + ' ' * spaceleft
                sys.stdout.write((message+'\r') % bar)
```

```
                        sys.stdout.flush()

            return _func_with_progress
```

2. Then we need a function that actually does something for which we might want to report progress. For the sake of this example, it will be just a simple function that waits a specified amount of time:

```
import time

@withprogressbar
def wait(seconds):
    """Waits ``seconds`` seconds and returns how long it waited."""
    start = time.time()
    step = seconds / 100.0
    for i in range(1, 101):
        time.sleep(step)
        yield i  # Send % of progress to withprogressbar

    # Return how much time passed since we started,
    # which is in fact how long we waited for real.
    return time.time() - start
```

3. Now calling the decorated function should tell us how long it has waited and display a progress bar while waiting:

```
print('WAITED', wait(5))
```

4. While the script is running, you should see your progress bar and the final result, looking something like this:

```
$ python /tmp/progress.py
[====================================] 100%
WAITED 5.308781862258911
```

How it works...

All the work is done by the `withprogressbar` function. It acts as a decorator, so we can apply it to any function with the `@withprogressbar` syntax.

That is very convenient because the code that reports progress is isolated from the code actually doing the work, which allows us to reuse it in many different cases.

To make a decorator that interacts with the decorated function while the function itself is running, we relied on Python generators:

```
gen = func(*args, **kwargs)
while True:
    try:
        progress = next(gen)
    except StopIteration as exc:
        sys.stdout.write('\n')
        return exc.value
    else:
        # display the progressbar
```

When we call the decorated function (in our example, the `wait` function), we will be in fact calling _func_with_progress from our decorator. The first thing that function will do is call the decorated function:

```
gen = func(*args, **kwargs)
```

As the decorated function contains a `yield progress` statement, any time it wants to display some progress (`yield i` from within the `for` loop in `wait`), the function will return `generator`.

Any time the generator faces a `yield progress` statement, we will receive it back as the return value of the next function applied to the generator:

```
progress = next(gen)
```

We can then display our progress and call `next(gen)` again so that the decorated function can move forward and return a new progress (the decorated function is currently paused at `yield` and won't process until we call `next` on it—that's why our whole code is wrapped in `while True:`, to let the function continue forever, until it finishes what it has to do).

Once the decorated function finished all the work it had to do, it will raise a `StopIteration` exception, which will contain the value returned by the decorated function in the `.value` attribute.

As we want to propagate any returned value to the caller, we just return that value ourselves. This is especially important if the function that was decorated is supposed to return some result of the work it did, such as a `download(url)` function that is supposed to return a reference to the downloaded file.

Before returning, we print a new line:

```
sys.stdout.write('\n')
```

This ensures that anything that follows the progress bar won't overlap with the progress bar itself, but will be printed on a new line.

Then we are left with just displaying the progress bar itself. The core of the progress bar part of the recipe is based on just two lines of code:

```
sys.stdout.write((message+'\r') % bar)
sys.stdout.flush()
```

These two lines will ensure that our message is printed on the screen without moving to a new line like `print` normally does. Instead, this will move back to the beginning of the same line. Try replacing that `'\r'` with `'\n'` and you'll immediately see the difference. With `'\r'`, you see a single progress bar moving from 0-100%, while with `'\n'`, you will see many progress bars being printed.

The call to `sys.stdout.flush()` is then required to ensure that the progress bar is actually displayed, as usually output is only flushed on a new line, and as we are just printing the same line over and over, it wouldn't get flushed unless we did it explicitly.

Now that we know how to draw a progress bar and update it, the rest of the function is involved in computing the progress bar to display:

```
message = '[%s] {}%%'.format(progress)
bar_width = max_width - len(message) + 3   # Add 3 characters to cope for
the %s and %%

filled = int(round(bar_width / 100.0 * progress))
spaceleft = bar_width - filled
bar = '=' * filled + ' ' * spaceleft
```

First, we compute `message`, which is what we want to show on screen. The message is computed without the progress bar itself, for the progress bar, we are leaving a `%s` placeholder so that we can fill it later on.

We do this so that we know how much space is left for the bar itself after we displayed the surrounding brackets and the percentage. That value is `bar_width`, which is computed by subtracting from the maximum screen width (retrieved with `shutil.get_terminal_size()` at the beginning of our function) from the size of our message. The three extra characters we have to add will address the space that was consumed by `%s` and `%%` in our message, which won't actually be there once the message is displayed to screen, as the `%s` will be replaced by the bar itself and the `%%` will resolve to a single `%`.

Once we know how much space is available for the bar itself, we compute how much of that space should be filled with `'='` (the already completed part of the work) and how much should be filled with empty space, `' '` (the part of the work that is yet to come). This is achieved by computing the size of the screen to fill and match the percentage of our progress:

```
filled = int(round(bar_width / 100.0 * progress))
```

Once we know how much to fill with `'='`, the rest is just empty spaces:

```
spaceleft = bar_width - filled
```

So, we can build our bar with filled equal signs and `spaceleft` empty spaces:

```
bar = '=' * filled + ' ' * spaceleft
```

Once the bar is ready, it will be injected into the message that is displayed onscreen through the usage of the `%` string formatting operator:

```
sys.stdout.write((message+'\r') % bar)
```

If you noticed, I mixed two types of string formatting (`str.format` and `%`). I did so because I think it makes what's going on with the formatting clearer, instead of having to properly account for escaping on each formatting step.

Message boxes

While less common nowadays, there is still a lot of value in being able to create interactive character-based user interfaces, especially when just a simple message dialog with an OK button or an OK/cancel dialog is needed; you can achieve a better result by directing the user's attention to them through a nice-looking text dialog.

Getting ready

The `curses` library is only included, in Python for Unix systems, so Windows users might need a solution, such as CygWin or the Linux Subsystem for Windows, to be able to have a Python setup that includes `curses` support.

How to do it...

For this recipe, perform the following steps:

1. We will make a `MessageBox.show` method which we can use to show a message box whenever we need it. The `MessageBox` class will be able to show message boxes with just OK or OK/cancel buttons:

```python
import curses
import textwrap
import itertools


class MessageBox(object):
    @classmethod
    def show(cls, message, cancel=False, width=40):
        """Show a message with an Ok/Cancel dialog.

        Provide ``cancel=True`` argument to show a cancel button
        too.
        Returns the user selected choice:

            - 0 = Ok
            - 1 = Cancel
        """
        dialog = MessageBox(message, width, cancel)
        return curses.wrapper(dialog._show)

    def __init__(self, message, width, cancel):
        self._message = self._build_message(width, message)
        self._width = width
        self._height = max(self._message.count('\n')+1, 3) + 6
        self._selected = 0
        self._buttons = ['Ok']
        if cancel:
            self._buttons.append('Cancel')

    def _build_message(self, width, message):
        lines = []
```

```
        for line in message.split('\n'):
            if line.strip():
                lines.extend(textwrap.wrap(line, width-4,
                            replace_whitespace=False))
            else:
                lines.append('')
        return '\n'.join(lines)

    def _show(self, stdscr):
        win = curses.newwin(self._height, self._width,
                        (curses.LINES - self._height) // 2,
                        (curses.COLS - self._width) // 2)
        win.keypad(1)
        win.border()
        textbox = win.derwin(self._height - 1, self._width - 3,
                        1, 2)
        textbox.addstr(0, 0, self._message)
        return self._loop(win)

    def _loop(self, win):
        while True:
            for idx, btntext in enumerate(self._buttons):
                allowedspace = self._width // len(self._buttons)
                btn = win.derwin(
                    3, 10,
                    self._height - 4,
                    (((allowedspace-10)//2*idx) + allowedspace*idx
                        + 2)
                )
                btn.border()
                flag = 0
                if idx == self._selected:
                    flag = curses.A_BOLD
                btn.addstr(1, (10-len(btntext))//2, btntext, flag)
            win.refresh()

            key = win.getch()
            if key == curses.KEY_RIGHT:
                self._selected = 1
            elif key == curses.KEY_LEFT:
                self._selected = 0
            elif key == ord('\n'):
                return self._selected
```

2. Then we can use it through the `MessageBox.show` method:

```
MessageBox.show('Hello World,\n\npress enter to continue')
```

3. We can even use it to check for user choices:

```
if MessageBox.show('Are you sure?\n\npress enter to confirm',
                   cancel=True) == 0:
    print("Yeah! Let's continue")
else:
    print("That's sad, hope to see you soon")
```

How it works...

The message box is based on the `curses` library, which allows us to draw text-based graphics on the screen. When we use the dialog box, we will enter a full-screen text graphic mode, and as soon as we exit it, we will recover our previous terminal state.

That allows us to interleave the `MessageBox` class in more complex programs without having to write the whole program with `curses`. This is allowed by the `curses.wrapper` function that is used in the `MessageBox.show` class method to wrap the `MessageBox._show` method that actually shows the box.

The message to show is prepared in the `MessageBox` initializer, through the `MessageBox._build_message` method, to ensure that it wraps when it's too long and that multiple lines of text are properly handled. The height of the message box depends on the length of the message and the resulting number of lines, plus six lines that we always include to add borders (which consume two lines) and the buttons (which consume four lines).

The `MessageBox._show` method then creates the actual box window, adds a border to it, and displays the message within it. Once the message is displayed, we enter `MessageBox._loop`, which will wait for the user choice between OK and cancel.

The `MessageBox._loop` method draws all the required buttons with their own borders through the `win.derwin` function. Each button is 10-characters wide and 3-characters tall, and will display itself depending on the value of `allowedspace`, which reserves an equal portion of the box space to each button. Then, once the button box is drawn, it will check whether the currently displayed button is the selected one; if it is, then the label of the button is displayed with bold text. This allows the user to know the currently selected choice.

Once both buttons are drawn, we call `win.refresh()` to actually display on screen what we've just drawn.

Then we wait for the user to press any key to update the screen accordingly; the left/right arrow keys will switch between the OK/cancel choices, and *Enter* will confirm the current choice.

If the the user changes the selected button (by pressing the left or right keys), we loop again and redraw the buttons. We only need to redraw the buttons because the rest of the screen has not changed; the window border and the message are still the same, so there is no need to draw over them. The content of the screen is always preserved unless a `win.erase()` method is called, so we never need to redraw parts of the screen we don't need to update.

By being smart about this, we could also avoid redrawing the buttons themselves. This is because only the cancel/OK text needs to be redrawn when it changes from bold to normal and vice versa.

Once the user presses the *Enter* key, we quit the loop and return the currently selected choice between OK and cancel. That allows the caller to act according to the user choice.

Input box

When writing console-based software, it is sometimes necessary to ask users to provide long text inputs that can't easily be provided through command options.

There are few examples of this in the Unix world, such as editing `crontab` or tweaking multiple configuration options at once. Most of them rely on starting a fully-fledged third-party editor, such as **nano** or **vim**, but it's possible to easily roll a solution that in many cases will suffice with just the Python standard library, such that our tools can ask long or complex user input.

Getting ready

The `curses` library is only included in Python for Unix systems, so Windows users might need a solution, such as CygWin or the Linux Subsystem for Windows, to be able to have a Python setup that includes `curses` support.

How to do it...

For this recipe, perform the following steps:

1. The Python standard library provides a `curses.textpad` module that has the foundation of a multiline text editor with `emacs`, such as key bindings. We just need to extend it a little to add some required behaviors and fixes:

```python
import curses
from curses.textpad import Textbox, rectangle


class TextInput(object):
    @classmethod
    def show(cls, message, content=None):
        return curses.wrapper(cls(message, content)._show)

    def __init__(self, message, content):
        self._message = message
        self._content = content

    def _show(self, stdscr):
        # Set a reasonable size for our input box.
        lines, cols = curses.LINES - 10, curses.COLS - 40

        y_begin, x_begin = (curses.LINES - lines) // 2,
                            (curses.COLS - cols) // 2
        editwin = curses.newwin(lines, cols, y_begin, x_begin)
        editwin.addstr(0, 1, "{}: (hit Ctrl-G to submit)"
         .format(self._message))
        rectangle(editwin, 1, 0, lines-2, cols-1)
        editwin.refresh()

        inputwin = curses.newwin(lines-4, cols-2, y_begin+2,
        x_begin+1)
        box = Textbox(inputwin)
        self._load(box, self._content)
        return self._edit(box)

    def _load(self, box, text):
        if not text:
            return
        for c in text:
            box._insert_printable_char(c)

    def _edit(self, box):
        while True:
```

```
            ch = box.win.getch()
            if not ch:
                continue
            if ch == 127:
                ch = curses.KEY_BACKSPACE
            if not box.do_command(ch):
                break
            box.win.refresh()
        return box.gather()
```

2. Then we can read input from the user:

```
result = TextInput.show('Insert your name:')
print('Your name:', result)
```

3. We can even ask it to edit an existing text:

```
result = TextInput.show('Insert your name:',
                        content='Some Text\nTo be edited')
print('Your name:', result)
```

How it works...

Everything starts with the `TextInput._show` method, which prepares two windows; the first draws the help text (`'Insert your name:'` in our example) and a border box for the text area.

Once those are drawn, it creates a new window dedicated to `Textbox` as the textbox will be freely inserting, removing, and editing the content of that window.

If we have existing content (`content=` argument), the `TextInput._load` function takes care of inserting it into the textbox before moving forward with editing. Each character in the provided content is injected into the textbox window through the `Textbox._insert_printable_char` function.

Then we can finally enter the edit loop (the `TextInput._edit` method), where we listen for key presses and react accordingly. Actually, most of the work is already done for us by `Textbox.do_command`, so we just need to forward the pressed key to it to insert the characters into our text or react to a special command. The only special part of this method is that we check for character 127, which is *Backspace*, and replace it with `curses.KEY_BACKSPACE`, as not all terminals send the same codes when the *Backspace* key is pressed. Once the character is handled by `do_command`, we can refresh the window so that any new text appears and we loop again.

When the user presses *Ctrl + G*, the editor will consider the text complete and will quit the edit loop. Before doing so, we call `Textbox.gather` to fetch the entire contents of the text editor and send it back to the caller.

One thing to note is that the content is actually fetched from the content of the `curses` window. So, it actually includes all the empty space you can see on your screen. For this reason, the `Textbox.gather` method will strip empty space to avoid sending you back a response that is mostly empty space surrounding your text. This is quite clear if you try to write something that includes multiple empty lines; they will all be stripped together with the rest of the empty space.

Filesystem and Directories

4

In this chapter, we will cover following recipes:

- Traversing folders—recursively traversing a path in the filesystem and inspecting its contents
- Working with paths—building paths in a system-independent way
- Expanding filenames—finding all files that match a specific pattern
- Getting file information—detecting the properties of a file or directory
- Named temporary files—working with temporary files that you need to access from other processes too
- Memory and disk buffer—spooling a temporary buffer to disk if it's bigger than a threshold
- Managing filename encoding—working with the encoding of filenames
- Copying a directory—copying the content of a whole directory
- Safely replacing a file's content—how to replace the content of a file safely in case of failures

Introduction

Working with files and directories is natural with most software and something we, as users, do every day, but as a developer, you will quickly find that it can be more complex than expected, especially when multiple platforms have to be supported or encodings are involved.

The Python standard library has many powerful tools to work with files and directories. At first, it might be hard to spot those across the `os`, `shutil`, `stat`, and `glob` functions, but once you are aware of all the pieces, it's clear that the standard library provides a great set of tools to work with files and directories.

ersing folders

ννnen working with a path in the filesystem, it's common the need to find all files contained directly or in subfolders. Think about copying a directory or computing its size; in both cases, you will need to fetch the complete list of files included in the directory you want to copy, or for which you want to compute the size.

How to do it...

The steps for this recipe are as follows:

1. The `os.walk` function in the `os` module is meant to traverse a directory recursively, its usage is not immediate, but with little effort, we can wrap it into a convenient generator of all the contained files:

```
import os

def traverse(path):
    for basepath, directories, files in os.walk(path):
        for f in files:
            yield os.path.join(basepath, f)
```

2. Then, we can just iterate over `traverse` and apply whatever operation we need on top of it:

```
for f in traverse('.'):
    print(f)
```

How it works...

The `os.walk` function navigates the directory and all its subfolders. For each directory that it finds, it returns three values: the directory itself, the subdirectories it contains, and the files it contains. Then, it will move into the subdirectories of the directory it just provided and return the same three values for the subdirectory.

This means that in our recipe, `basepath` is always the current directory that is being inspected, `directories` are its subdirectories, and `files` are the files that it contains.

By iterating over the list of files contained within the current directory and joining their names with the directory path itself, we can get the path of all files contained in the directory. As `os.walk` will then move into all the subdirectories, we will be able to return all the files that are directly or indirectly within the required path.

Working with paths

Python was originally created as a system management language. It was originally meant to write scripts for the Unix system, so navigating the disk has always been one of the core parts of the language, but in the most recent versions of Python, this was extended further with the `pathlib` module, which makes it very convenient and easy to build paths that refer to files or directories, without having to care about the system we are running on.

Since writing multiplatform software can be bothersome, it's very important to have intermediate layers that abstract the conventions of the underlying system and allow us to write code that will work everywhere.

Especially when working with paths, the differences between how Unix and Windows systems treating paths can be problematic. The fact that one system uses / and the other \ to separate the parts of the path is bothersome by itself, but Windows also has the concept of drivers while Unix systems don't, so we need something that allows us to abstract these differences and manage paths easily.

How to do it...

Perform the following steps for this recipe:

1. The `pathlib` library allows us to build paths from the parts that constitute it, by properly doing the right thing based on the system you are on:

```
>>> import pathlib
>>>
>>> path = pathlib.Path('somefile.txt')
>>> path.write_text('Hello World')  # Write some text into file.
11
>>> print(path.resolve())  # Print absolute path
/Users/amol/wrk/pythonstlcookbook/somefile.txt
>>> path.read_text()  # Check the file content
'Hello World'
>>> path.unlink()  # Destroy the file
```

2. The interesting part is that the same actions would lead to the same exact result on Windows, even though `path.resolve()` would have printed a slightly different result:

```
>>> print(path.resolve())  # Print absolute path
C:\\wrk\\pythonstlcookbook\\somefile.txt
```

3. Once we have a `pathlib.Path` instance, we can even move around the filesystem by using the / operator:

```
>>> path = pathlib.Path('.')
>>> path = path.resolve()
>>> path
PosixPath('/Users/amol/wrk/pythonstlcookbook')
>>> path = path / '..'
>>> path.resolve()
PosixPath('/Users/amol/wrk')
```

The previous code works on both Windows and Linux/macOS and leads to the expected result, even though I wrote it on a Unix-like system.

There's more...

`pathlib.Path` actually builds a different object depending on the system we are in. On POSIX systems, it will result in a `pathlib.PosixPath` object, while on Windows systems, it will lead to a `pathlib.WindowsPath` object.

It is not possible to build `pathlib.WindowsPath` on a POSIX system, because it's implemented on top of Windows system calls, which are not available on Unix systems. In case you need to work with Windows paths on a POSIX system (or with POSIX paths on a Windows system), you can rely on `pathlib.PureWindowsPath` and `pathlib.PurePosixPath`.

Those two objects won't implement features to actually access the files (read, write, link, resolve absolute paths, and so on), but they will allow you to perform simple operations that are only related to manipulating the path itself.

Expanding filenames

In the everyday use of our system, we are used to providing paths, such as `*.py`, to identify all the Python files, so it's not a surprise that our users expect to be able to do the same when they provide one or more files to our software.

Usually, wildcards are expanded by the shell itself, but suppose you are reading them from a configuration file or you want to write a tool that clears the `.pyc` files (a cache of compiled Python bytecode) in your current project, then the Python standard library has what you need.

How to do it...

The steps for this recipe are:

1. `pathlib` is able to perform many operations on the path you provided. One of them is resolving wildcards:

   ```
   >>> list(pathlib.Path('.').glob('*.py'))
   [PosixPath('conf.py')]
   ```

2. It also supports resolving wildcards recursively:

   ```
   >>> list(pathlib.Path('.').glob('**/*.py'))
   [PosixPath('conf.py'), PosixPath('venv/bin/cmark.py'),
    PosixPath('venv/bin/rst2html.py'), ...]
   ```

Getting file information

When users provide a path you really don't know what the path refers to. Is it a file? Is it a directory? Does it even exist?

Retrieving file information allows us to fetch details about the provided path, such as whether it points to a file and how big that file is.

How to do it...

Perform the following steps for this recipe:

1. Using `.stat()` on any `pathlib.Path` will provide most details about a path:

   ```
   >>> pathlib.Path('conf.py').stat()
   os.stat_result(st_mode=33188,
                  st_ino=116956459,
                  st_dev=16777220,
                  st_nlink=1,
                  st_uid=501,
                  st_gid=20,
                  st_size=9306,
                  st_atime=1519162544,
                  st_mtime=1510786258,
                  st_ctime=1510786258)
   ```

The returned details refer to:

- `st_mode`: File type, flags, and permissions
- `st_ino`: Filesystem node storing the file
- `st_dev`: Device where the file is stored
- `st_nlink`: Number of references (hyperlinks) to this file
- `st_uid`: User owning the file
- `st_gid`: Group owning the file
- `st_size`: Size of the file in bytes
- `st_atime`: Last time the file was accessed
- `st_mtime`: Last time the file was modified
- `st_ctime`: Time the file was created on Windows, time the metadata was modified on Unix

2. If we want to see other details, such as whether the path exists or whether it's a directory, we can rely on these specific methods:

```
>>> pathlib.Path('conf.py').exists()
True
>>> pathlib.Path('conf.py').is_dir()
False
>>> pathlib.Path('_build').is_dir()
True
```

Named temporary files

Usually when working with temporary files, we don't care where they are stored. We need to create them, store some content there, and get rid of them when we are done. Most of the time, we use temporary files when we want to store something that is too big to fit in memory, but sometimes you need to be able to provide a file to another tool or software, and a temporary file is a great way to avoid the need to know where to store such a file.

In that situation, we need to know the path that leads to the temporary file so that we can provide it to the other tool.

That's where `tempfile.NamedTemporaryFile` can help. Like all other `tempfile` forms of temporary files, it will be created for us and will be deleted automatically as soon as we are done working with it, but different from the other types of temporary files, it will have a known path that we can provide to other programs who will be able to read and write from that file.

How to do it...

`tempfile.NamedTemporaryFile` will create the temporary file:

```
>>> from tempfile import NamedTemporaryFile
>>>
>>> with tempfile.NamedTemporaryFile() as f:
...     print(f.name)
...
/var/folders/js/ykgc_8hj10n1fmh3pzdkw2w40000gn/T/tmponbsaf34
```

The fact that the `.name` attribute leads to the full file path on disk allows us to provide it to other external programs:

```
>>> with tempfile.NamedTemporaryFile() as f:
...     os.system('echo "Hello World" > %s' % f.name)
...     f.seek(0)
...     print(f.read())
...
0
0
b'Hello World\n'
```

Memory and disk buffer

Sometimes, we need to keep certain data in a buffer, such as a file we downloaded from the internet or some data we are generating on the fly.

As the size of such data is not always predictable, is usually not a good idea to keep it all in memory.

If you are downloading a big 32 GB file from the internet that you need to process (such as decompress or parse), it will probably exhaust all your memory if you try to store it into a string before processing it.

That's why it's usually a good idea to rely on `tempfile.SpooledTemporaryFile`, which will keep the content in memory until it reaches its maximum size and will then move it to a temporary file if it's bigger than the maximum allowed size.

That way, we can have the benefit of keeping an in-memory buffer of our data, without the risk of exhausting all the memory, because as soon as the content is too big, it will be moved to disk.

How to do it...

Like the other `tempfile` object, creating `SpooledTemporaryFile` is enough to make the temporary file available. The only additional part is to provide the maximum allowed size, `max_size=`, after which the content will be moved to disk:

```
>>> with tempfile.SpooledTemporaryFile(max_size=30) as temp:
...     for i in range(3):
...         temp.write(b'Line of text\n')
...
...     temp.seek(0)
...     print(temp.read())
...
b'Line of text\nLine of text\nLine of text\n'
```

How it works...

`tempfile.SpooledTemporaryFile` has an `internal` `_file` property that keeps the real data stored in a `BytesIO` store until it can fit in memory, and then moves it to a real file once it gets bigger than `max_size`.

You can easily see this behavior by printing the value of `_file` while you are writing data:

```
>>> with tempfile.SpooledTemporaryFile(max_size=30) as temp:
...     for i in range(3):
...         temp.write(b'Line of text\n')
...         print(temp._file)
...
<_io.BytesIO object at 0x10d539ca8>
<_io.BytesIO object at 0x10d539ca8>
<_io.BufferedRandom name=4>
```

Managing filename encoding

Working with filesystems in a reliable way is not as easy as it might seem. Our system must have a specific encoding to represent text and usually that means that everything we create is handled in that encoding, including filenames.

The problem is that there is no strong guarantee on the encoding of filenames. Suppose you attach an external hard drive, what's the encoding of filenames on that drive? Well, it will depend on the encoding the system had at the time the files were created.

Usually, to cope with this problem, software tries the system encoding and if it fails, it prints some placeholders (have you ever seen a filename full of ? just because your system couldn't understand the name of the file?), which usually allows us to see that there is a file, and in many cases even open it, even though we might not know how it's actually named.

To make everything more complex, there is a big difference between Windows and Unix systems regarding how they treat filenames. On Unix systems, paths are fundamentally just bytes; you don't really care about their encoding as you just read and write a bunch of bytes. While on Windows, filenames are actually text.

In Python, filenames are usually stored as `str`. They are text that needs to be encoded/decoded somehow.

How to do it...

Whenever we process a filename, we should decode it according to the expected filesystem encoding. If we fail (because it's not stored in the expected encoding), we must still be able to put it into `str` without corrupting it, so that we can open that file even though we can't read its name:

```
def decode_filename(fname):
    fse = sys.getfilesystemencoding()
    return fname.decode(fse, "surrogateescape")
```

How it works...

`decode_filename` tries to do two things: first of all, it asks Python what the expected filesystem encoding according to the OS is. Once that's known, it tries to decode the provided filename using that encoding. If it fails, it decodes it using `surrogateescape`.

What this actually means is *if you fail to decode it, decode it into fake characters that we are going to use just to be able to represent it as text.*

This is really convenient because that way we are able to manage the filename as text even thought we don't know its encoding, and when it is encoded back to bytes with `surrogateescape`, it will lead back to its original sequence of bytes.

When the filename is encoded in the same encoding as our system, it's easy to see how we are able to decode it to `str` and also print it to read its content:

```
>>> utf8_filename_bytes = 'ùtf8.txt'.encode('utf8')
>>> utf8_filename = decode_filename(utf8_filename_bytes)
>>> type(utf8_filename)
<class 'str'>
>>> print(utf8_filename)
ùtf8.txt
```

If the encoding is instead one that is not our system encoding (that is, the file came from a very old external drive), we can't really read what's written inside, but we are still able to decode it to strings, so that we can keep it in a variable and provide it to any function that might need to work with that file:

```
>>> latin1_filename_bytes = 'làtìn1.txt'.encode('latin1')
>>> latin1_filename = decode_filename(latin1_filename_bytes)
>>> type(latin1_filename)
<class 'str'>
>>> latin1_filename
'l\udce0t\udcecn1.txt'
```

`surrogateescape` means being able to tell Python *I don't care whether the data is garbage, just pass the unknown bytes along as they are*.

Copying a directory

Making copies of a directory's contents is something we can do easily, but what if I told you that a tool such as `cp` (the command to copy files on GNU systems) is around 1,200 lines of code?

Obviously, the `cp` implementation is not Python-based, it has evolved over decades, and it takes care of far more than you probably need, but still rolling your own code to copy a directory recursively takes far more than you would expect.

Luckily for us, the Python standard library provides utilities to perform the most common operations out of the box and this is one of them.

How to do it...

The steps for this recipe are as follows:

1. The `copydir` function can rely on `shutil.copytree` to do most of the work:

```
import shutil

def copydir(source, dest, ignore=None):
    """Copy source to dest and ignore any file matching ignore
        pattern."""
    shutil.copytree(source, dest, ignore_dangling_symlinks=True,
                    ignore=shutil.ignore_patterns(*ignore) if
                    ignore else None)
```

2. Then, we can easily use it to copy the contents of any directory and even limit it to only the relevant parts. We are going to copy a directory that contains three files, out of which we really only want to copy the `.pdf` file:

```
>>> import glob
>>> print(glob.glob('_build/pdf/*'))
['_build/pdf/PySTLCookbook.pdf', '_build/pdf/PySTLCookbook.rtc',
'_build/pdf/PySTLCookbook.stylelog']
```

3. Our destination doesn't currently exist, so it contains nothing:

```
>>> print(glob.glob('/tmp/buildcopy/*'))
[]
```

4. Once we do `copydir`, it will be created and contains what we expect:

```
>>> copydir('_build/pdf', '/tmp/buildcopy', ignore=('*.rtc',
'*.stylelog'))
```

5. Now, the target directory exists and contains the content we expect:

```
>>> print(glob.glob('/tmp/buildcopy/*'))
['/tmp/buildcopy/PySTLCookbook.pdf']
```

How it works...

`shutil.copytree` will retrieve the content of the provided directory through `os.listdir`. For every entry returned by `listdir`, it will check whether it's a file or a directory.

e, it will copy it through the `shutil.copy2` function (it's actually possible to
ue used function by providing a `copy_function` argument), if it's a
᠁ory, `copytree` itself is called recursively.

The `ignore` argument is then used to build a function that, once called, will return all the
files that need to be ignored given a provided pattern:

```
>>> f = shutil.ignore_patterns('*.rtc', '*.stylelog')
>>> f('_build', ['_build/pdf/PySTLCookbook.pdf',
                  '_build/pdf/PySTLCookbook.rtc',
                  '_build/pdf/PySTLCookbook.stylelog'])
{'_build/pdf/PySTLCookbook.stylelog', '_build/pdf/PySTLCookbook.rtc'}
```

So, `shutil.copytree` will copy all the files apart from `ignore_patterns`, which will
make it skip.

The last `ignore_dangling_symlinks=True` argument ensures that in the case of broken
`symlinks`, we just skip the file instead of crashing.

Safely replacing file's content

Replacing the content of a file is a very slow operation. Compared to replacing the content
of a variable, it's usually a few times slower; when we write something to disk, it takes time
before it's actually flushed and time before the content is actually written to disk. It's not an
atomic operation, so if our software faces any issues while saving a file, there is a good
chance that the file might end up being half-written and our users don't have a way to
recover the consistent state of their data.

There is a pattern commonly used to solve this kind of issue, which is based on the fact that
writing a file is a slow, expensive, error-prone operation, but renaming a file is an atomic,
fast, and cheap operation.

How to do it...

You need to perform the following recipes:

1. Much like `open` can be used as a context manager, we can easily roll out a
   `safe_open` function that allows us to open a file for writing in a safe way:

   ```
   import tempfile, os

   class safe_open:
   ```

```
        def __init__(self, path, mode='w+b'):
            self._target = path
            self._mode = mode

        def __enter__(self):
            self._file = tempfile.NamedTemporaryFile(self._mode,
delete=False)
            return self._file

        def __exit__(self, exc_type, exc_value, traceback):
            self._file.close()
            if exc_type is None:
                os.rename(self._file.name, self._target)
            else:
                os.unlink(self._file.name)
```

2. Using `safe_open` as a context manager allows us to write to the file pretty much like we would normally:

```
with safe_open('/tmp/myfile') as f:
    f.write(b'Hello World')
```

3. And the content will be properly saved once we quit the context:

```
>>> print(open('/tmp/myfile').read())
Hello World
```

4. The major difference is that in case of a crash in our software or a system failure while we are writing, we won't end up with a half-written file, but we will preserve any previous state of the file. In this example, we crash midway through trying to write `Replace the hello world, expect to write some more`:

```
with open('/tmp/myfile', 'wb+') as f:
    f.write(b'Replace the hello world, ')
    raise Exception('but crash meanwhile!')
    f.write(b'expect to write some more')
```

5. With a normal `open`, the result would be just `"Replace the hello world, "`:

```
>>> print(open('/tmp/myfile').read())
Replace the hello world,
```

6. While using `safe_open`, the file will only contain the new data if the whole write process succeeded:

```
with safe_open('/tmp/myfile') as f:
    f.write(b'Replace the hello world, ')
    raise Exception('but crash meanwhile!')
    f.write(b'expect to write some more')
```

7. In all other cases, the file will still retain its previous state:

```
>>> print(open('/tmp/myfile').read())
Hello World
```

How it works...

`safe_open` relies on `tempfile` to create a new file where the write operations actually happen. Any time we write to `f` in our context, we are actually writing to the temporary file.

Then, only when the context exists (`exc_type` is none in `safe_open.__exit__`), we actually swap the old file with the new one we just wrote, using `os.rename`.

If everything works as expected, we should have the new file with all its content updated.

If any of the steps fails, we just write some or no data to a temporary file and get rid of it through `os.unlink`.

Our previous file, in this case, was never touched and thus still retains its previous state.

5
Date and Time

In this chapter, we will cover the following recipes:

- Time-zone-aware datetime—retrieving a reliable value for the current datetime
- Parsing dates—how to parse dates according to the ISO 8601 format
- Saving dates—how to store datetimes
- From timestamp to datetime—converting to and from timestamps
- Displaying dates in a user format—formatting dates according to our user language
- Going to tomorrow—how to compute a datetime that refers to tomorrow
- Going to next month—how to compute a datetime that refers to next month
- Weekdays—how to build a date that refers to the nth Monday/Friday of the month
- Workdays—how to get workdays in a time range
- Combining dates and times—making a datetime out of a date and time

Introduction

Dates are a part of our lives and we are used to handling times and dates as a basic process. Even a small kid knows what time it is or what *tomorrow* means. But, try to talk to someone on the other side of the world and suddenly the concepts of *tomorrow*, *midnight*, and so on start to become very complex.

When you say tomorrow, are you talking about your tomorrow or mine? If you schedule a process that should run at midnight, which midnight is it?

To make everything harder, we have leap seconds, odd time zones, daylight savings, and so on. When you try to approach dates in software, especially in software as a service that might be used by people around the world, suddenly it becomes clear that dates are a complex affair.

This chapter includes some recipes that, while being short, can save you headaches and bugs when working with user-provided dates.

Time-zone-aware datetime

Python datetimes are usually *naive*, which means they don't know which time zone they refer to. This can be a major problem because, given a datetime, it's impossible to know when it actually refers to.

The most common error in working with dates in Python is trying to get the current datetime through `datetime.datetime.now()`, as all `datetime` methods work with naive dates, it's impossible to know which time that value represents.

How to do it...

Perform the following steps for this recipe:

1. The only reliable way to retrieve the current datetime is by using `datetime.datetime.utcnow()`. Independently of where the user is and how the system is configured, it will always return the UTC time. So we need to make it time-zone-aware to be able to decline it to any time zone in the world:

```
import datetime

def now():
    return
datetime.datetime.utcnow().replace(tzinfo=datetime.timezone.utc)
```

2. Once we have a time-zone-aware current time, it is possible to convert it to any other time zone, so that we can display to our users the value in their own time zone:

```
def astimezone(d, offset):
    return
d.astimezone(datetime.timezone(datetime.timedelta(hours=offset)))
```

3. Now, given I'm currently in the UTC+01:00 time zone, I can grab the current time-zone-aware time for UTC and then display it in my own time zone:

```
>>> d = now()
>>> print(d)
2018-03-19 21:35:43.251685+00:00
```

```
>>> d = astimezone(d, 1)
>>> print(d)
2018-03-19 22:35:43.251685+01:00
```

How it works...

All Python datetimes, by default, come without any time zone specified, but by setting `tzinfo`, we can make them aware of the time zone they refer to.

If we just grab our current time (`datetime.datetime.now()`), there is no easy way for us to know from within our software which time zone we are grabbing the time from. The only time zone we can always rely on is UTC, for that reason. Whenever retrieving the current time, it's best always to rely on `datetime.datetime.utcnow()`.

Once we have a date for UTC, as we know it's actually for the UTC time zone, we can easily attach the `datetime.timezone.utc` time zone (the only one that Python provides out of the box) and make it time-zone-aware.

The `now` function does that: it grabs the datetime and makes it time-zone-aware.

As our datetime is now time-zone-aware, from that moment on, we can rely on the `datetime.datetime.astimezone` method to convert to any time zone we want. So, if we know that our user is on UTC+01:00, we can display the datetime with the user's local value instead of showing a UTC value.

That's exactly what the `astimezone` function does. Once a datetime and an offset from UTC are provided, it returns a date that refers to a local time zone based on that offset.

There's more...

You might have noticed that while this solution works, it lacks more advanced features. For example, I'm currently on UTC+01:00, but according to my country's Daylight Savings policy, I might be on UTC+02:00. Also, we only support offsets based on an integer hour, and while that's the most common case, there are time zones, such as India's or Iran's, that have a half-hour offset.

While we can extend our support for time zones to include these oddities, for more advanced cases you should probably rely on the `pytz` package, which ships time zones for the full IANA time zone database.

Parsing dates

When receiving a datetime from another software or from a user, it will probably be in a string format. Formats such as JSON don't even define how a date should be represented, but it's usually a best practice to provide those in the ISO 8601 format.

The ISO 8601 format is usually defined as `[YYYY]-[MM]-[DD]T[hh]:[mm]:[ss]+-[TZ]`, for example `2018-03-19T22:00+0100` would refer to March 19 at 10 P.M. on the UTC+01:00 time zone.

ISO 8601 conveys all the information you need to represent a date and time, so it's a good way to marshal a datetime and send it across a network.

Sadly, it has many oddities (for example, the `+00` time zone can also be written as `Z`, or you can omit the `:` between hours, minutes, and seconds), so parsing it might sometimes cause trouble.

How to do it...

Here are the steps to follow:

1. Due to all the variants ISO 8601 allows, there is no easy way to throw it to `datetime.datetime.strptime` and get back a datetime for all case; we must coalesce all possible formats to a single one and then parse that one:

```python
import datetime

def parse_iso8601(strdate):
    date, time = strdate.split('T', 1)
    if '-' in time:
        time, tz = time.split('-')
        tz = '-' + tz
    elif '+' in time:
        time, tz = time.split('+')
        tz = '+' + tz
    elif 'Z' in time:
        time = time[:-1]
        tz = '+0000'
    date = date.replace('-', '')
    time = time.replace(':', '')
    tz = tz.replace(':', '')
    return datetime.datetime.strptime('{}T{}{}'.format(date, time,
tz),
                                      "%Y%m%dT%H%M%S%z")
```

2. The previous implementation of `parse_iso8601` copes with most possible ISO 8601 representations:

```
>>> parse_iso8601('2018-03-19T22:00Z')
datetime.datetime(2018, 3, 19, 22, 0, tzinfo=datetime.timezone.utc)
>>> parse_iso8601('2018-03-19T2200Z')
datetime.datetime(2018, 3, 19, 22, 0, tzinfo=datetime.timezone.utc)
>>> parse_iso8601('2018-03-19T22:00:03Z')
datetime.datetime(2018, 3, 19, 22, 0, 3,
tzinfo=datetime.timezone.utc)
>>> parse_iso8601('20180319T22:00:03Z')
datetime.datetime(2018, 3, 19, 22, 0, 3,
tzinfo=datetime.timezone.utc)
>>> parse_iso8601('20180319T22:00:03+05:00')
datetime.datetime(2018, 3, 19, 22, 0, 3,
tzinfo=datetime.timezone(datetime.timedelta(0, 18000)))
>>> parse_iso8601('20180319T22:00:03+0500')
datetime.datetime(2018, 3, 19, 22, 0, 3,
tzinfo=datetime.timezone(datetime.timedelta(0, 18000)))
```

How it works...

The basic idea of `parse_iso8601` is that whatever dialect of ISO 8601 is received before parsing it, we will transform it into the form of `[YYYY][MM][DD]T[hh][mm][ss]+-[TZ]`.

The hardest part is detecting the time zone, as that can be separated by +, –, or can even be Z. Once the time zone is extracted, we can just get rid of all examples of – in the date and all instances of : in times.

Note that before extracting the time zone we separated the time from the date, as both the date and the time zone might contain the – character, and we don't want our parser to get confused.

There's more...

Parsing dates can become very complex. While our `parse_iso8601` will work when interacting with most systems that serve a date in string format (such as JSON), you will quickly face cases where it falls short due to all the ways a datetime can be expressed.

For example, we might receive back a value such as `2 weeks ago` or `July 4, 2013 PST`. Trying to parse all these cases is not very convenient and can get complicated pretty quickly. In case you have to handle these special cases, you should probably rely on an external package such as `dateparser`, `dateutil`, or `moment`.

Saving dates

Sooner or later, we all have to save a date somewhere, sending it to a database or saving it into a file. Maybe we will be converting it into JSON to send it to another software.

Many database systems do not track time zones. Some of them have a configuration option that states what time zone they should work with, but in most cases, the date you provide will be saved as is.

This leads to unexpected bugs or behaviors in many cases. Suppose you were a good boy scout and properly did all the work required to receive a datetime preserving its time zone. Now you have a datetime of `2018-01-15 15:30:00 UTC+01:00` and, once you store it in your database, `UTC+01:00` will easily be lost, even if you store it in a file yourself, storing and restoring the time zone is usually a bothersome work.

For this reason, you should always ensure you convert your datetimes to UTC before storing them somewhere, that will always guarantee that, independently from which time zone the datetime came from, it will always represent the right time when you load it back.

How to do it...

The steps for this recipe are as follows:

1. To save a datetime, we want a function that ensures that datetime always refers to UTC before actually storing it:

```
import datetime

def asutc(d):
    return d.astimezone(datetime.timezone.utc)
```

2. The `asutc` function can be used with any datetime to ensure it's moved to UTC before actually storing it:

```
>>> now = datetime.datetime.now().replace(
...     tzinfo=datetime.timezone(datetime.timedelta(hours=1))
... )
```

```
>>> now
datetime.datetime(2018, 3, 22, 0, 49, 45, 198483,
                        tzinfo=datetime.timezone(datetime.timedelta(0,
3600)))
>>> asutc(now)
datetime.datetime(2018, 3, 21, 23, 49, 49, 742126,
tzinfo=datetime.timezone.utc)
```

How it works...

The functioning of this recipe is pretty straightforward, through the `datetime.datetime.astimezone` method, the date is always converted to its UTC representation.

This ensures it will work for both where your storage keeps track of time zones (as the date will still be time-zone-aware, but the time zone will be UTC) and when your storage doesn't preserve time zones (as a UTC date without a time zone still represents the same UTC date as if the delta was zero).

From timestamps to datetimes

Timestamps are the representation of a date in the number of seconds from a specific moment. Usually, as the value that a computer can represent is limited in size, that is normally taken from January 1st, 1970.

If you ever received a value such as 1521588268 as a datetime representation, you might be wondering how that can be converted into an actual datetime.

How to do it...

Most recent Python versions introduced a method to quickly convert datetimes back and forth from timestamps:

```
>>> import datetime
>>> ts = 1521588268

>>> d = datetime.datetime.utcfromtimestamp(ts)
>>> print(repr(d))
datetime.datetime(2018, 3, 20, 23, 24, 28)

>>> newts = d.timestamp()
```

```
>>> print(newts)
1521584668.0
```

There's more...

As pointed out in the recipe introduction, there is a limit to how big a number can be for a computer. For that reason, it's important to note that while `datetime.datetime` can represent practically any date, a timestamp can't.

For example, trying to represent a datetime from `1300` will succeed but it will fail to convert it to a timestamp:

```
>>> datetime.datetime(1300, 1, 1)
datetime.datetime(1300, 1, 1, 0, 0)
>>> datetime.datetime(1300, 1, 1).timestamp()
Traceback (most recent call last):
  File "<stdin>", line 1, in <module>
OverflowError: timestamp out of range
```

A timestamp is only able to represent dates starting from January 1st, 1970.

The same is true also in the reverse direction for faraway dates, while `253402214400` represents the timestamp for December 31, 9999, trying to create a datetime from a date later than that value will fail:

```
>>> datetime.datetime.utcfromtimestamp(253402214400)
datetime.datetime(9999, 12, 31, 0, 0)
>>> datetime.datetime.utcfromtimestamp(253402214400+(3600*24))
Traceback (most recent call last):
  File "<stdin>", line 1, in <module>
ValueError: year is out of range
```

A datetime is only able to represent dates from the year 1 to 9999.

Displaying dates in user format

When displaying dates from software, it's easy to confuse users if they don't know the format you are going to rely on.

We already know that time zones play an important role and that when displaying a time we always want to show it as time-zone-aware, but even dates can have their ambiguities. If you write 3/4/2018, will it be April 3rd or March 4th?

For this reason, you usually have two choices:

- Go for the international format (2018-04-03)
- Localize the date (April 3, 2018)

When possible, it's obviously better to be able to localize the date format, so that our users will see a value that they can easily recognize.

How to do it...

This recipe requires the following steps:

1. The `locale` module in the Python standard library provides a way to get formatting for the localization supported by your system. By using it, we can format dates in any way allowed by the target system:

```
import locale
import contextlib


@contextlib.contextmanager
def switchlocale(name):
    prev = locale.getlocale()
    locale.setlocale(locale.LC_ALL, name)
    yield
    locale.setlocale(locale.LC_ALL, prev)


def format_date(loc, d):
    with switchlocale(loc):
        fmt = locale.nl_langinfo(locale.D_T_FMT)
        return d.strftime(fmt)
```

2. Calling `format_date` will properly give the output as a string representation of the date in the expected `locale` module:

```
>>> format_date('de_DE', datetime.datetime.utcnow())
'Mi 21 Mär 00:08:59 2018'
>>> format_date('en_GB', datetime.datetime.utcnow())
'Wed 21 Mar 00:09:11 2018'
```

How it works...

The `format_date` function is divided into two major parts.

The first is provided by the `switchlocale` context manager, which is in charge of enabling the requested `locale` (locales are process-wide), giving back control to the wrapped block of code and then restoring the original `locale`. This way, we can use the requested `locale` only within the context manager and not influence any other part of our software.

The second is what happens within the context manager itself. Using `locale.nl_langinfo`, the date-and-time format string (`locale.D_T_FMT`) is requested to the currently enabled `locale`. That gives back a string that tells us how to format a datetime in the currently active `locale`. The returned string will be something like `'%a %e %b %X %Y'`.

Then the date itself is formatted according to the retrieved format string through `datetime.strftime`.

Note that the returned string will usually contain the `%a` and `%b` formatters, which represent the *current weekday* and *current month* names. As the name of a weekday or month changes for each language, the Python interpreter will emit the name of the weekday or month in the currently enabled `locale`.

So, we not only formatted the date the way the user expected, but the resulting output will also be in the user's language.

There's more...

While this solution seems very convenient, it's important to note that it relies on switching `locale` on the fly.

Switching `locale` is a very expensive operation, so if you have a lot of values to format (such as a `for` loop or thousand of dates), it might be far too slow.

Also switching `locale` is not thread-safe, so you won't be able to apply this recipe in multithreaded software, unless all the switching of `locale` happens before other threads are started.

If you want to handle localization in a robust and thread-safe way, you might want to check the babel package. Babel has support for the localization of dates and numbers, and it works in a way that doesn't require setting a global state, thus behaving properly even in threaded environments.

Going to tomorrow

When you have a date, it's common to need to apply math to that date. For example maybe you want to move to tomorrow or to yesterday.

Datetimes support math operations, such as adding or subtracting to them, but when time is involved, it's not easy to get the exact number of seconds you need to add or subtract to move to the next or previous day.

For this reason, this recipe will show off an easy way to move to the next or previous day from any given date.

How to do it...

For this recipe, here are the steps:

1. The `shiftdate` function will allow us to move to a date by any number of days:

```python
import datetime

def shiftdate(d, days):
    return (
        d.replace(hour=0, minute=0, second=0, microsecond=0) +
        datetime.timedelta(days=days)
    )
```

2. Using it is as simple as just providing the days you want to add or remove:

```python
>>> now = datetime.datetime.utcnow()
>>> now
datetime.datetime(2018, 3, 21, 21, 55, 5, 699400)
```

3. We can use it to go to tomorrow:

```python
>>> shiftdate(now, 1)
datetime.datetime(2018, 3, 22, 0, 0)
```

4. Or to go to yesterday:

```
>>> shiftdate(now, -1)
datetime.datetime(2018, 3, 20, 0, 0)
```

5. Or even to go into the next month:

```
>>> shiftdate(now, 11)
datetime.datetime(2018, 4, 1, 0, 0)
```

How it works...

Usually what we want when moving datetime is to go to the beginning of a day. Suppose you want to find all events that happen tomorrow out of a list of events, you really want to search for `day_after_tomorrow > event_time >= tomorrow` as you want to find all events that happened from tomorrow at midnight up to the day after tomorrow at midnight.

So, simply changing the day itself won't work, because our datetime also has a time associated with it. If we just add a day to the date, we will actually end up being somewhere in the range of hours that are included in tomorrow.

That's the reason why the `shiftdate` function always replaces the time of the provided date with midnight.

Once the date has been moved to midnight, we just add to it a `timedelta` equal to the number of specified days. If this number is negative, we will just move back in time as `D + -1 == D -1`.

Going to next month

Another frequent need when moving dates is to be able to move the date to the next or previous month.

If you read the *Going to tomorrow* recipe, you will see many similarities with this recipe even though there are some additional changes that are required when working with months that are not needed when working with days, as months have a variable duration.

How to do it...

Perform the following steps for this recipe:

1. The `shiftmonth` function will allow us to move our date back and forth by any number of months:

```
import datetime

def shiftmonth(d, months):
    for _ in range(abs(months)):
        if months > 0:
            d = d.replace(day=5) + datetime.timedelta(days=28)
        else:
            d = d.replace(day=1) - datetime.timedelta(days=1)
    d = d.replace(day=1, hour=0, minute=0, second=0, microsecond=0)
    return d
```

2. Using it is as simple as just providing the months you want to add or remove:

```
>>> now = datetime.datetime.utcnow()
>>> now
datetime.datetime(2018, 3, 21, 21, 55, 5, 699400)
```

3. We can use it to go to the next month:

```
>>> shiftmonth(now, 1)
datetime.datetime(2018, 4, 1, 0, 0)
```

4. Or back to the previous month:

```
>>> shiftmonth(now, -1)
datetime.datetime(2018, 2, 1, 0, 0)
```

5. Or even to move by any number of months:

```
>>> shiftmonth(now, 10)
datetime.datetime(2019, 1, 1, 0, 0)
```

How it works...

If you tried to compare this recipe with the *Going to tomorrow* one, you would notice that this one got far more complex even though its purpose is very similar.

Just as when moving across days we are interested in moving at a specific point in time during the day (usually the beginning), when moving months, we don't want to end up being in a random day and time in the new month.

That explains the last part of our recipe, where for any datetime resulting from our math expression, we reset the time to midnight of the first day of the month:

```
d = d.replace(day=1, hour=0, minute=0, second=0, microsecond=0)
```

Like for the days recipe, this allows us to check for conditions, such as `two_month_from_now > event_date >= next_month`, as we will catch all events from midnight of the first day up to 23:59 of the last day.

The part you might be wondering about is the `for` loop.

Differently from when we have to move by days (which all have an equal duration of 24 hours), when moving by months, we need to account for the fact that each of them will have a different duration.

This is why, when moving forward, we set the current date to be the 5th of the month and then we add 28 days. Adding 28 days by itself wouldn't suffice as it would only work for February, and if you are wondering, adding 31 days won't work either, because in the case of February, you would be moving by two months instead of just one.

That is why we set the current date to be the 5th of the month because we want to pick a day from which we know for sure that adding 28 days to it will move us into the next month.

So, for example, picking the 1st of the month would work, because March 1st + 28 days = March 29th, so we would still be in March. While March 5th + 28 days = April 2nd, April 5th + 28 days = May 3rd, and Feb 5th + 28 days = March 5th. So for any given month, we are always moving into the the next one when adding 28 days to the 5th.

The fact that we always move on to a different day won't really matter as that day will always be replaced with the 1st of the month.

As there isn't any fixed amount of days we can move that ensure we always move exactly into the next month, we can't move just by adding `days * months`, so we have to do this in a `for` loop and continuously move into the next month a `months` number of times.

When moving back, things get far easier. As all months begin with the first of the month, we can just move there and then subtract one day. We will always end up being on the last day of the previous month.

Weekdays

Building a date for the 20th of the month or for the 3rd week of the month is pretty straightforward, but what if you have to build the date for the 3rd Monday of the month?

How to do it...

Go through these steps:

1. To approach this problem, we are going to actually generate all the month days that match the requested weekday:

```
import datetime

def monthweekdays(month, weekday):
    now = datetime.datetime.utcnow()
    d = now.replace(day=1, month=month, hour=0, minute=0, second=0,
                    microsecond=0)
    days = []
    while d.month == month:
        if d.isoweekday() == weekday:
            days.append(d)
        d += datetime.timedelta(days=1)
    return days
```

2. Then, once we have a list of those, grabbing the nth day is just a matter of indexing the resulting list. For example, to grab the Mondays from March:

```
>>> monthweekdays(3, 1)
[datetime.datetime(2018, 3, 5, 0, 0),
 datetime.datetime(2018, 3, 12, 0, 0),
 datetime.datetime(2018, 3, 19, 0, 0),
 datetime.datetime(2018, 3, 26, 0, 0)]
```

3. So grabbing the 3rd Monday of March would be:

```
>>> monthweekdays(3, 1)[2]
datetime.datetime(2018, 3, 19, 0, 0)
```

How it works...

At the beginning of the recipe, we create a date for the first day of the requested month. Then we just move forward one day at a time until the month finishes and we set aside all days that match the requested weekday.

The weekdays go from one for Monday to seven for Sunday.

Once we have all the Mondays, Fridays, or whatever days of the month, we can just index the resulting list to grab only the ones we are actually interested in.

Workdays

In many management applications, you only have to consider workdays, and Saturdays and Sundays won't matter. You are not working during those days, so from a work point of view, they don't exist.

So when computing days included in a given timespan for a project management or work-related application, you can ignore those days.

How to do it...

We want to grab the list of days between two dates as far as they are working days:

```
def workdays(d, end, excluded=(6, 7)):
    days = []
    while d.date() < end.date():
        if d.isoweekday() not in excluded:
            days.append(d)
        d += datetime.timedelta(days=1)
    return days
```

For example, if it's March 22nd, 2018, which is a Thursday, and I want to know the working days up to the next Monday (which is March 26th), I can easily ask for `workdays`:

```
>>> workdays(datetime.datetime(2018, 3, 22), datetime.datetime(2018, 3,
26))
[datetime.datetime(2018, 3, 22, 0, 0),
 datetime.datetime(2018, 3, 23, 0, 0)]
```

So we know that two days are left: Thursday itself and Friday.

In case you are in a part of the world where you work on Sunday and maybe don't on Fridays, the `excluded` argument can be used to signal which days should be excluded from working days.

How it works...

The recipe is pretty straightforward, we just start from the provided date (d), add one day at a time and loop until we reach `end`.

We consider the provided arguments to be datetimes, thus we loop comparing only the date, as we don't want to randomly include and exclude the last day depending on times provided in d and `end`.

This allows `datetime.datetime.utcnow()` to provide us with the first argument without having to care about when the function was called. Only the dates themselves will be compared, without their times.

Combining dates and times

Sometimes you will have separated dates and times. This is particularly frequent when they are entered by a user. From an interaction point of view, it's usually easier to pick a date and then pick a time than to pick a date and a time together. Or you might be combining inputs from two different sources.

In all those cases, you will end up with a date and a time that you want to combine in a single `datetime.datetime` instance.

How to do it...

The Python standard library provides support for such operations out of the box, so having any two of those:

```
>>> t = datetime.time(13, 30)
>>> d = datetime.date(2018, 1, 11)
```

We can easily combine them into a single entity:

```
>>> datetime.datetime.combine(d, t)
datetime.datetime(2018, 1, 11, 13, 30)
```

There's more...

If your `time` instance has a time zone (`tzinfo`), combining the date with the time will also preserve it:

```
>>> t = datetime.time(13, 30, tzinfo=datetime.timezone.utc)
>>> datetime.datetime.combine(d, t)
datetime.datetime(2018, 1, 11, 13, 30, tzinfo=datetime.timezone.utc)
```

If your time doesn't have a time zone, you can still specify one when combining the two values:

```
>>> t = datetime.time(13, 30)
>>> datetime.datetime.combine(d, t, tzinfo=datetime.timezone.utc)
```

Providing a time zone when combining is only supported for Python 3.6+. If you are working with a previous Python version, you will have to set the time zone into the time value.

6
Read/Write Data

In this chapter, we will cover the following recipes:

- Reading and writing text data—reading text encoded in any encoding from a file
- Reading lines of text—reading a text file divided line by line
- Reading and writing binary data—reading binary-structured data from a file
- Zipping a directory—reading and writing a compressed ZIP archive
- Pickling and shelving—how to save Python objects on disk
- Reading configuration files—how to read configuration files in the `.ini` format
- Writing XML/HTML content—generating XML/HTML content
- Reading XML/HTML content—parsing XML/HTML content from a file or string
- Reading and writing CSV—reading and writing CSV spreadsheet-like files
- Reading and writing to a relational database—loading and saving data into a `SQLite` database

Introduction

The input for your software will come from various sources: command-line options, the standard input, the network, and, frequently, files. Reading from an input itself is rarely the problem when dealing with external sources of data; some input might require a bit more setup, some are more straightforward, but generally it's just a matter of opening it and then reading from it.

The problem arises with what to do with the data that we read. There are thousands of formats out there, each with its own complexities, some are text-based and some are binaries. In this chapter, we will set recipes to deal with the most common formats that you will probably have to face during your life as a developer.

Reading and writing text data

When reading a text file, we already know we should open it in text mode, which is the default Python mode. In this mode, Python will try to decode the content of the file according to what `locale.getpreferredencoding` returns as being the preferred encoding for our system.

Sadly, the fact that any type of encoding is the preferred encoding for our system has nothing to do with what encoding might have been used to save the contents of the file. As it might be a file that someone else wrote, or even if we write it ourselves, the editor might have saved it in any encoding.

So the only solution is to specify the encoding that should be used to decode the file.

How to do it...

The `open` function that Python provides accepts an `encoding` argument that can be used to properly encode/decode the contents of a file:

```python
# Write a file with latin-1 encoding
with open('/tmp/somefile.txt', mode='w', encoding='latin-1') as f:
    f.write('This is some latin1 text: "è già ora"')

# Read back file with latin-1 encoding.
with open('/tmp/somefile.txt', encoding='latin-1') as f:
    txt = f.read()
    print(txt)
```

How it works...

Once the `encoding` option is passed to `open`, the resulting object file will know that any string provided to `file.write` must be encoded to the specified encoding before storing the actual bytes into the file. This is also true for `file.read()`, which will fetch the bytes from the file and decode them with the specified encoding before returning them to you.

This allows you to read/write content in files with any encoding independently from the one that your system declares as the favorite one.

There's more...

If you're wondering how it might be possible to read a file for which the encoding is unknown, well, that's a far more complex problem.

The fact is that unless the file provides some guidance in a header, or something equivalent, that can tell you the type of encoding on the content, there is no reliable way to know how a file might be encoded.

You might try multiple different types of encoding and check which one is able to decode the content (doesn't throw `UnicodeDecodeError`), but the fact that a set of bytes decodes to an encoding doesn't guarantee that it decodes to the right result. For example, the `'ì'` character encoded to `utf-8` decodes perfectly in `latin-1`, but results in a totally different thing:

```
>>> 'ì'.encode('utf-8').decode('latin-1')
'Ã¬'
```

If you really want to try guessing the type-encoding of the content, you might want to try a library, such as `chardet`, that is able to detect most common types of encoding. If the length of the data to decode is long and varied enough, it will frequently succeed in detecting the right encoding.

Reading lines of text

When working with text files, the easiest way to process them is usually by line; each line of text is a separate entity and we can build them back by joining all lines by `'\n'` or `'\r\n'` depending on the system, thus it would be very convenient to have all the lines of a text file available in a list.

There is a very convenient way to grab lines out of a text file that Python makes instantly available.

How to do it...

As the `file` object itself is an iterable, we can directly build a list out of it:

```
with open('/var/log/install.log') as f:
    lines = list(f)
```

How it works...

`open` acts as a context manager, returning the resulting object file. It's very convenient to rely on the context manager as, when we are done with our file, we need to close it and using `open` as a context manager will actually do that for us as soon as we quit the body of `with`.

The interesting part is that `file` is actually an iterable. When you iterate over a file, you get back the lines that are contained within it. So applying `list` to it will build a list of all the lines and we can then navigate the resulting list as we wish.

Reading and writing binary data

Reading text data is already pretty complex as it requires decoding the contents of a file, but reading binary data can be far more complex as it requires parsing the bytes and their contents to reconstruct the original data that was saved within the file.

In some cases, you might even have to cope with byte-ordering because, when saving a number into a text file, the order the bytes will be written in really depends on the system that is writing that file.

Suppose we want to read the beginning of the TCP header, the specific source and destination port, sequence number, and acknowledgment number, which is represented as follows:

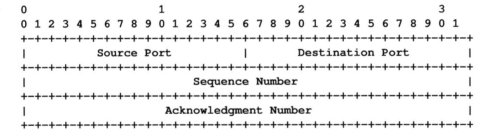

How to do it...

The steps for this recipe are as follows:

1. Given a file that contains a dump of a TCP packet (on my computer, I saved it as `/tmp/packet.dump`), we can try to read it as binary data and parse its contents.

The Python `struct` module is the perfect tool for reading binary-structured data and we can use it to parse our TCP packet as we know the size of each piece:

```
>>> import struct
>>> with open('/tmp/packet.dump', 'rb') as f:
...     data = struct.unpack_from('>HHLL', f.read())
>>> data
(50291, 80, 2778997212, 644363807)
```

Being an HTTP connection, the result is what we would expect: `Source Port: 50291, Destination Port: 80, Sequence Number: 2778997212`, and `Acknowledgment Number: 644363807`.

2. The same can be done to write back the binary data by using `struct.pack`:

```
>>> with open('/tmp/packet.dump', 'wb') as f:
...     data = struct.pack('>HHLL', 50291, 80, 2778997212,
644363807)
...     f.write(data)
>>> data
b'\xc4s\x00P\xa5\xa4!\xdc&h6\x1f'
```

How it works...

First of all, we opened the file in *binary mode* (the `rb` argument). This tells Python to avoid trying to decode the contents of the file as if it was text; the content is returned as it is in a `bytes` object.

Then the data we read with `f.read()` is passed to `struct.unpack_from`, which is able to decode binary data as a set of numbers, strings, and so on. In our case, we used > to specify that the data we are reading is in big-endian ordering (like all network-related data) and then `HHLL` to state that we want to read two unsigned 16-bit numbers and two unsigned 32-bit numbers (the ports and the sequence/acknowledgment numbers).

As we used `unpack_from`, any other remaining data is just ignored after the four specified numbers are consumed.

The same applies to writing binary data. We opened the file in binary mode, packaged the four numbers into a bytes object through `struct.pack`, and wrote them to the file.

There's more...

The `struct.pack` and `struct.unpack` functions support many options and formatters to define what data should be written/read and how it should be written/read.

The most common formatters for byte order are the following:

Character	Byte order
=	native
<	little-endian
>	big-endian

If none of those is specified, the data will be encoded in your system native byte order and will be aligned as it's naturally aligned in your system memory. It's strongly discouraged to save data this way as the only system guaranteed to be able to read it back is the one that saved it.

For the data itself, each type of data is represented by a single character, and each character defines the kind of data (integer, float, string) and its size:

Format	C type	Python type	Size (bytes)
x	pad byte	no value	
c	char	bytes of length 1	1
b	signed char	integer	1
B	unsigned char	integer	1
?	_Bool	bool	1
h	short	integer	2
H	unsigned short	integer	2
i	int	integer	4
I	unsigned int	integer	4
l	long	integer	4
L	unsigned long	integer	4
q	long long	integer	8
Q	unsigned long long	integer	8
n	ssize_t	integer	
N	size_t	integer	
e	half precision float	float	2
f	float	float	4

Format	C type	Python type	Size (bytes)
d	double	float	8
s	char[]	bytes	
p	char[]	bytes	
P	void *	integer	

Zipping a directory

Archive files are a good way to distribute whole directories as if they were a single file and to reduce the size of the distributed files.

Python has built-in support for creating ZIP archive files, which can be leveraged to compress a whole directory.

How to do it...

The steps for this recipes are as follows:

1. The `zipfile` module allows us to create compressed ZIP archives made up of multiple files:

```python
import zipfile
import os

def zipdir(archive_name, directory):
    with zipfile.ZipFile(
        archive_name, 'w', compression=zipfile.ZIP_DEFLATED
    ) as archive:
        for root, dirs, files in os.walk(directory):
            for filename in files:
                abspath = os.path.join(root, filename)
                relpath = os.path.relpath(abspath, directory)
                archive.write(abspath, relpath)
```

2. Using `zipdir` is as simple as providing a name for the `.zip` file that should be created and a path for the directory that should be archived:

```python
zipdir('/tmp/test.zip', '_build/doctrees')
```

3. In this case, I compressed the directory that contains the document trees for this book. Once the archive is ready, we can verify its content by opening it with `zipfile` again and listing the contained entries:

```
>>> with zipfile.ZipFile('/tmp/test.zip') as archive:
...     for n in archive.namelist():
...         print(n)
algorithms.doctree
concurrency.doctree
crypto.doctree
datastructures.doctree
datetimes.doctree
devtools.doctree
environment.pickle
filesdirs.doctree
gui.doctree
index.doctree
io.doctree
multimedia.doctree
```

How it works...

`zipfile.ZipFile` is first opened in write mode with the `ZIP_DEFLATED` compression (which means compress the data with the standard ZIP format) as a context. That allows us to perform changes to the archive and then flush them and close the archive automatically as soon as we exit the body of the context manager.

Within the context, we rely on `os.walk` to traverse the whole directory and all its subdirectories and find all the contained files.

For each file found in each directory, we build two paths: the absolute one and the relative one.

The absolute one is required to tell `ZipFile` from where to read the data that needs to be added to the archive, and the relative one is used to give a proper name to the data we are writing into the archive. This way, each file we write into the archive will be named as it was on our disk, but instead of being stored with its full path (`/home/amol/pystlcookbook/_build/doctrees/io.doctree`), it will be stored with the relative path (`_build/doctrees/io.doctree`), so that in case the archive is decompressed, the file will be created relative to the directory we are decompressing into, instead of ending up with a long pointless path that resembles the one that the file had on my computer.

Once the path of the file and the name that should be used to store it are ready, they are provided to `ZipFile.write` to actually write the file into the archive.

Once all the files are written, we exit the context manager and the archive is finally flushed.

Pickling and shelving

If there is a lot of information that your software needs or if you want to preserve history across different runs, there is little choice apart from saving it somewhere and loading it back on the next run.

Manually saving and loading back data can be tedious and error-prone, especially if the data structures are complex.

For this reason, Python provides a very convenient module, `shelve`, that allows us to save and restore Python objects of any kind as far as it's possible to `pickle` them.

How to do it...

Perform the following steps for this recipe:

1. `shelf`, implemented by `shelve`, can be opened like any other file in Python. Once opened, it's possible to read and write keys into it like a dictionary:

```
>>> with shelve.open('/tmp/shelf.db') as shelf:
...     shelf['value'] = 5
...
```

2. Values stored into `shelf` can be read back as a dictionary, too:

```
>>> with shelve.open('/tmp/shelf.db') as shelf:
...     print(shelf['value'])
...
5
```

3. Complex values, or even custom classes, can be stored in `shelve`:

```
>>> class MyClass(object):
...     def __init__(self, value):
...         self.value = value
...
>>> with shelve.open('/tmp/shelf.db') as shelf:
...     shelf['value'] = MyClass(5)
```

```
...
>>> with shelve.open('/tmp/shelf.db') as shelf:
...     print(shelf['value'])
...
<__main__.MyClass object at 0x101e90d30>
>>> with shelve.open('/tmp/shelf.db') as shelf:
...     print(shelf['value'].value)
...
5
```

How it works...

The shelve module is implemented as a context manager that manages a dbm database.

When the context is entered, the database is opened, and the contained objects become accessible because shelf was a dictionary.

Each object is stored into the database as a pickled object. That means that before storing it, each object is encoded with pickle and results in a serialized string:

```
>>> import pickle
>>> pickle.dumps(MyClass(5))
b'\x80\x03c__main__\nMyClass\nq\x00)\x81q\x01}'
b'q\x02X\x05\x00\x00\x00valueq\x03K\x05sb.'
```

That allows shelve to store any kind of Python object, even custom classes, as far as they are available again at the time the object is read back.

Then, when the context is exited, all the keys of shelf that were changed are written back to disk by calling shelf.sync when shelf is closed.

There's more...

A few things need attention when working with shelve.

First of all, shelve doesn't track mutations. If you store a mutable object (such as dict or list) in shelf, any change you do to it won't be saved. Only changes to the root keys of shelf itself are tracked:

```
>>> with shelve.open('/tmp/shelf.db') as shelf:
...     shelf['value'].value = 10
...
>>> with shelve.open('/tmp/shelf.db') as shelf:
```

```
...     print(shelf['value'].value)
...
5
```

This just means that you need to reassign any value you want to mutate:

```
>>> with shelve.open('/tmp/shelf.db') as shelf:
...     myvalue = shelf['value']
...     myvalue.value = 10
...     shelf['value'] = myvalue
...
>>> with shelve.open('/tmp/shelf.db') as shelf:
...     print(shelf['value'].value)
...
10
```

`shelve` doesn't allow concurrent read/writes from multiple processes or threads. You must wrap the `shelf` access with a lock (such as by using `fcntl.flock`) if you want to access the same `shelf` from multiple processes.

Reading configuration files

When your software has too many options to simply pass them all through the command line, or when you want to ensure that your users don't have to manually provide them every time they start the application, loading those options from a configuration file is one of the most widespread solutions.

Configuration files should be easy to read and write for humans, as they will be working with them quite often, and one of the most common requirements is for them to allow comments, so that the user can place comments in the configuration to write down why some options were set or how some values were computed. This way, when the user comes back to the configuration file in six months, they will still know the reasons for those options.

For these reasons, usually relying on JSON or machine-machine formats to configure options doesn't work very well, so a configuration-specific format is best.

One of the longest-living configuration formats is the `.ini` file, which allows us to declare multiple sections with the `[section]` syntax and to set options with the `name = value` syntax.

A resulting configuration file will look as follows:

```
[main]
debug = true
path = /tmp
frequency = 30
```

Another great advantage is that we can easily read `.ini` files from Python.

How to do it...

The steps for this recipe are:

1. Most of the work of loading and parsing `.ini` can be done by the `configparser` module itself, but we are going to extend it to implement per-section default values and converters:

```python
import configparser


def read_config(config_text, schema=None):
    """Read options from ``config_text`` applying given
``schema``"""
    schema = schema or {}

    cfg = configparser.ConfigParser(
        interpolation=configparser.ExtendedInterpolation()
    )
    try:
        cfg.read_string(config_text)
    except configparser.MissingSectionHeaderError:
        config_text = '[main]\n' + config_text
        cfg.read_string(config_text)

    config = {}
    for section in schema:
        options = config.setdefault(section, {})
        for option, option_schema in schema[section].items():
            options[option] = option_schema.get('default')
    for section in cfg.sections():
        options = config.setdefault(section, {})
```

```
                section_schema = schema.get(section, {})
                for option in cfg.options(section):
                    option_schema = section_schema.get(option, {})
                    getter = 'get' + option_schema.get('type', '')
                    options[option] = getattr(cfg, getter)(section, option)
            return config
```

2. Using the provided function is as easy as providing a configuration and a schema that should be used to parse it:

```
config_text = '''
debug = true

[registry]
name = Alessandro
surname = Molina

[extra]
likes = spicy food
countrycode = 39
'''

config = read_config(config_text, {
    'main': {
        'debug': {'type': 'boolean'}
    },
    'registry': {
        'name': {'default': 'unknown'},
        'surname': {'default': 'unknown'},
        'middlename': {'default': ''},
    },
    'extra': {
        'countrycode': {'type': 'int'},
        'age': {'type': 'int', 'default': 0}
    },
    'more': {
        'verbose': {'type': 'int', 'default': 0}
    }
})
```

The resulting configuration dictionary, `config`, will contain all the options provided in the configuration or declared in the schema, converted to the type specified in the schema:

```
>>> import pprint
>>> pprint.pprint(config)
{'extra': {'age': 0, 'countrycode': 39, 'likes': 'spicy food'},
 'main': {'debug': True},
 'more': {'verbose': 0},
```

```
'registry': {'middlename': 'unknown',
             'name': 'Alessandro',
             'surname': 'Molina'}}
```

How it works...

The `read_config` function does three major things:

- Allows us to parse plain lists of options without sections. This allows us to parse simple `config` files:

```
option1 = value1
option2 = value2
```

- Applies default values for all options declared in the configuration's `default` schema.
- Converts all values to the `type` provided in the schema.

The first feature is provided by trapping any `MissingSectionHeaderError` exception raised during parsing and automatically adding a `[main]` section if it's missing. All the options provided without any section will be recorded under the `main` section.

Providing default values is instead done by doing a first pass through all the sections and options declared in the schema and setting them to the value provided in their `default` or to `None` if no default value is provided.

In a second pass, all the default values are then overridden with the actual values stored in the configuration when those exist.

During this second pass, for each value being set, the `type` for that option is looked up in the schema. A string such as `getboolean` or `getint` is built by prefixing the type with the `get` word. This results in being the name of the `configparser` method that needs to be used to parse the configuration option into the requested type.

If no `type` was provided, an empty string is used. That results in the plain `.get` method being used, which reads the values as text. So not providing a `type` means treating the option as a normal string.

All the fetched and converted options are then stored in a dictionary, which makes it easier to access the converted values through the `config[section][name]` notation without needing to always call an accessor, such as `.getboolean`.

There's more...

The `interpolation=configparser.ExtendedInterpolation()` argument provided to the `ConfigParser` object also enables an interpolation mode that allows us to refer to values from other sections into the configuration file.

This is convenient to avoid having to repeat the same values over and over, for example, when providing multiple paths that should all start from the same root:

```
[paths]
root = /tmp/test01
images = ${root}/images
sounds = ${root}/sounds
```

Also, the syntax allows us to refer to options in other sections:

```
[main]
root = /tmp/test01

[paths]
images = ${main:root}/images
sounds = ${main:root}/sounds
```

Another convenient feature of `ConfigParser` is that if you want to make an option available in all sections, you can just specify it in the special `[DEFAULT]` section.

That will make the option available in all other sections unless it's explicitly overwritten in the section itself:

```
>>> config = read_config('''
... [DEFAULT]
... option = 1
...
... [section1]
...
... [section2]
... option = 5
... ''')
>>> config
{'section1': {'option': '1'},
 'section2': {'option': '5'}}
```

Writing XML/HTML content

Writing SGML-based languages is generally not very hard, most languages provide utilities to work with them, but if the document gets too big, it's easy to get lost when trying to build the tree of elements programmatically.

Ending up with hundreds of `.addChild` or similar calls all after each other makes it really hard to understand where we were in the document and what part of it we are currently editing.

Thankfully, by joining the Python `ElementTree` module with context managers, we can have a solution that allows our code structure to match the structure of the XML/HTML we are trying to generate.

How to do it...

For this recipe, perform the following steps:

1. We can create an `XMLDocument` class that represents the tree of an XML/HTML document and have `XMLDocumentBuilder` assist in actually building the document by allowing us to insert tags and text:

```python
import xml.etree.ElementTree as ET
from contextlib import contextmanager


class XMLDocument:
    def __init__(self, root='document', mode='xml'):
        self._root = ET.Element(root)
        self._mode = mode

    def __str__(self):
        return ET.tostring(self._root, encoding='unicode',
method=self._mode)

    def write(self, fobj):
        ET.ElementTree(self._root).write(fobj)

    def __enter__(self):
        return XMLDocumentBuilder(self._root)

    def __exit__(self, exc_type, value, traceback):
        return
```

```
class XMLDocumentBuilder:
    def __init__(self, root):
        self._current = [root]

    def tag(self, *args, **kwargs):
        el = ET.Element(*args, **kwargs)
        self._current[-1].append(el)
        @contextmanager
        def _context():
            self._current.append(el)
            try:
                yield el
            finally:
                self._current.pop()
        return _context()

    def text(self, text):
        if self._current[-1].text is None:
            self._current[-1].text = ''
        self._current[-1].text += text
```

2. We can then use our XMLDocument to build the document we want. For example, we can build web pages in HTML mode:

```
doc = XMLDocument('html', mode='html')

with doc as _:
    with _.tag('head'):
        with _.tag('title'): _.text('This is the title')
    with _.tag('body'):
        with _.tag('div', id='main-div'):
            with _.tag('h1'): _.text('My Document')
            with _.tag('strong'): _.text('Hello World')
            _.tag('img', src='http://via.placeholder.com/150x150')
```

3. XMLDocument supports casting to string, so to see the resulting XML, we can just print it:

```
>>> print(doc)
<html>
    <head>
        <title>This is the title</title>
    </head>
    <body>
        <div id="main-div">
            <h1>My Document</h1>
            <strong>Hello World</strong>
            <img src="http://via.placeholder.com/150x150">
```

```
        </div>
      </body>
    </html>
```

As you can see, the structure of our code matches the nesting of the actual XML document, so it's easy to see that anything within _.tag('body') is the content of our body tag.

Writing the resulting document to an actual file can be done by relying on the XMLDocument.write method:

```
doc.write('/tmp/test.html')
```

How it works...

The actual document generation is performed by xml.etree.ElementTree, but if we had to generate the same document with plain xml.etree.ElementTree, it would have resulted in a bunch of el.append calls:

```
root = ET.Element('html')
head = ET.Element('head')
root.append(head)
title = ET.Element('title')
title.text = 'This is the title'
head.append(title)
```

This makes it really hard to have any understanding of where we are. In this example, we were just building a structure, <html><head><title>This is the title</title></head></html>, but it was already pretty hard to follow that title was inside head and so on. For a more complex document, it would become impossible.

So while our XMLDocument preserves the root of the document tree and provides support for casting it to string and writing it to a file, the actual work is done by XMLDocumentBuilder.

XMLDocumentBuilder keeps a stack of nodes to track where we are in the tree (XMLDocumentBuilder._current). The tail of that list will always tell us which tag we're currently inside.

Calling XMLDocumentBuilder.text will add text to the currently active tag:

```
doc = XMLDocument('html', mode='html')
with doc as _:
    _.text('Some text, ')
    _.text('and even more')
```

The preceding code will result in `<html>Some text, and even more</html>` being generated.

The `XMLDocumentBuilder.tag` method will add a new tag within the currently active tag:

```
doc = XMLDocument('html', mode='html')
with doc as _:
    _.tag('input', type='text', placeholder='Name?')
    _.tag('input', type='text', placeholder='Surname?')
```

This leads to the following:

```
<html>
    <input placeholder="Name?" type="text">
    <input placeholder="Surname?" type="text">
</html>
```

The interesting part is that the `XMLDocumentBuilder.tag` method also returns a context manager. On entry, it will set the entered tag as the currently active one and on exit, it will recover the previously active node.

That allows us to nest `XMLDocumentBuilder.tag` calls and generate a tree of tags:

```
doc = XMLDocument('html', mode='html')
with doc as _:
    with _.tag('head'):
        with _.tag('title') as title: title.text = 'This is a title'
```

This leads to the following:

```
<html>
    <head>
        <title>This is a title</title>
    </head>
</html>
```

The actual document node can be grabbed through `as`, so in previous examples we were able to grab the `title` node that was just created and set a text for it, but `XMLDocumentBuilder.text` would have worked too because the `title` node was now the active element once we entered its context.

There's more...

There is one trick that I frequently apply when using this recipe. It makes it a bit harder to understand what's going on, on the Python side, and that's the reason why I avoided doing it while explaining the recipe itself, but it makes the HTML/XML structure even more readable by getting rid of most Python *noise*.

If you assign the XMLDocumentBuilder.tag and XMLDocumentBuilder.text methods to some short names, you can nearly disappear the fact that you are calling Python functions and make the XML structure more relevant:

```
doc = XMLDocument('html', mode='html')
with doc as builder:
    _ = builder.tag
    _t = builder.text

    with _('head'):
        with _('title'): _t('This is the title')
    with _('body'):
        with _('div', id='main-div'):
            with _('h1'): _t('My Document')
            with _('strong'): _t('Hello World')
            _('img', src='http://via.placeholder.com/150x150')
```

Written this way, the only things you actually see are the HTML tags and their content, which makes the document structure more obvious.

Reading XML/HTML content

Reading HTML or XML files allows us to parse web pages' content and to read documents or configurations described in XML.

Python has a built-in XML parser, the ElementTree module which is perfect for parsing XML files, but when HTML is involved, it chokes quickly due to the various quirks of HTML.

Consider trying to parse the following HTML:

```
<html>
    <body class="main-body">
        <p>hi</p>
        <img><br>
        <input type="text" />
    </body>
</html>
```

You will quickly face errors:

```
xml.etree.ElementTree.ParseError: mismatched tag: line 7, column 6
```

Luckily, it's not too hard to adapt the parser to handle at least the most common HTML files, such as self-closing/void tags.

How to do it...

You need to perform the following steps for this recipe:

1. ElementTree by default uses expat to parse documents, and then relies on xml.etree.ElementTree.TreeBuilder to build the DOM of the document.

   We can replace XMLParser based on expat with our own parser based on HTMLParser and have TreeBuilder rely on it:

```python
import xml.etree.ElementTree as ET
from html.parser import HTMLParser


class ETHTMLParser(HTMLParser):
    SELF_CLOSING = {'br', 'img', 'area', 'base', 'col', 'command',
                    'embed', 'hr', 'input', 'keygen', 'link',
                    'menuitem', 'meta', 'param',
                    'source', 'track', 'wbr'}

    def __init__(self, *args, **kwargs):
        super(ETHTMLParser, self).__init__(*args, **kwargs)
        self._builder = ET.TreeBuilder()
        self._stack = []

    @property
    def _last_tag(self):
        return self._stack[-1] if self._stack else None
```

```
    def _handle_selfclosing(self):
        last_tag = self._last_tag
        if last_tag in self.SELF_CLOSING:
            self.handle_endtag(last_tag)

    def handle_starttag(self, tag, attrs):
        self._handle_selfclosing()
        self._stack.append(tag)
        self._builder.start(tag, dict(attrs))

    def handle_endtag(self, tag):
        if tag != self._last_tag:
            self._handle_selfclosing()
        self._stack.pop()
        self._builder.end(tag)

    def handle_data(self, data):
        self._handle_selfclosing()
        self._builder.data(data)

    def close(self):
        return self._builder.close()
```

2. Using this parser, we can finally handle our HTML document with success:

```
text = '''
<html>
    <body class="main-body">
        <p>hi</p>
        <img><br>
        <input type="text" />
    </body>
</html>
'''

parser = ETHTMLParser()
parser.feed(text)
root = parser.close()
```

3. We can verify that our `root` node actually contains our original HTML document by printing it back:

```
>>> print(ET.tostring(root, encoding='unicode'))
<html>
    <body class="main-body">
        <p>hi</p>
        <img /><br />
        <input type="text" />
```

```
            </body>
          </html>
```

4. The resulting `root` document can then be navigated like any other tree of
   `ElementTree.Element`:

```
def print_node(el, depth=0):
    print(' '*depth, el)
    for child in el:
        print_node(child, depth + 1)

>>> print_node(root)
 <Element 'html' at 0x102799a48>
  <Element 'body' at 0x102799ae8>
   <Element 'p' at 0x102799a98>
   <Element 'img' at 0x102799b38>
   <Element 'br' at 0x102799b88>
   <Element 'input' at 0x102799bd8>
```

How it works...

To build the tree of `ElementTree.Element` objects representing the HTML document, we used two classes together: `HTMLParser` to read the HTML text, and `TreeBuilder` to build the tree of `ElementTree.Element` objects.

Every time `HTMLParser` faces an open or closed tag, it will call `handle_starttag` and `handle_endtag`. When we face those, we notify `TreeBuilder` that a new element must be started and then that the element must be closed.

Concurrently, we keep track of the last tag that was started (so the tag we're currently in) in `self._stack`. This way, we can know the currently opened tag that hasn't yet been closed. Every time we face a new open tag or a closed tag, we check whether the last open tag was a self-closing tag; if it was, we close it before opening or closing the new tag.

This automatically converts code. Consider the following:

```
<br><p></p>
```

It will be converted to the following:

```
In::
<br></br><p></p>
```

As a new open tag was found, after facing a self-closing tag (`<br>`), the `<br>` tag is automatically closed.

It also handles code such as the following:

```
<body><br></body>
```

The preceding code is converted into the following:

```
<body><br></br></body>
```

As a different closing tag (`</body>`) is faced right after the `<br>` self-closing tag, `<br>` is automatically closed.

Even when `handle_data` is called, while processing text inside a tag, if the last open tag was a self-closing one, the self-closing tag is automatically closed:

```
<p><br>Hello World</p>
```

The `Hello World` text is considered as being the content of `<p>` instead of being the content of `<br>` because the code was converted to the following:

```
<p><br></br>Hello World</p>
```

Finally, once the full document is parsed, calling `ETHTMLParser.close()` will terminate the tree built by `TreeBuilder` and will return the resulting root `Element`.

There's more...

The proposed recipe shows how to use `HTMLParser` to adapt the XML parsing utilities to cope with HTML, which is more flexible in rules when compared with XML.

While this solution handles mostly commonly written HTML, it won't cover all possible cases. HTML supports some oddities that are sometimes used, such as attributes without any value:

```
<input disabled>
```

Or attributes without quotes:

```
<input type=text>
```

And even some attributes with content but without any closing tag:

```
<li>Item 1
<li>Item 2
```

Even though most of these formats are supported, they are rarely used (with maybe the exception of attributes without any value, which our parser will just report as having a value of None), so in most cases, they won't cause trouble. But if you really need to parse HTML supporting all the possible oddities, it's surely easier to use an external library, such as lxml or html5lib, that tries to behave as much like a browser as possible when facing oddities.

Reading and writing CSV

CSV is considered one of the best exchange formats for tabular data; nearly all spreadsheet tools support reading and writing CSV, and it's easy to edit it with any plain text editor as it's easy for humans to understand.

Just split and set the values with a comma and you have practically written a CSV document.

Python has very good built-in support for reading CSV files, and we can easily write or read CSV data through the csv module.

We will see how it's possible to read and write a table:

```
"ID","Name","Surname","Language"
1,"Alessandro","Molina","Italian"
2,"Mika","Häkkinen","Suomi"
3,"Sebastian","Vettel","Deutsch"
```

How to do it...

Let's see the steps for this recipe:

1. First of all, we will see how to write the specified table:

```
import csv

with open('/tmp/table.csv', 'w', encoding='utf-8') as f:
    writer = csv.writer(f, quoting=csv.QUOTE_NONNUMERIC)
    writer.writerow(("ID","Name","Surname","Language"))
    writer.writerow((1,"Alessandro","Molina","Italian"))
    writer.writerow((2,"Mika","Häkkinen","Suomi"))
    writer.writerow((3,"Sebastian","Vettel","Deutsch"))
```

2. The `table.csv` file will contain the same table that we saw previously, and we can read it back using any of the `csv` readers. The most convenient one, when your CSV file has headers, is `DictReader`, which will read each row in a dictionary with the headers as the keys:

```
with open('/tmp/table.csv', 'r', encoding='utf-8', newline='') as
f:
    reader = csv.DictReader(f)
    for row in reader:
        print(row)
```

3. Iterating over `DictReader` will consume the rows, which should print the same data we wrote:

```
{'Surname': 'Molina', 'Language': 'Italian', 'ID': '1', 'Name':
'Alessandro'}
{'Surname': 'Häkkinen', 'Language': 'Suomi', 'ID': '2', 'Name':
'Mika'}
{'Surname': 'Vettel', 'Language': 'Deutsch', 'ID': '3', 'Name':
'Sebastian'}
```

There's more...

CSV files are plain text files, with a few limitations. For example, nothing tells us how a newline should be encoded (\r\n or \n) and nothing tells us which encoding should be used, `utf-8` or `ucs-2`. In theory, CSV doesn't even state that it must be comma-separated; a lot of software will write it separated by : or ;.

That's why you should pay attention to the `encoding` provided to the `open` function when reading CSV files. In our example, we knew for sure that `utf8` was used, because we wrote the file ourselves, but in other cases, there would be no guarantee that any specific encoding was used.

In case you are not sure how the CSV file is formatted, you can try to use the `csv.Sniffer` object, which, when applied to the text contained in the CSV file, will try to detect the dialect that was used.

Once the dialect is known, you can pass it to `csv.reader` to tell the reader to parse the file using that dialect.

Reading/writing a database

Python is often referred to as a language that has *batteries included*, thanks to its very complete standard library, and one of the best features it provides is reading and writing from a full-featured relational database.

Python ships with the SQLite library built in, meaning that we can save and read database files stored by SQLite.

The usage is pretty straightforward and most of it actually just involves sending SQL for execution.

How to do it...

For this recipes, the steps are as follows:

1. Using the sqlite3 module, it's possible to create a new database file, create a table, and insert entries into it:

```
import sqlite3


with sqlite3.connect('/tmp/test.db') as db:
    try:
        db.execute('''CREATE TABLE people (
            id INTEGER PRIMARY KEY AUTOINCREMENT NOT NULL,
            name TEXT,
            surname TEXT,
            language TEXT
        )''')
    except sqlite3.OperationalError:
        # Table already exists
        pass

    sql = 'INSERT INTO people (name, surname, language) VALUES (?,
?, ?)'
    db.execute(sql, ("Alessandro", "Molina", "Italian"))
    db.execute(sql, ("Mika", "Häkkinen", "Suomi"))
    db.execute(sql, ("Sebastian", "Vettel", "Deutsch"))
```

2. The `sqlite3` module also provides support for `cursors`, which allow us to stream the results of a query from the database to your own code:

```
with sqlite3.connect('/tmp/test.db') as db:
    db.row_factory = sqlite3.Row
    cursor = db.cursor()
    for row in cursor.execute('SELECT * FROM people WHERE language
                               != :language',
                               {'language': 'Italian'}):
        print(dict(row))
```

3. The previous snippet will print all rows stored in our database as `dict`, with the keys matching column names, and the values matching the value of each column in the row:

```
{'name': 'Mika', 'language': 'Suomi', 'surname': 'Häkkinen', 'id':
2}
{'name': 'Sebastian', 'language': 'Deutsch', 'surname': 'Vettel',
'id': 3}
```

How it works...

`sqlite3.connect` is used to open a database file; the returned object can then be used to perform any query against it, being an insertion or a selection.

The `.execute` method is then used to run any SQL against the opened database. The SQL to run is provided as a plain string.

When performing queries, it's usually a bad idea to provide values directly in SQL, especially if those values were provided by the user.

Imagine we write the following:

```
cursor.execute('SELECT * FROM people WHERE language != %s' % ('Italian',)):
```

What would have happened if instead of `Italian`, the user provided the string `'Italian" OR 1=1 OR "'`? Instead of filtering the results, the user would have got access to the full content of the table. It's easy to see how this can become a security issue if the query is filtered by user ID and the table contains data from multiple users.

Also in case of `executescript` commands, the user would be able to rely on the same behavior to actually execute any SQL code, thereby injecting code into our own application.

For this reason, `sqlite3` provides a way to pass arguments to the SQL queries and escape their content, so that even if the user provided malicious input, nothing bad would happen.

The `?` placeholders in our `INSERT` statements and the `:language` placeholder in our `SELECT` statement exist exactly for this purpose: to rely on `sqlite` escaping behavior.

The two are equivalent and it's your choice which one you use. One works with tuples while the other works with dictionaries.

When consuming results from the database, they are then provided through `Cursor`. You can think of a cursor as something streaming data from the database. Each row is read only when you need to access it, thereby avoiding the need to load all rows in memory and transfer them all in a single shot.

While this is not a major problem for common cases, it can cause issues when a lot of data is read, up to the point where the system might kill your Python script because it's consuming too much memory.

By default, reading rows from a cursor returns tuples, with values in the same order the columns were declared. By using `db.row_factory = sqlite3.Row`, we ensure that the cursor returns rows as `sqlite3.Row` objects.

They are far more convenient than tuples, because while they can be indexed like tuples (you can still write `row[0]`), they also support accessing through column names (`row['name']`). Our snippet relies on the fact that `sqlite3.Row` objects can be converted to dictionaries to print all the row values with their column names.

There's more...

The `sqlite3` module supports many additional features, such as transactions, custom types, and in-memory databases.

Custom types allow us to read structured data as Python objects, but my favorite feature is support for in-memory databases.

Using an in-memory database is very convenient when writing test suites for your software. If you write software that relies on the `sqlite3` module, make sure you write tests connecting to a `":memory:"` database. That will make your tests faster and will avoid piling up test database files on your disk every time you run tests.

Algorithms 7

In this chapter, we will cover the following recipes:

- Searching, sorting, filtering—high-performance searching in sorted containers
- Getting the nth element of any iterable—grabbing the nth element of any iterable, generators too
- Grouping similar items—splitting an iterable into groups of similar items
- Zipping—merging together data from multiple iterables into a single iterable
- Flattening a list of lists—converting a list of lists into a flat list
- Producing permutations and—computing all possible permutations of a set of elements
- Accumulating and reducing—applying binary functions to iterables
- Memoizing—speeding up computation by caching functions
- Operators to functions—how to keep references to callables for a Python operator
- Partials—reducing the number of arguments of a function by preapplying some
- Generic functions—functions that are able to change behavior according to the provided argument type
- Proper decoration—properly decorating a function to avoid missing its signature and docstring
- Context managers—automatically running code whenever you enter and exit a block of code
- Applying variable context managers—how a variable number of context managers can be applied

Introduction

When writing software, there are a whole bunch of things that you will find yourself doing over and over independently from the type of application you are writing.

Apart from whole features that you might have to reuse across different applications (such as login, logging, and authorization), there are a bunch of little building blocks that you can reuse across any kind of software.

This chapter will try to gather a bunch of recipes that can be used as reusable snippets to achieve very common operations that you might have to perform independently from your software's purpose.

Searching, sorting, filtering

Searching for an element is a very common need in programming. Looking up an item in a container is basically the most frequent operation that your code will probably do, so it's very important that it's quick and reliable.

Sorting is frequently connected to searching, as it's often possible to involve smarter lookup solutions when you know your set is sorted, and sorting means continuously searching and moving items until they are in sorted order. So they frequently go together.

Python has built-in functions to sort containers of any type and look up items in them, even with functions that are able to leverage the sorted sequence.

How to do it...

For this recipe, the following steps are to be performed:

1. Take the following set of elements:

```
>>> values = [ 5, 3, 1, 7 ]
```

2. Looking up an element in the sequence can be done through the in operator:

```
>>> 5 in values
True
```

3. Sorting can be done through the `sorted` function:

```
>>> sorted_value = sorted(values)
>>> sorted_values
[ 1, 3, 5, 7 ]
```

4. Once we have a sorted container, we can actually use the `bisect` module to find contained entries faster:

```
def bisect_search(container, value):
    index = bisect.bisect_left(container, value)
    return index < len(container) and container[index] == value
```

5. `bisect_search` can be used to know whether an entry is in the list, much like the `in` operator did:

```
>>> bisect_search(sorted_values, 5)
True
```

6. But, the advantage is that it can be a lot faster for many sorted entries:

```
>>> import timeit
>>> values = list(range(1000))
>>> 900 in values
True
>>> bisect_search(values, 900)
True
>>> timeit.timeit(lambda: 900 in values)
timeit.timeit(lambda: bisect_search(values, 900))
13.61617108999053
>>> timeit.timeit(lambda: bisect_search(values, 900))
0.872136551013682
```

So, the `bisect_search` function is 17 times faster than a plain lookup in our example.

How it works...

The `bisect` module uses dichotomic searching to look for the point of insertion of an element in a sorted container.

If an element exists in the array, its insertion position is exactly where the element is (as it should go exactly where it is):

```
>>> values = [ 1, 3, 5, 7 ]
>>> bisect.bisect_left(values, 5)
2
```

If the element is missing, it will return the position of the next, immediately bigger element:

```
>>> bisect.bisect_left(values, 4)
2
```

This means we will get a position even for elements that do not exist in our container. That's why we compare the element at the returned position with the element that we were looking for. If the two are different, it means that the nearest element was returned and so the element itself was not found.

For the same reason, if the element is not found and it's bigger than the biggest value contained in the container, the length of the container itself is returned (as the element should go at the end), so we need to also ensure that we `index < len(container)` to check for elements that were not in the container.

There's more...

So far, we've only sorted and looked up the entries themselves, but in many cases you will have complex objects where you are interested in sorting and searching for a specific property of an object.

For example, you might have a list of people and you want to sort by their names:

```
class Person:
    def __init__(self, name, surname):
        self.name = name
        self.surname = surname
    def __repr__(self):
        return '<Person: %s %s>' % (self.name, self.surname)

people = [Person('Derek', 'Zoolander'),
          Person('Alex', 'Zanardi'),
          Person('Vito', 'Corleone')
          Person('Mario', 'Rossi')]
```

Sorting those people by name can be done by relying on the `key` argument of the `sorted` function, which specifies a callable that should return the value for which the entry should be sorted:

```
>>> sorted_people = sorted(people, key=lambda v: v.name)
[<Person: Alex Zanardi>, <Person: Derek Zoolander>,
 <Person: Mario Rossi>, <Person: Vito Corleone>]
```

Sorting through a `key` function is much faster than sorting through a comparison function. Because the `key` function only needs to be called once per item (then the result is preserved), while the `comparison` function needs to be called over and over every time that there are two items that need to be compared. So, if computing the value for which we should sort is expensive, the `key` function approach can achieve significant performance improvements.

Now the problem is that `bisect` doesn't allow us to provide a key, so to be able to use `bisect` on the people list, we would have to first build a `keys` list where we can apply the `bisect`:

```
>>> keys = [p.name for p in people]
>>> bisect_search(keys, 'Alex')
True
```

This requires one more pass through the list to build the `keys` list, so it's only convenient if you have to look up multiple entries (or the same entry multiple times), otherwise a linear search across the list will be faster.

Note that you would have to build the `keys` list even to be able to use the `in` operator. So, if you want to search for a property without building an ad hoc list, you will have to rely on filtering as `filter` or list comprehensions.

Getting the nth element of any iterable

Randomly accessing to containers is something we are used to doing frequently and without too many issues. For most container types, it's even a very cheap operation. When working with generic iterables and generators on the other side, it's not as easy as we would expect and it often ends up with us converting them to lists or ugly `for` loops.

The Python standard library actually has ways to make this very straightforward.

How to do it...

The `itertools` module is a treasure of valuable functions when working with iterables, and with minor effort it's possible to get the nth item of any iterable:

```
import itertools

def iter_nth(iterable, nth):
    return next(itertools.islice(iterable, nth, nth+1))
```

Given a random iterable, we can use it to grab the element we want:

```
>>> values = (x for x in range(10))
>>> iter_nth(values, 4)
4
```

How it works...

The `itertools.islice` function is able to take a slice of any iterable. In our specific case, we want the slice that goes from the element we are looking for to the next one.

Once we have the slice containing the element we were looking for, we need to extract that item from the slice itself.

As `islice` acts on iterables, it returns an iterable itself. This means we can use `next` to consume it, and as the item we were looking for is actually the first of the slice, using `next` will properly return the item we were looking for.

In case the item is out of bounds (for example, we look for the fourth item out of just three), a `StopIteration` error is raised and we can trap it like we would for `IndexError` in normal lists.

Grouping similar items

Sometimes you might face a list of entries that has multiple, repeated entries and you might want to group the similar ones based on some kind of property.

For example, here is a list of names:

```
names = [('Alex', 'Zanardi'),
         ('Julius', 'Caesar'),
         ('Anakin', 'Skywalker'),
         ('Joseph', 'Joestar')]
```

We might want to build a group of all people whose names start with the same character, so we can keep our phone book in alphabetical order instead of having names randomly scattered here and there.

How to do it...

The `itertools` module is again a very powerful tool that provides us with the foundations we need to handle iterables:

```
import itertools

def group_by_key(iterable, key):
    iterable = sorted(iterable, key=key)
    return {k: list(g) for k,g in itertools.groupby(iterable, key)}
```

Given our list of names, we can apply a key function that grabs the first character of the name so that all entries will be grouped by it:

```
>>> group_by_key(names, lambda v: v[0][0])
{'A': [('Alex', 'Zanardi'), ('Anakin', 'Skywalker')],
 'J': [('Julius', 'Caesar'), ('Joseph', 'Joestar')]}
```

How it works...

The core of the function here is provided by `itertools.groupby`.

This function moves the iterator forward, grabs the item, and adds it to the current group. When an item with a different key is faced, a new group is created.

So, in fact, it will only group nearby entries that share the same key:

```
>>> sample = [1, 2, 1, 1]
>>> [(k, list(g)) for k,g in itertools.groupby(sample)]
[(1, [1]), (2, [2]), (1, [1, 1])]
```

As you can see, there are three groups instead of the expected two, because the first group of 1 is immediately interrupted by number 2, and so we end up with two different groups of 1.

We sort the elements before grouping them, the reason being that sorting ensures that equal elements are all near to one another:

```
>>> sorted(sample)
[1, 1, 1, 2]
```

At that point, the grouping function will create the correct amount of groups because there is a single chunk for each equivalent element:

```
>>> sorted_sample = sorted(sample)
>>> [(k, list(g)) for k,g in itertools.groupby(sorted_sample)]
[(1, [1, 1, 1]), (2, [2])]
```

We frequently work with complex objects in real life, so the `group_by_key` function also accepts a `key` function. That will state for which key the elements should be grouped.

As sorted accepts a key function when sorting, we know that all our elements will be sorted for that key before grouping and so we will return the right number of groups.

Finally, as `groupby` returns an iterator or iterators (each group within the top iterable is an iterator too), we cast each group to a list and build a dictionary out of the groups so that they can be easily accessed by `key`.

Zipping

Zipping means attaching two different iterables to create a new one that contains values from both.

This is very convenient when you have multiple tracks of values that should proceed concurrently. Imagine you had names and surnames and you want to just get a list of people:

```
names = [ 'Sam', 'Axel', 'Aerith' ]
surnames = [ 'Fisher', 'Foley', 'Gainsborough' ]
```

How to do it...

We want to zip together names and surnames:

```
>>> people = zip(names, surnames)
>>> list(people)
[('Sam', 'Fisher'), ('Axel', 'Foley'), ('Aerith', 'Gainsborough')]
```

How it works...

Zip will make a new iterable where each item in the newly-created iterable is a collection that is made by picking one item for each one of the provided iterables.

So, `result[0] = (i[0], j[0])`, and `result[1] = (i[1], j[1])`, and so on. If `i` and `j` have different lengths, it will stop as soon as one of the two is exhausted.

If you want to proceed until you exhaust the longest one of the provided iterables instead of stopping on the shortest one, you can rely on `itertools.zip_longest`. Values from the iterables that were already exhausted will be filled with a default value.

Flattening a list of lists

When you have multiple nested lists, you often need to just iterate over all the items contained in the lists without much interest in the depth at which they are actually stored.

Say you have this list:

```
values = [['a', 'b', 'c'],
          [1, 2, 3],
          ['X', 'Y', 'Z']]
```

If you just want to grab all the items within it, you really don't want to iterate over the lists within the list and then on the items of each one of them. We just want the leaf items and we don't care at all that they are in a list within a list.

How to do it...

What we want to do is just join all the lists into a single iterable that will yield the items themselves, as we are talking about iterators, the `itertools` module has the right function that will allow us to chain all the lists as if they were a single one:

```
>>> import itertools
>>> chained = itertools.chain.from_iterable(values)
```

The resulting `chained` iterator will yield the underlying items, one by one, when consumed:

```
>>> list(chained)
['a', 'b', 'c', 1, 2, 3, 'X', 'Y', 'Z']
```

How it works...

The `itertools.chain` function is a very convenient one when you have to consume multiple iterables one after the other.

By default, it accepts those iterables as arguments, so we would have to do:

```
itertools.chain(values[0], values[1], values[2])
```

But, for convenience, `itertools.chain.from_iterable` will chain the entries contained in the provided argument instead of having to pass them explicitly one by one.

There's more...

If you know how many items the original lists contained and they have the same size, it's easy to apply the reverse operation.

We already know it's possible to merge entries from multiple sources using `zip`, so what we actually want to do is zip together the elements that were part of the same original list, so that we can go back from being `chained` to the original list of lists:

```
>>> list(zip(chained, chained, chained))
[('a', 'b', 'c'), (1, 2, 3), ('X', 'Y', 'Z')]
```

In this case, we had three items lists, so we had to provide `chained` three times.

This works because `zip` will sequentially consume one entry from each provided argument. So, as we are providing the same argument three times, we are in fact consuming the first three entries, then the next three, and then the last three.

If `chained` was a list instead of an iterator, we would have to create an iterator out of the list:

```
>>> chained = list(chained)
>>> chained ['a', 'b', 'c', 1, 2, 3, 'X', 'Y', 'Z']
>>> ichained = iter(chained)
>>> list(zip(ichained, ichained, ichained)) [('a', 'b', 'c'), (1, 2, 3),
('X', 'Y', 'Z')]
```

If we didn't use `ichained` but instead we used the original `chained`, the result would be pretty far from what we wanted:

```
>>> chained = list(chained)
>>> chained
['a', 'b', 'c', 1, 2, 3, 'X', 'Y', 'Z']
```

```
>>> list(zip(chained, chained, chained))
[('a', 'a', 'a'), ('b', 'b', 'b'), ('c', 'c', 'c'),
 (1, 1, 1), (2, 2, 2), (3, 3, 3),
 ('X', 'X', 'X'), ('Y', 'Y', 'Y'), ('Z', 'Z', 'Z')]
```

Producing permutations and combinations

Given a set of elements, if you ever felt the need to do something for each possible permutation of those elements, you might have wondered what the best way to generate all those permutations was.

Python has various functions in the `itertools` module that will help with permutations and combinations, the differences between those are not always easy to grasp, but once you investigate what they do, they will become clear.

How to do it...

The Cartesian product is usually what people think of when talking about combinations and permutations.

1. Given a set of elements, A, B, and C, we want to extract all possible couples of two elements, AA, AB, AC, and so on:

   ```
   >>> import itertools
   >>> c = itertools.product(('A', 'B', 'C'), repeat=2)
   >>> list(c)
   [('A', 'A'), ('A', 'B'), ('A', 'C'),
    ('B', 'A'), ('B', 'B'), ('B', 'C'),
    ('C', 'A'), ('C', 'B'), ('C', 'C')]
   ```

2. In case you want to omit the duplicated entries (AA, BB, CC), you can just use permutations:

   ```
   >>> c = itertools.permutations(('A', 'B', 'C'), 2)
   >>> list(c)
   [('A', 'B'), ('A', 'C'),
    ('B', 'A'), ('B', 'C'),
    ('C', 'A'), ('C', 'B')]
   ```

3. You might even want to ensure that the same couple doesn't happen twice (such as `AB` versus `BA`), in such a case, `itertools.combinations` might be what you are looking for:

```
>>> c = itertools.combinations(('A', 'B', 'C'), 2)
>>> list(c)
[('A', 'B'), ('A', 'C'), ('B', 'C')]
```

So most needs of combining values from a set can be easily solved through the function provided by the `itertools` module.

Accumulating and reducing

List comprehensions and `map` are very convenient tools when you need to apply a function to all elements of an iterable and get back the resulting values. But those are mostly meant to apply unary functions and keep a collection of the transformed values (such as add `1` to all numbers), but if you want to apply functions that should receive more than one element at the time, they don't fit very well.

The reduction and accumulation functions instead are meant to receive multiple values from the iterable and return a single value (in the case of reduction) or multiple values (in the case of accumulation).

How to do it...

The steps for this recipe are as follows:

1. The most simple example of reduction is summing all items in an iterable:

```
>>> values = [ 1, 2, 3, 4, 5 ]
```

2. This is something that can easily be done by `sum`, but for the sake of this example, we will use `reduce`:

```
>>> import functools, operator
>>> functools.reduce(operator.add, values)
15
```

3. If instead of having a single final result, you want to keep the results of the intermediate steps, you can use `accumulate`:

```
>>> import itertools
>>> list(itertools.accumulate(values, operator.add))
[1, 3, 6, 10, 15]
```

There's more...

`accumulate` and `reduce` are not limited to mathematical uses. While those are the most obvious examples, they are very flexible functions and their purpose changes depending uniquely on the function they are going to apply.

For example, if you have multiple lines of text, you can also use `reduce` to compute the total sum of all text:

```
>>> lines = ['this is the first line',
...          'then there is one more',
...          'and finally the last one.']
>>> functools.reduce(lambda x, y: x + len(y), [0] + lines)
69
```

Or, if you have multiple dictionaries you need to collapse:

```
>>> dicts = [dict(name='Alessandro'), dict(surname='Molina'),
...          dict(country='Italy')]
>>> functools.reduce(lambda d1, d2: {**d1, **d2}, dicts)
{'name': 'Alessandro', 'surname': 'Molina', 'country': 'Italy'}
```

It's even a very convenient way to access deeply nested dictionaries:

```
>>> import operator
>>> nesty = {'a': {'b': {'c': {'d': {'e': {'f': 'OK'}}}}}}
>>> functools.reduce(operator.getitem, 'abcdef', nesty)
'OK'
```

Memoizing

When running a function over and over, avoiding the cost to call that function can greatly speed up the resulting code.

Think of a `for` loop or a recursive function that maybe has to call that function dozens of times. If instead of calling it, it could preserve the known results of a previous call to the function, it could make code much faster.

The most common example for memoizing is the Fibonacci sequence. The sequence is computed by adding the first two numbers, then the second number is added to the result, and so on.

This means that in the sequence 1, 1, 2, 3, 5, computing 5 required us to compute 3 + 2, which required us to compute 2 + 1, which required us to compute 1 + 1.

Doing the Fibonacci sequence in a recursive manner is the most obvious approach as it leads to 5 = `fib(n3)` + `fib(n2)`, which was made of 3 = `fib(n2)` + `fib(n1)`, so you can easily see that we had to compute `fib(n2)` twice. Memoizing the result of `fib(n2)` would allow us to perform such computation only once and then reuse the result on the next call.

How to do it...

Here are the steps for this recipe:

1. Python provides an LRU cache built-in, which we can use for memoization:

```
import functools

@functools.lru_cache(maxsize=None)
def fibonacci(n):
    '''inefficient recursive version of Fibonacci number'''
    if n > 1:
        return fibonacci(n-1) + fibonacci(n-2)
    return n
```

2. We can then use the function to compute the full sequence:

```
fibonacci_seq = [fibonacci(n) for n in range(100)]
```

3. The result will be a list with all the Fibonacci numbers up to the 100th:

```
>>> print(fibonacci_seq)
[0, 1, 1, 2, 3, 5, 8, 13, 21 ...
```

The difference in performance is huge. If we use the `timeit` module to time our function, we can easily see how much memoizing helped with performance.

4. When the memoized version of the `fibonacci` function is used, the computation ends in less than a millisecond:

```
>>> import timeit
>>> timeit.timeit(lambda: [fibonacci(n) for n in range(40)],
number=1)
0.000033469987101
```

5. Then if we remove `@functools.lru_cache()`, which implemented the memoization, the timing changes radically:

```
>>> timeit.timeit(lambda: [fibonacci(n) for n in range(40)],
number=1)
89.14927123498637
```

So it's easy to see how memoization changed the performance to fractions of a second from 89 seconds.

How it works...

Whenever the function is invoked, `functools.lru_cache` saves the returned value together with the provided arguments.

The next time the function will be called, the arguments are searched in the saved arguments and, if they are found, the previously returned value is provided instead of calling the function.

This, in fact, changes the cost of calling our function to being just the cost of a lookup in a dictionary.

So the first time we call `fibonacci(5)`, it gets computed, then next time it will be called, it will do nothing and the value previously stored for 5 will be returned. As `fibonacci(6)` has to call `fibonacci(5)` to be able to compute, it's easy to see how we provided a major performance benefit for any `fibonacci(n)` where n>5.

Also as we wanted the whole sequence, the saving is not just for a single call, but for each call in the list comprehension following the first one that needs a memoized value.

The `lru_cache` function was born as a **least recently used** (**LRU**) cache, so by default, it will keep around only the `128` most recent, but by passing `maxsize=None`, we can use it as a standard cache and discard the LRU part of it. All calls will be cached forever without a limit.

Purely for the Fibonacci case, you will notice that setting `maxsize` to any value greater than 3 changes nothing, as each Fibonacci number only requires the previous two calls to be able to compute.

Operators to functions

Suppose you want to create a simple calculator. The first step is parsing the formula the user is going to write to be able to perform it. The basic formula is made of an operator and two operands, so you have, in practice, a function and its arguments.

But given +, −, and so on, how can we have our parser return the associated functions? Usually to sum two numbers, we just write n1 + n2, but we can't pass around + itself to be called with any n1 and n2.

This is because + is an operator and not a function, but underlying that it's still just a function in CPython that gets executed.

How to do it...

We can use the `operator` module to get a callable that represents any Python operator that we can store or pass around:

```python
import operator

operators = {
    '+': operator.add,
    '-': operator.sub,
    '*': operator.mul,
    '/': operator.truediv
}

def calculate(expression):
    parts = expression.split()

    try:
        result = int(parts[0])
    except:
        raise ValueError('First argument of expression must be numberic')

    operator = None
    for part in parts[1:]:
        try:
```

```
            num = int(part)
            if operator is None:
                raise ValueError('No operator proviede for the numbers')
        except ValueError:
            if operator:
                raise ValueError('operator already provided')
            operator = operators[part]
        else:
            result = operator(result, num)
            operator = None

    return result
```

Our `calculate` function acts as a very basic calculator (without operators precedence, real numbers, negative numbers, and so on):

```
>>> print(calculate('5 + 3'))
8
>>> print(calculate('1 + 2 + 3'))
6
>>> print(calculate('3 * 2 + 4'))
10
```

How it works...

So, we were able to store functions for the four mathematical operators in the `operators` dictionary and look them up based on the text that was encountered in the expression.

In `calculate`, the expression is split by space, so 5 + 3 becomes `['5', '+', '3']`. Once we have the three elements of the expression (the two operands and the operator), we can just iterate over the parts and when we encounter the +, look it up in the `operators` dictionary to get back the associated function that should be called, which is `operator.add`.

The `operator` module contains functions for the most common Python operators, from comparisons (`operator.gt`) to dot-based attribute access (`operator.attrgetter`).

Most of the provided functions are meant to be paired with `map`, `sorted`, `filter`, and so on.

Partials

We already know that we can apply unary functions to multiple elements using `map`, and apply binary functions using `reduce`.

There is a whole set of functions that accepts a callable in Python and applies it to a set of items.

The major problem is that frequently the callable we want to apply might have a slightly different signature, and while we can solve the issue by wrapping the callable into another callable that adapts the signature, this is not very convenient if you just want to apply a function to a set of items.

For example, if you want to multiply all numbers in a list by 3, there is no function that multiplies a given argument by 3.

How to do it...

We can easily adapt `operator.mul` to be a unary function and then pass it to `map` to apply it to the whole list:

```
>>> import functools, operator
>>>
>>> values = range(10)
>>> mul3 = functools.partial(operator.mul, 3)
>>> list(map(mul3, values))
[0, 3, 6, 9, 12, 15, 18, 21, 24, 27]
```

As you can see, `operator.mul` was called with 3 and the item as its arguments, and thus returned `item*3`.

How it works...

We created a new `mul3` callable through `functools.partial`. This callable just calls `operator.mul`, passing 3 as the first argument and then passing any argument provided to the callable to `operator.mul` as the second, third, and so on arguments.

So, in the end, doing `mul3(5)` means `operator.mul(3, 5)`.

This is because `functools.partial` creates a new function out of a provided function hardwiring the provided arguments.

It is, of course, also possible to pass keyword arguments, so that instead of hardwiring the first argument, we can set any argument.

The resulting function is then applied to all numbers through `map`, which leads to creating a new list with all the numbers from 0 to 10 multiplied by 3.

Generic functions

Generic functions are one of my favorite features of the standard library. Python is a very dynamic language and through duck-typing, you will frequently be able to write code that works in many different conditions (it doesn't matter if you receive a list or a tuple), but in some cases, you will really need to have two totally different code bases depending on the received input.

For example, we might want to have a function that prints content of the provided dictionary in a human-readable format, but we want it also to work properly on lists of tuples and report errors for unsupported types.

How to do it...

The `functools.singledispatch` decorator allows us to implement a generic dispatch based on argument type:

```python
from functools import singledispatch

@singledispatch
def human_readable(d):
    raise ValueError('Unsupported argument type %s' % type(d))

@human_readable.register(dict)
def human_readable_dict(d):
    for key, value in d.items():
        print('{}: {}'.format(key, value))

@human_readable.register(list)
@human_readable.register(tuple)
def human_readable_list(d):
    for key, value in d:
        print('{}: {}'.format(key, value))
```

Calling the three functions will properly dispatch the request to the right function:

```
>>> human_readable({'name': 'Tifa', 'surname': 'Lockhart'})
name: Tifa
surname: Lockhart

>>> human_readable([('name', 'Nobuo'), ('surname', 'Uematsu')])
name: Nobuo
surname: Uematsu

>>> human_readable(5)
Traceback (most recent call last):
    File "<stdin>", line 1, in <module>
    File "<stdin>", line 2, in human_readable
ValueError: Unsupported argument type <class 'int'>
```

How it works...

The function decorated with @singledispatch actually gets replaced by a check for the argument type.

Each call to human_readable.register will record into a registry which callable should be used for each argument type:

```
>>> human_readable.registry
mappingproxy({
    <class 'list'>: <function human_readable_list at 0x10464da60>,
    <class 'object'>: <function human_readable at 0x10464d6a8>,
    <class 'dict'>: <function human_readable_dict at 0x10464d950>,
    <class 'tuple'>: <function human_readable_list at 0x10464da60>
})
```

Whenever the decorated function gets called, it will instead look up the type of the argument in the registry and will forward the call to the associated function for execution.

The function decorated with @singledispatch should always be the generic implementation, the one that should be used in case the argument is not explicitly supported.

In our example, this just throws an error, but frequently it will instead try to provide an implementation that works in most cases.

Then the specific implementations can be registered with `@function.register` to cover the cases that the primary function couldn't cover or to actually implement the behavior if the primary function just throws an error.

Proper decoration

Decorators are usually not straightforward for anyone who faces them for the first time, but once you get used to them, they become a very convenient tool to extend a function's behavior or implement a lightweight form of aspect-oriented programming.

But even once decorators become natural and part of everyday development, they have subtleties that are not obvious until you face them for the first time.

It might not be immediately obvious when you are applying a `decorator`, but by using them, you are changing the signature of the `decorated` function, up to the point that the name of the function itself and its documentation are lost:

```
def decorator(f):
    def _f(*args, **kwargs):
        return f(*args, **kwargs)
    return _f


@decorator
def sumtwo(a, b):
    """Sums a and b"""
    return a + back
```

The `sumtwo` function was decorated with `decorator`, but now, if we try to access the function documentation or name, they won't be accessible anymore:

```
>>> print(sumtwo.__name__)
'_f'
>>> print(sumtwo.__doc__)
None
```

Even though we provided a docstring for `sumtwo` and we know for sure that it was named `sumtwo`, we need to ensure that our decorations are properly applied and preserve properties of the original functions.

How to do it...

You need to perform the following steps for this recipe:

1. The Python standard library provides a `functools.wraps` decorator that can be applied to decorators to have them preserve the properties of the decorated functions:

   ```
   from functools import wraps


   def decorator(f):
       @wraps(f)
       def _f(*args, **kwargs):
           return f(*args, **kwargs)
       return _f
   ```

2. Here we apply the decorator to a function:

   ```
   @decorator
   def sumthree(a, b):
       """Sums a and b"""
       return a + back
   ```

3. As you can see, it will properly retain the name and docstring of the function:

   ```
   >>> print(sumthree.__name__)
   'sumthree'
   >>> print(sumthree.__doc__)
   'Sums a and b'
   ```

   If the decorated function had custom attributes, those will be copied to the new function too.

There's more...

`functools.wraps` is a very convenient tool and does its best to ensure that the decorated function looks exactly like the original one.

But while the properties of the function can easily be copied, the signature of the function itself is not as easy to copy.

So inspecting our decorated function arguments won't return the original arguments:

```
>>> import inspect
>>> inspect.getfullargspec(sumthree)
FullArgSpec(args=[], varargs='args', varkw='kwargs', defaults=None,
            kwonlyargs=[], kwonlydefaults=None, annotations={})
```

So the reported arguments are just *args and **kwargs instead of a and b. To access the real arguments, we must dive into the underlying functions through the __wrapped__ attribute:

```
>>> inspect.getfullargspec(sumthree.__wrapped__)
FullArgSpec(args=['a', 'b'], varargs=None, varkw=None, defaults=None,
            kwonlyargs=[], kwonlydefaults=None, annotations={})
```

Luckily, the standard library provides an inspect.signature function that does this for us:

```
>>> inspect.signature(sumthree)
(a, b)
```

So, it's better to rely on inspect.signature whenever we want to check arguments of a function to be able to support both decorated and undecorated functions.

Applying decorations can also collide with other decorators. The most common example is classmethod:

```
class MyClass(object):
    @decorator
    @classmethod
    def dosum(cls, a, b):
        return a+b
```

Trying to decorate classmethod won't usually work:

```
>>> MyClass.dosum(3, 3)
Traceback (most recent call last):
  File "<stdin>", line 1, in <module>
    return f(*args, **kwargs)
TypeError: 'classmethod' object is not callable
```

You need to make sure that @classmethod is always the last applied decorator, to ensure it will work as expected:

```
class MyClass(object):
    @classmethod
    @decorator
    def dosum(cls, a, b):
        return a+b
```

At that point, the classmethod will work as expected:

```
>>> MyClass.dosum(3, 3)
6
```

There are so many decorator-related quirks that the Python environment has libraries that try to implement decoration properly for everyday usage. If you don't want to think about how to handle them, you might want to try the wrapt library, which will take care of most decoration oddities for you.

Context managers

Decorators can be used to ensure that something is executed when you enter and exit a function, but in some cases, you might want to ensure that something is always executed at the beginning and end of a block of code without having to move it to its own function or without rewriting those parts that should be executed every time.

Context managers exist to solve this need, factoring out code that you would have to rewrite over and over in place of try:except:finally: clauses.

The most common usage of context managers is probably the closing context manager, which ensures that files get closed once the developer is done working with them, but the standard library makes it easy to write new ones.

How to do it...

For this recipe, the following steps are to be performed:

1. contextlib provides features related to context managers, contextlib.contextmanager can make it very easy to write context managers:

```
@contextlib.contextmanager
def logentrance():
```

```
print('Enter')
yield
print('Exit')
```

2. Then the context manager created can be used like any other context manager:

```
>>> with logentrance():
>>>     print('This is inside')
Enter
This is inside
Exit
```

3. Exceptions raised within the wrapped block will be propagated to the context manager, so it's possible to handle them with a standard try:except:finally: clause and do any proper cleanup:

```
@contextlib.contextmanager
def logentrance():
    print('Enter')
    try:
        yield
    except:
        print('Exception')
        raise
    finally:
        print('Exit')
```

4. The changed context manager will be able to log exceptions without interfering with the exception propagation:

```
>>> with logentrance():
        raise Exception('This is an error')
Enter
Exception
Exit
Traceback (most recent call last):
    File "<stdin>", line 1, in <module>
        raise Exception('This is an error')
Exception: This is an error
```

Applying variable context managers

When using context managers, you must rely on the `with` statement to apply them. While it's possible to apply more than one context manager per statement by separating them with commas, it's not as easy to apply a variable number of them:

```
@contextlib.contextmanager
def first():
    print('First')
    yield

@contextlib.contextmanager
def second():
    print('Second')
    yield
```

The context managers that we want to apply must be known when writing the code:

```
>>> with first(), second():
>>>     print('Inside')
First
Second
Inside
```

But what if sometimes we only want to apply the `first` context manager, and sometimes we want to apply both?

How to do it...

`contextlib.ExitStack` serves various purposes, one of which is to allow us to apply a variable number of context managers to a block.

For example, we might want to apply both context managers only when we are printing an even number in a loop:

```
from contextlib import ExitStack

for n in range(5):
    with ExitStack() as stack:
        stack.enter_context(first())
        if n % 2 == 0:
            stack.enter_context(second())
        print('NUMBER: {}'.format(n))
```

The result will be that the `second` is only added to the context, and thus invoked for even numbers:

```
First
Second
NUMBER: 0
First
NUMBER: 1
First
Second
NUMBER: 2
First
NUMBER: 3
First
Second
NUMBER: 4
```

As you can see, for 1 and 3, only `First` is printed.

Of course, when exiting the context declared through the `ExitStack` context manager, all the context managers registered within the `ExitStack` will be exited too.

Cryptography

In this chapter, we will cover the following recipes:

- Asking for passwords—when asking for a password in a terminal-based software, make sure you don't leak it.
- Hashing passwords—how can passwords be stored without a risk of leaking them?
- Verifying a file's integrity—how to check that a file transferred over a network wasn't corrupted.
- Verify a message's integrity—how to check that a message you are sending to another software hasn't been altered.

Introduction

While cryptography is generally perceived as a complex field, there are tasks based on it that are part of our everyday lives as software developers, or at least they should be, to ensure a minimum level of security in our code base.

This chapter tries to cover recipes for most of the common tasks that you will have to face every day that can help to make your software resilient to attacks.

While software written in Python will hardly suffer from exploitation, such as buffer overflows (unless there are bugs in the interpreter or compiled libraries you rely on), there are still a whole bunch of cases where you might be leaking information that must remain undisclosed.

Asking for passwords

In terminal-based programs, it's common to ask for passwords from our users. It's usually a bad idea to do so from command options, as on Unix-like systems, they will be visible to anyone with access to the shell who is able to run a `ps` command to get the list of processes, and to anyone willing to run a `history` command to get the list of recently executed commands.

While there are ways to tweak the command arguments to hide them from the list of processes, it's always best to ask for passwords interactively so that no trace of them is left.

But, asking for them interactively is not enough, unless you also ensure they are not displayed while typing, otherwise anyone looking at your screen can grab all your passwords.

How to do it...

Luckily, the Python standard library provides an easy way to input passwords from a prompt without showing them back:

```
>>> import getpass
>>> pwd = getpass.getpass()
Password:
>>> print(pwd)
'HelloWorld'
```

How it works...

The `getpass.getpass` function will use the `termios` library on most systems to disable the echoing back of the characters written by the user. To avoid messing with the rest of the application input, it will be done within a new file descriptor for the terminal.

On systems that do not support this, it will use more basic calls to read characters directly from `sys.stdin` without echoing them back.

Hashing passwords

Avoiding storing passwords in plain text is a known best practice, as software usually only needs to check whether the password provided by the user is correct, and the hash of the password can be stored and compared with the hash of the provided password. If the two hashes match, the passwords are equal; if they don't, the provided password is wrong.

Storing passwords is a pretty standard practice, and usually they are stored as a hash plus some salt. The salt is a randomly generated string that is joined with the password before hashing. Being randomly generated, it ensures that even hashes of equal passwords get different results.

The Python standard library provides a pretty complete set of hashing functions, some of them very well-suited to storing passwords.

How to do it...

Python 3 introduced key derivation functions, which are especially convenient when storing passwords. Both `pbkdf2` and `scrypt` are provided. While `scrypt` is more robust against attacks as it's both memory- and CPU-heavy, it only works on systems that provide OpenSSL 1.1+. While `pbkdf2` works on any system, in worst cases a Python-provided fallback is used.

So, while from a security point of view `scrypt` would be preferred, we will rely on `pbkdf2` due to its wider availability and the fact that it's been available since Python 3.4 (`scrypt` is only available on Python 3.6+):

```
import hashlib, binascii, os

def hash_password(password):
    """Hash a password for storing."""
    salt = hashlib.sha256(os.urandom(60)).hexdigest().encode('ascii')
    pwdhash = hashlib.pbkdf2_hmac('sha512', password.encode('utf-8'),
                                  salt, 100000)
    pwdhash = binascii.hexlify(pwdhash)
    return (salt + pwdhash).decode('ascii')

def verify_password(stored_password, provided_password):
    """Verify a stored password against one provided by user"""
    salt = stored_password[:64]
    stored_password = stored_password[64:]
    pwdhash = hashlib.pbkdf2_hmac('sha512',
                                  provided_password.encode('utf-8'),
```

```
                    salt.encode('ascii'),
                    100000)
   pwdhash = binascii.hexlify(pwdhash).decode('ascii')
   return pwdhash == stored_password
```

The two functions can be used to hash the user-provided password for storage on disk or into a database (`hash_password`) and to verify the password against the stored one when a user tries to log back in (`verify_password`):

```
>>> stored_password = hash_password('ThisIsAPassWord')
>>> print(stored_password)
cdd5492b89b64f030e8ac2b96b680c650468aad4b24e485f587d7f3e031ce8b63cc7139b18
aba02e1f98edbb531e8a0c8ecf971a61560b17071db5eaa8064a87bcb2304d89812e1d07fe
bfea7c73bda8fbc2204e0407766197bc2be85eada6a5
>>> verify_password(stored_password, 'ThisIsAPassWord')
True
>>> verify_password(stored_password, 'WrongPassword')
False
```

How it works...

There are two functions involved here:

- `hash_password`: Encodes a provided password in a way that is safe to store on a database or file
- `verify_password`: Given an encoded password and a plain text one provided by the user, it verifies whether the provided password matches the encoded (and thus saved) one

`hash_password` actually does multiple things; it doesn't just hash the password.

The first thing it does is generate some random salt that should be added to the password. That's just the `sha256` hash of some random bytes read from `os.urandom`. It then extracts a string representation of the hashed salt as a set of hexadecimal numbers (`hexdigest`).

The salt is then provided to `pbkdf2_hmac` together with the password itself to hash the password in a randomized way. As `pbkdf2_hmac` requires bytes as its input, the two strings (password and salt) are previously encoded in pure bytes. The salt is encoded as plain ASCII as the hexadecimal representation of a hash will only contain the 0-9 and A-F characters. While the password is encoded as `utf-8`, it could contain any character. (Is there anyone with emojis in their passwords?)

The resulting `pbkdf2` is a bunch of bytes, as we want to store it into a database; we use `binascii.hexlify` to convert the bunch of bytes into their hexadecimal representation in a string format. `hexlify` is a convenient way to convert bytes to strings without losing data. It just prints all the bytes as two hexadecimal digits, so the resulting data will be twice as big as the original data, but apart from that, it's exactly the same as the converted data.

At the end, the function joins together the hash with its salt. As we know that the `hexdigest` of a `sha256` hash (the salt) is always 64 characters long. By joining them together, we can grab back the salt by reading the first 64 characters of the resulting string.

This will permit `verify_password` to verify the password and to verify whether the salt used to encode it is required.

Once we have our password, `verify_password` can then be used to verify provided passwords against it. So it takes two arguments: the hashed password and the new password that should be verified.

The first thing `verify_password` does is extract the salt from the hashed password (remember, we placed it as the first 64 characters of the string resulting from `hash_password`).

The extracted salt and the password candidate are then provided to `pbkdf2_hmac` to compute their hash and then convert it into a string with `binascii.hexlify`. If the resulting hash matches with the hash part of the previously stored password (the characters after the salt), it means that the two passwords match.

If the resulting hash doesn't match, it means that the provided password is wrong. As you can see, it's very important that we made the salt and the password available together, because we need it to be able to verify the password, and a different salt would result in a different hash and thus we'd never be able to verify the password.

Verifying a file's integrity

If you've ever downloaded a file from a public network, you might have noticed that their URLs are frequently in the form of `http://files.host.com/somefile.tar.gz#md5=3b3f5b2327421800ef00c38ab5ad81a6`.

That's because the download might go wrong and the data you got might be partially corrupted. So the URL includes an MD5 hash that you can use to verify that the downloaded file is fine through the `md5sum` tool.

The same applies when you download a file from a Python script. If the file provided has an MD5 hash for verification, you might want to check whether the retrieved file is valid and, in cases where it is not, then you can retry downloading it again.

How to do it...

Within `hashlib`, there are multiple supported hashing algorithms, and probably the most widespread one is `md5`, so we can rely on `hashlib` to verify our downloaded file:

```
import hashlib

def verify_file(filepath, expectedhash, hashtype='md5'):
    with open(filepath, 'rb') as f:
        try:
            filehash = getattr(hashlib, hashtype)()
        except AttributeError:
            raise ValueError(
                'Unsupported hashing type %s' % hashtype
            ) from None

        while True:
            data = f.read(4096)
            if not data:
                break
            filehash.update(data)

    return filehash.hexdigest() == expectedhash
```

Our file can then be downloaded and verified with `verify_file`.

For example, I might download the `wrapt` distribution from the **Python Package Index (PyPI)** and I might want to verify that it was correctly downloaded.

The file name would be `wrapt-1.10.11.tar.gz#sha256=d4d560d479f2c21e1b5443bbd15fe7ec4b37fe7e53d335d3b9b0a7b1226fe3c6` on which I could run my `verify_file` function:

```
>>> verify_file(
...     'wrapt-1.10.11.tar.gz',
...     'd4d560d479f2c21e1b5443bbd15fe7ec4b37fe7e53d335d3b9b0a7b1226fe3c6',
...     'sha256
... )
True
```

How it works...

The first thing the function does is open the file in binary mode. As all hash functions require bytes and we don't even know the content of the file, reading it in binary mode is the most convenient solution.

Then, it checks whether the requested hashing algorithm is available in `hashlib`. That's done through `getattr` by trying to grab `hashlib.md5`, `hashlib.sha256`, and so on. If the algorithm is not supported, it won't be a valid `hashlib` attribute (as it won't exist in the module) and will throw `AttributeError`. To make those easier to understand, they are trapped and a new `ValueError` is raised that states clearly that the algorithm is not supported.

Once the file is opened and the algorithm is verified, an empty hash gets created (notice that right after `getattr`, the parenthesis will lead to the creation of the returned hash).

We start with an empty one because the file might be very big, and we don't want to read the complete file and throw it at the hashing function at once.

Instead, we start with an empty hash and we read the file in chunks of 4 KB, then each chunk is fed to the hashing algorithm to update the hash.

Finally, once we have the hash computed, we grab its representation as hexadecimal numbers and compare it to the one provided to the function.

If the two match, the file was properly downloaded.

Verifying a message's integrity

When sending messages through a public network or storages accessible to other users and systems, we need to know whether the message contains the original content or whether it was intercepted and modified by anyone.

That's a typical form of a man-in-the-middle attack and it's something that can modify anything in our content, which is stored in a place that other people can read too, such as an unencrypted network or a disk on a shared system.

The HMAC algorithm can be used to guarantee that a message wasn't altered from its original state and it's frequently used to sign digital documents to ensure their integrity.

A good scenario for HMAC might be a password-reset link; those links usually include a parameter about the user for whom the password should be reset: `http://myapp.com/reset-password?user=myuser@email.net`.

But anyone might replace the user argument and reset other people's passwords. So, we want to ensure that the link we provide wasn't actually modified, since it was sent by attaching an HMAC to it.

That will result in something such as: `http://myapp.com/reset-password?user=myuser@email.netsignature=8efc6e7161004cfb09d05af69cc0af86bb5edb5e88bd477ba545a9929821f582`.

Furthermore, any attempt at modifying the user will make the signature invalid, thus making it impossible to reset other people's passwords.

Another use case is deploying REST APIs to authenticate and verify requests. Amazon Web Services uses HMAC as an authentication system for its web services. When you register, an access key and a secret are provided to you. Any request you make must be hashed with HMAC, using the secret key to ensure that you are actually the user stated in the request (as you owned its secret key), and the request itself wasn't changed in any way because details of it are hashed with HMAC too.

The HMAC signature is frequently involved in cases where your software has to send messages to itself or receive messages from a verified partner that can own a secret key.

How to do it...

For this recipe, the following steps are to be performed:

1. The standard library provides an `hmac` module that, combined with the hashing functions provided in `hashlib`, can serve the purpose of computing the message's authentication code for any provided message:

```python
import hashlib, hmac, time

def compute_signature(message, secret):
    message = message.encode('utf-8')
    timestamp = str(int(time.time()*100)).encode('ascii')

    hashdata = message + timestamp
    signature = hmac.new(secret.encode('ascii'),
                         hashdata,
                         hashlib.sha256).hexdigest()
    return {
```

```
            'message': message,
            'signature': signature,
            'timestamp': timestamp
        }


def verify_signature(signed_message, secret):
    timestamp = signed_message['timestamp']
    expected_signature = signed_message['signature']
    message = signed_message['message']

    hashdata = message + timestamp
    signature = hmac.new(secret.encode('ascii'),
                         hashdata,
                         hashlib.sha256).hexdigest()
    return signature == expected_signature
```

2. Our functions can then be used to compute a signed message and we can check that a signed message wasn't altered in any way:

```
>>> signed_msg = compute_signature('Hello World', 'very_secret')
>>> verify_signature(signed_msg, 'very_secret')
True
```

3. If you try to change the message field of the signed message, it won't be valid anymore, and only the real message will match the signature:

```
>>> signed_msg['message'] = b'Hello Boat'
>>> verify_signature(signed_msg, 'very_secret')
False
```

How it works...

Our purpose is to ensure that any given message can't be changed in any way or it will invalidate the signature attached to the message.

So the `compute_signature` function, given a message and a private secret key, returns all the data that the signed message should include when it's sent to the receiver. The sent data includes the message itself, the signature, and a timestamp. The timestamp is included because, in many cases, it's a good idea to ensure that the message is a recent one. If you are receiving an API request signed with HMAC or a cookie that you just set, you might want to ensure that you are handling a recent message and not one that was sent an hour ago. The timestamp can't be tampered with as it's included in the signature together with the message, and its presence makes it harder for attackers to guess the secret key, as two identical messages will result in having two different signatures, thanks to the timestamp.

Once the message and the timestamp are known, the `compute_signature` function hands them to `hmac.new`, together with the secret key, to compute the signature itself. For convenience, the signature is represented as the characters that compose the hexadecimal numbers that represent the bytes the signature is made of. This ensures that it can be transferred as plain text in HTTP headers or some similar manner.

Once we have our signed message as returned by `compute_signature`, this can be stored somewhere and, when loading it back, we can use `verify_signature` to check that it wasn't tampered with.

The `verify_signature` function takes the same steps as `compute_signature`. The signed message includes the message itself, the timestamp, and the signature. So `verify_signature` grabs the message and the timestamp and joins them with the secret key to compute the signature. If the computed signature matches the signature provided in the signed message, it means the message wasn't altered in any way. Otherwise, even a minor change to the message or to the timestamp will make the signature invalid.

9
Concurrency

In this chapter, we will cover the following recipes:

- ThreadPools—running tasks concurrently through a pool of threads
- Coroutines—interleaving the execution of code through coroutines
- Processes—dispatching work to multiple subprocesses
- Futures—futures represent a task that will complete in the future
- Scheduled tasks—setting a task to run at a given time, or every few seconds
- Sharing data between processes—managing variables that are accessible across multiple processes

Introduction

Concurrency is the ability to run two or more tasks in the same time span, whether they are parallel or not. Python provides many tools to implement concurrency and asynchronous behaviors: threads, coroutines, and processes. While some of them don't allow real parallelism due to their design (coroutines), or due to a Global Interpreter Lock (threads), they are very easy to use and can be leveraged to perform parallel I/O operations or to interleave functions with minimum effort. When real parallelism is required, multiprocessing is easy enough in Python to be a viable solution for any kind of software.

This chapter will cover the most common ways to achieve concurrency in Python, will show you how to perform asynchronous tasks that will wait in the background for certain conditions, and how to share data between processes.

ThreadPools

Threads have been, historically, the most common way to achieve concurrency within software.

In theory, when the system allows, these threads can achieve real parallelism, but in Python, the **Global Interpreter Lock (GLI)** doesn't allow threads actually to leverage multicore systems, as the lock will allow a single Python operation to proceed at any given time.

For this reason, threads are frequently undervalued in Python, but in fact, even when the GIL is involved, they can be a very convenient solution to run I/O operations concurrently.

While using coroutines, we would need a `run` loop and some custom code to ensure that the I/O operation proceeds in parallel. Using threads, we can run any kind of function within a thread and, if that function does some kind of I/O, such as reading from a socket or from a disk, the other threads will proceed in the meantime.

One of the major drawbacks of threads is the cost of spawning them. That's frequently stated as one of the reasons why coroutines can be a better solution, but there is a way to avoid paying that cost whenever you need a thread: `ThreadPool`.

A `ThreadPool` is a set of threads that is usually started when your application starts and sits there doing nothing until you actually have some work to dispatch. This way, when we have a task that we want to run into a separate thread, we just have to send it to `ThreadPool`, and `ThreadPool` will assign it to the first available thread out of all the threads that it owns. As those threads are already there and running, we don't have to pay the cost to spawn a thread every time we have work to do.

How to do it...

The steps for this recipe are as follows:

1. To showcase how `ThreadPool` works, we will need two operations that we want to run concurrently. One will fetch a URL from the web, which might take some time:

```python
def fetch_url(url):
    """Fetch content of a given url from the web"""
    import urllib.request
    response = urllib.request.urlopen(url)
    return response.read()
```

2. The other will just wait for a given condition to be true, looping over and over until it's done:

```
def wait_until(predicate):
    """Waits until the given predicate returns True"""
    import time
    seconds = 0
    while not predicate():
        print('Waiting...')
        time.sleep(1.0)
        seconds += 1
    print('Done!')
    return seconds
```

3. Then we will just fire the download for `https://httpbin.org/delay/3`, which will take 3 seconds, and concurrently wait for the download to complete.

4. To do so, we will run the two tasks in a `ThreadPool` (of four threads), and we will wait for both of them to complete:

```
>>> from multiprocessing.pool import ThreadPool
>>> pool = ThreadPool(4)
>>> t1 = pool.apply_async(fetch_url,
args=('https://httpbin.org/delay/3',))
>>> t2 = pool.apply_async(wait_until, args=(t1.ready, ))
Waiting...
>>> pool.close()
>>> pool.join()
Waiting...
Waiting...
Waiting...
Done!
>>> print('Total Time:', t2.get())
Total Time: 4
>>> print('Content:', t1.get())
Content: b'{"args":{},"data":"","files":{},"form":{},
            "headers":{"Accept-Encoding":"identity",
            "Connection":"close","Host":"httpbin.org",
            "User-Agent":"Python-urllib/3.5"},
            "origin":"99.199.99.199",
            "url":"https://httpbin.org/delay/3"}\n'
```

How it works...

`ThreadPool` is made of two major components: a bunch of threads and a bunch of queues. When the pool is created, a few orchestration threads are started together with as many worker threads as you specified at pool initialization.

The worker threads will be in charge of actually running the tasks you dispatch to them, while the orchestration threads will be in charge of managing the worker threads, doing things such as telling them to quit when the pool is closed, or restarting them when they crash.

If no number of worker threads is provided, `TaskPool` will just start as many threads as the amount of cores on your system as returned by `os.cpu_count()`.

Once the threads are started, they will just sit there waiting to consume something from the queue containing the work that is to be done. As soon as the queue has an entry, the worker thread will wake up and consume it, starting the work.

Once the work is done, the job and its result are put back into the results queue so that whoever was waiting for them can fetch them.

So, when we created `TaskPool`, we actually started four workers that began waiting for anything to do from the tasks queue:

```
>>> pool = ThreadPool(4)
```

Then, once we provided work for the `TaskPool`, we actually queued up two functions into the tasks queue, and as soon as a worker became available, it fetched one of them and started running it:

```
>>> t1 = pool.apply_async(fetch_url, args=('https://httpbin.org/delay/3',))
```

Meanwhile, `TaskPool` returns an `AsyncResult` object, which has two interesting methods: `AsyncResult.ready()`, which tells us whether the result is ready (the task finished), and `AsyncResult.get()`, which returns the result once it's available.

The second function we queued up was the one that would wait for a specific predicate to be `True`, and in this case, we provided `t1.ready`, which is the ready method of the previous `AsyncResult`:

```
>>> t2 = pool.apply_async(wait_until, args=(t1.ready, ))
```

This means that the second task will complete once the first one completes, as it will wait until `t1.ready() == True`.

Once both of the tasks are running, we tell `pool` that we have nothing more to do, so that it can quit once it's finished what it's doing:

```
>>> pool.close()
```

And we wait for `pool` to quit:

```
>>> pool.join()
```

This way, we will wait for both tasks to complete and then we will quit all the threads started by `pool`.

Once we know that all tasks are completed (because `pool.join()` returned), we can grab the results and print them:

```
>>> print('Total Time:', t2.get())
Total Time: 4
>>> print('Content:', t1.get())
Content: b'{"args":{},"data":"","files":{},"form":{},
          "headers":{"Accept-Encoding":"identity",
          "Connection":"close","Host":"httpbin.org",
          "User-Agent":"Python-urllib/3.5"},
          "origin":"99.199.99.199",
          "url":"https://httpbin.org/delay/3"}\n'
```

If we had more work to do, we would avoid running the `pool.close()` and `pool.join()` methods, so that we could send more work to `TaskPool`, which would get done as soon as there was a thread free.

There's more...

`ThreadPool` is particularly convenient when you have multiple entries to which you need to apply the same operation over and over. Suppose you have a list of four URLs that you need to download:

```
urls = [
    "https://httpbin.org/delay/1",
    "https://httpbin.org/delay/2",
    "https://httpbin.org/delay/3",
    "https://httpbin.org/delay/4"
]
```

Fetching them in a single thread would take a lot of time:

```
def fetch_all_urls():
    contents = []
    for url in urls:
        contents.append(fetch_url(url))
    return contents
```

We can test the time by running the function through the `timeit` module:

```
>>> import timeit
>>> timeit.timeit(fetch_all_urls, number=1)
12.116707602981478
```

If we could do so using a separate thread for each function, it would only take the time of the slowest one to fetch all the provided URLs, as the download would proceed concurrently for all of them.

`ThreadPool` actually provides us with the `map` method that does exactly that: it applies a function to a list of arguments:

```
def fetch_all_urls_theraded():
    pool = ThreadPool(4)
    return pool.map(fetch_url, urls)
```

The result will be a list containing the results returned by each call and we can easily test that this will be much faster than our original example:

```
>>> timeit.timeit(fetch_all_urls_theraded, number=1)
4.660976745188236
```

Coroutines

Threads are the most common way to implement concurrency in most languages and use cases, but they are expensive in terms of cost, and while `ThreadPool` can be a good solution for cases when thousands of threads are involved, it's usually unreasonable to involve thousands of threads. Especially when long-lived I/O is involved, you might easily reach thousands of operations running concurrently (think of the amount of concurrent HTTP requests an HTTP server might have to handle) and most of those tasks will be sitting doing nothing, just waiting for data from the network or from the disk most of the time.

In those cases, asynchronous I/O is the preferred approach. Compared to synchronous blocking I/O where your code is sitting there waiting for the read or write operation to complete, asynchronous I/O allows a task that needs data to initiate the read operation, switch to doing something else, and once the data is available, go back to what it was doing.

In some cases, the notification of available data might come in the form of a signal, which would interrupt the concurrently running code, but, more commonly, asynchronous I/O is implemented through the usage of a selector (such as `select`, `poll`, or `epoll`) and an event loop that will resume the function waiting for the data as soon as the selector is notified that the data is available.

This actually leads to interleaving functions that are able to run for a while, reach a point where they need some I/O, and pass control to another function that will give it back as soon as it needs to perform some I/O too. Functions whose execution can be interleaved by suspending and resuming them are called **coroutines**, as they run cooperatively.

How to do it...

In Python, coroutines are implemented through the `async def` syntax and are executed through an `asyncio` event loop.

For example, we might write a function that runs two coroutines that count down from a given number of seconds, printing their progress. That would easily allow us to see that the two coroutines are running concurrently, as we would see output from one interleaved with output from the other:

```
import asyncio

async def countdown(identifier, n):
    while n > 0:
        print('left:', n, '({})'.format(identifier))
        await asyncio.sleep(1)
        n -= 1

async def main():
    await asyncio.wait([
        countdown("A", 2),
        countdown("B", 3)
    ])
```

Once an event loop is created and we run `main` within it, we will see the two functions running:

```
>>> loop = asyncio.get_event_loop()
>>> loop.run_until_complete(main())
left:  2  (A)
left:  3  (B)
left:  1  (A)
left:  2  (B)
left:  1  (B)
```

Once the execution has completed, we can close the event loop as we won't need it anymore:

```
>>> loop.close()
```

How it works...

The core of our coroutines world is the **event loop**. It's not possible to run coroutines (or, at least, it gets very complicated) without an event loop, so the first thing our code does is create an event loop:

```
>>> loop = asyncio.get_event_loop()
```

Then we ask the event loop to wait until a provided coroutine is completed:

```
loop.run_until_complete(main())
```

The `main` coroutine only starts two `countdown` coroutines and waits for their completion. That's done by using `await` and, in that, the `asyncio.wait` function is in charge of waiting for a bunch of coroutines:

```
await asyncio.wait([
    countdown("A", 2),
    countdown("B", 3)
])
```

`await` is important here, because we are talking about coroutines, so unless they are explicitly awaited, our code would immediately move forward, and thus, even though we called `asyncio.wait`, we would not be waiting.

In this case, we are waiting for the two countdowns to complete. The first countdown will start from 2 and will be identified by the character A, while the second countdown will start from 3 and will be identified by B.

The `countdown` function by itself is very simple. It's just a function that loops forever and prints how much there is left to wait.

Between each loop it waits one second, so that it waits the expected number of seconds:

```
await asyncio.sleep(1)
```

You might be wondering why we are using `asyncio.sleep` instead of `time.sleep`, and the reason is that, when working with coroutines, you must ensure that every other function that will block is a coroutine too. That way, you know that while your function is blocked, you would let the other coroutines move forward.

By using `asyncio.sleep`, we let the event loop move the other `countdown` function forward while the first one is waiting and, thus, we properly interleave the execution of the two functions.

This can be verified by checking the output. When `asyncio.sleep` is used, the output will be interleaved between the two functions:

```
left 2 (A)
left 3 (B)
left 1 (A)
left 2 (B)
left 1 (B)
```

When `time.sleep` is used, the first coroutine will have to complete fully before the second one can move forward:

```
left 2 (A)
left 1 (A)
left 3 (B)
left 2 (B)
left 1 (B)
```

So, a general rule when working with coroutines is that whenever you are going to call something that will block, make sure that it's a coroutine too, or you will lose the concurrency property of coroutines.

There's more...

We already know that the most important benefit of coroutines is that the event loop is able to pause their execution while they are waiting for I/O operations to let other coroutines proceed. While there is currently no built-in implementation of HTTP protocol with support for coroutines, it's easy enough to roll out a back version to reproduce our example of downloading a website concurrently to track how long it's taking.

As for the `ThreadPool` example, we will need the `wait_until` function that will wait for any given predicate to be true:

```
async def wait_until(predicate):
    """Waits until the given predicate returns True"""
    import time
    seconds = 0
    while not predicate():
        print('Waiting...')
        await asyncio.sleep(1)
        seconds += 1
    print('Done!')
    return seconds
```

We will also need a `fetch_url` function to download the content of the URL. As we want this to run as a coroutine, we can't rely on `urllib`, or it would block forever instead of passing control back to the event loop. So, we will have to read the data using `asyncio.open_connection`, which works at pure TCP level and thus will require us to implement HTTP support ourselves:

```
async def fetch_url(url):
    """Fetch content of a given url from the web"""
    url = urllib.parse.urlsplit(url)
    reader, writer = await asyncio.open_connection(url.hostname, 80)
    req = ('GET {path} HTTP/1.0\r\n'
            'Host: {hostname}\r\n'
            '\r\n').format(path=url.path or '/', hostname=url.hostname)
    writer.write(req.encode('latin-1'))
    while True:
        line = await reader.readline()
        if not line.strip():
            # Read until the headers, from here on is the actualy response.
            break
    return await reader.read()
```

At this point, it's possible to interleave the two coroutines and see that the download proceeds concurrently with the waiting, and that it completes in the expected time:

```
>>> loop = asyncio.get_event_loop()
>>> t1 = asyncio.ensure_future(fetch_url('http://httpbin.org/delay/3'))
>>> t2 = asyncio.ensure_future(wait_until(t1.done))
>>> loop.run_until_complete(t2)
Waiting...
Waiting...
Waiting...
Waiting...
Done!
>>> loop.close()
>>> print('Total Time:', t2.result())
Total Time: 4
>>> print('Content:', t1.result())
Content: b'{"args":{},"data":"","files":{},"form":{},
           "headers":{"Connection":"close","Host":"httpbin.org"},
           "origin":"93.147.95.71",
           "url":"http://httpbin.org/delay/3"}\n'
```

Processes

Threads and coroutines are concurrency models that coexist with the Python GIL and the leverage execution time left available by I/O operations to allow other tasks to continue. With modern multicore systems, it's great to be able to use the full power that the system provides by involving real parallelism and distributing the work across all the cores that are available.

The Python standard library provides very refined tools to work with multiprocessing, which is a great solution to leverage parallelism on Python. As multiprocessing will lead to multiple separate interpreters, the GIL won't get in the way, and compared to threads and coroutines, it might even be easier to reason with them as totally isolated processes that need to cooperate, rather than to think of multiple threads/coroutines within same system sharing the underlying memory state.

The major cost in managing processes is usually the spawn cost and the complexity of having to ensure you don't fork subprocesses in any odd condition, leading to unwanted data in memory being copied or file descriptors being reused.

multiprocessing.ProcessPool can be a very good solution to all these problems, as starting one at the beginning of our software will ensure that we don't have to pay any particular cost when we have a task to submit to a subprocess. Furthermore, by creating the processes only once at the beginning, we can guarantee a predictable (and mostly empty) state of the software being copied to create the subprocesses.

How to do it...

Pretty much like in the *ThreadPool* recipe, we will need two functions that will act as our tasks running concurrently in the processes.

In the case of processes, we don't need to perform I/O actually to run concurrently, so our tasks could be doing anything. What I'm going to use is the computing of the Fibonacci series while printing out progress, so that we can see how the output of the two processes will interleave:

```python
import os

def fib(n, seen):
    if n not in seen and n % 5 == 0:
        # Print out only numbers we didn't yet compute
        print(os.getpid(), '->', n)
        seen.add(n)

    if n < 2:
        return n
    return fib(n-2, seen) + fib(n-1, seen)
```

So, now we need to create the multiprocessing Pool that will run the fib function and spawn computation:

```
>>> from multiprocessing import Pool
>>> pool = Pool()
>>> t1 = pool.apply_async(fib, args=(20, set()))
>>> t2 = pool.apply_async(fib, args=(22, set()))
>>> pool.close()
>>> pool.join()
42588 -> 20
42588 -> 10
42588 -> 0
42589 -> 20
42588 -> 5
42589 -> 10
42589 -> 0
42589 -> 5
```

```
42588 -> 15
42589 -> 15
>>> t1.get()
6765
>>> t2.get()
17711
```

You can see how the process IDs of the two processes interleave, and once the job is completed, it's possible to get the results of both of them.

How it works...

When `multiprocessing.Pool` is created, a number of processes equal to the number of cores on the system (as stated by `os.cpu_count()`) is created through `os.fork` or by spawning a new Python interpreter, depending on what's supported by the underlying system:

```
>>> pool = Pool()
```

Once the new processes are started, they will all do the same thing: execute the `worker` function that loops forever consuming from the queue of jobs that were sent to `Pool` and running them one by one.

This means that if we create a `Pool` of two processes, we will have two workers. As soon as we ask `Pool` to perform something (through `Pool.apply_async`, `Pool.map`, or any other method), the jobs (functions and its arguments) are placed in `multiprocessing.SimpleQueue` from which the worker will fetch it.

Once `worker` fetches the task from the queue, it will run it. If multiple `worker` instances are running, each one of them will pick a task from the queue and run it.

Once the task has completed, the result of the function that was executed is pushed back into a results queue (together with the job itself to identify which task the result refers to), from which `Pool` will be able to consume the results and provide them back to the code that originally fired the tasks.

All this communication happens across multiple processes, so it can't happen in memory. Instead `multiprocessing.SimpleQueue`, which is underlying, uses `pipe`, each producer will write into `pipe`, and each consumer will read from `pipe`.

As `pipe` is only able to read and write bytes, the arguments we submit to `pool` and the results of the functions executed by `pool` are converted to bytes through the `pickle` protocol. That is able to marshal/unmarshal Python objects in as far as the same modules are available on both sides (sender and receiver).

So, we submit our requests to `Pool`:

```
>>> t1 = pool.apply_async(fib, args=(20, set()))
```

The `fib` function, `20`, and the empty set all get pickled and sent into the queue for one of the `Pool` workers to consume.

Meanwhile, while workers are picking up data and running the Fibonacci function, we join the pool, so that our primary process will block until all the processes on the pool have completed:

```
>>> pool.close()
>>> pool.join()
```

In theory, a process of the pool never completes (it runs forever, continuously looking for things to do in the queue). Before calling `join`, we `close` the pool. Closing the pool tells the pool to *exit all its processes once they finish what they are doing right now*.

Then, by immediately joining after `close`, we wait until the pool finishes what it's doing right now, which is serving our two requests.

As with threads, `multiprocessing.Pool` returns `AsyncResult` objects, which means we can check their completion through the `AsyncResult.ready()` method and we can grab the returned value, once it's ready, through `AsyncResult.get()`:

```
>>> t1.get()
6765
>>> t2.get()
17711
```

There's more...

`multiprocessing.Pool` works in nearly the same way as `multiprocessing.pool.ThreadPool`. In fact, they share a lot of their implementation as one is a subclass of the other.

But there are some major differences that are caused by the underlying technology used. One is based on threads and the other on subprocesses.

The major benefit of using processes is that the Python interpreter lock won't limit their parallelism, and they will be able to actually run in parallel with each other.

On the other side, there is a cost for that. Using processes is both more expensive in startup time (forking a process is usually slower than spawning a thread), and more expensive in terms of memory used, as each process will need to have its own state of memory. While a lot of this cost is reduced heavily on most systems through techniques such as copy on write, threads usually end up being a lot cheaper than processes.

For this reason, it's usually a good idea to start the process `pool` only at the beginning of your application, so that the additional cost of spawning processes is only paid once.

Processes are not only more expensive to start, but by contrast with threads, they don't share the state of the program; each process has its own state and memory. So it's not possible to share the data between `Pool` and the workers that will perform the tasks. All the data needs to be encoded through `pickle` and sent through `pipe` for the other end to consume. This has a huge cost compared to threads that can rely on a shared queue, especially when the data that has to be sent is big.

For this reason, it's usually a good idea to avoid involving processes when big files or data are involved in arguments or return values, as that data will have to be copied multiple times to reach its final destination. In that case, it's better to save the data on disk and pass around the path of the file.

Futures

When a background task is spawned, it might be running concurrently with your main flow forever and never complete its own job (such as the worker threads of a `ThreadPool`), or it might be something that will return a result to you sooner or later and you might be waiting for that result (such as a thread that downloads the content of a URL in the background).

These second types of task all share a common behavior: their result will be available in _future_. So, a result that will be available in the future is commonly referred to as `Future`. Programming languages don't all share the same exact definition of futures, and on Python `Future` is any function that will be completed in the future, typically returning a result.

`Future` is the callable itself, so it's unrelated to the technology that will be used actually to run the callable. You will need a way to let the execution of the callable proceed, and in Python, that's provided by `Executor`.

There are executors that can run the futures into threads, processes, or coroutines (in the case of coroutines, the loop itself is the executor).

How to do it...

To run a future, we will need an executor (either `ThreadPoolExecutor`, `ProcessPoolExecutor`) and the futures we actually want to run. For the sake of our example, we will use a function that returns the time it takes to load a web page so we can benchmarks multiple websites to see which one is the fastest:

```
import concurrent.futures
import urllib.request
import time

def benchmark_url(url):
    begin = time.time()
    with urllib.request.urlopen(url) as conn:
        conn.read()
    return (time.time() - begin, url)

class UrlsBenchmarker:
    def __init__(self, urls):
        self._urls = urls

    def run(self, executor):
        futures = self._benchmark_urls(executor)
        fastest = min([
            future.result() for future in
                concurrent.futures.as_completed(futures)
        ])
        print('Fastest Url: {1}, in {0}'.format(*fastest))

    def _benchmark_urls(self, executor):
        futures = []
        for url in self._urls:
            future = executor.submit(benchmark_url, url)
            future.add_done_callback(self._print_timing)
            futures.append(future)
        return futures

    def _print_timing(self, future):
```

```
        print('Url {1} downloaded in {0}'.format(
            *future.result()
        ))
```

Then we can create any kind of executor and have our `UrlsBenchmarker` run its futures within it:

```
>>> import concurrent.futures
>>> with concurrent.futures.ThreadPoolExecutor() as executor:
...     UrlsBenchmarker([
...             'http://time.com/',
...             'http://www.cnn.com/',
...             'http://www.facebook.com/',
...             'http://www.apple.com/',
...     ]).run(executor)
...
Url http://time.com/ downloaded in 1.0580978393554688
Url http://www.apple.com/ downloaded in 1.0482590198516846
Url http://www.facebook.com/ downloaded in 1.6707532405853271
Url http://www.cnn.com/ downloaded in 7.4976489543914795
Fastest Url: http://www.apple.com/, in 1.0482590198516846
```

How it works...

`UrlsBenchmarker` will fire a future for each URL through `UrlsBenchmarker._benchmark_urls`:

```
for url in self._urls:
    future = executor.submit(benchmark_url, url)
```

Each future will perform `benchmark_url`, which downloads the content of the given URL and returns the time it took to download it, along with the URL itself:

```
def benchmark_url(url):
    begin = time.time()
    # download url here...
    return (time.time() - begin, url)
```

Returning the URL itself is necessary, as `future` can know its return value, but not its arguments. So once we `submit` the function, we have lost which URL it is related to and by returning it together with the timing, we will always have the URL available whenever the timing is present.

Then for each `future`, a callback is added through `future.add_done_callback`:

```
future.add_done_callback(self._print_timing)
```

As soon as the future completes, it will call `UrlsBenchmarker._print_timing`, which prints the time it took to run the URL. This informs the user that the benchmark is proceeding and that it completed one of the URLs.

`UrlsBenchmarker._benchmark_urls` will then return `futures` for all the URLs that we had to benchmark in a list.

That list is then passed to `concurrent.futures.as_completed`. This will create an iterator that will return all `futures` in the order they completed and only when they are completed. So, we know that by iterating over it, we will only fetch `futures` that are already completed and we will block waiting for the completion of a new future as soon as the consumed all `futures` that already completed:

```
[
    future.result() for future in
        concurrent.futures.as_completed(futures)
]
```

So, the loop will only finish when all `futures` are complete.

The list of completed `futures` is consumed by a `list` comprehension that will create a list containing the results of those `futures`.

As the results are all in the (`time`, `url`) form, we can use `min` to grab the result with the minimum time, which is the URL that took less time to download.

This works because comparing two tuples compares the elements in order:

```
>>> (1, 5) < (2, 0)
True
>>> (2, 1) < (0, 5)
False
```

So, calling `min` on a list of tuples will grab the entry with the minimum value in the first element of the tuple:

```
>>> min([(1, 2), (2, 0), (0, 7)])
(0, 7)
```

The second element is only looked at when there are two first elements with the same value:

```
>>> min([(0, 7), (1, 2), (0, 3)])
(0, 3)
```

So, we grab the URL with the shortest timing (as the timing was the first of the entries in the tuple returned by the future) and print it as the fastest:

```
fastest = min([
    future.result() for future in
        concurrent.futures.as_completed(futures)
])
print('Fastest Url: {1}, in {0}'.format(*fastest))
```

There's more...

The futures executors are very similar to the worker pools provided by `multiprocessing.pool`, but they have some differences that might push you toward one direction or another.

The major difference is probably the way the workers are started. The pools start a fixed number of workers that are created and started all at the same time when the pool is created. So, creating the pool early moves the cost of spawning the workers at the beginning of the application. This means that the application can be quite slow to start because it might have to fork many processes according to the number of workers you requested or the number of cores your system has. Instead, the executor creates workers only when they are needed, and it's meant to evolve in the future to avoid making new workers when there are available ones.

So, executors are generally faster to start up at the expense of a bit more delay the first time a future is sent to it, while pools focus most of their cost on startup time. For this reason, if you have cases where you frequently need to create and destroy a pool of worker processes, the `futures` executor can be more efficient to work with.

Scheduled tasks

A common kind of background task is an action that should run by itself in the background at any given time. Typically, those are managed through a cron daemon or similar system tools by configuring the daemon to run a given Python script at the provided time.

When you have a primary application that needs to perform tasks cyclically (such as expiring caches, resetting password links, flushing a queue of emails to send, or similar tasks), it's not really viable to do so through a cron job as you would need to dump the data somewhere accessible to the other process: on disk, on a database, or any similarly shared storage.

Luckily, the Python standard library has an easy way to schedule tasks that are to be executed at any given time and joined with threads. It can be a very simple and effective solution for scheduled background tasks.

How to do it...

The `sched` module provides a fully functioning scheduled tasks executor that we can mix with threads to create a background scheduler:

```python
import threading
import sched
import functools


class BackgroundScheduler(threading.Thread):
    def __init__(self, start=True):
        self._scheduler = sched.scheduler()
        self._running = True
        super().__init__(daemon=True)
        if start:
            self.start()

    def run_at(self, time, action, args=None, kwargs=None):
        self._scheduler.enterabs(time, 0, action,
                                 argument=args or tuple(),
                                 kwargs=kwargs or {})

    def run_after(self, delay, action, args=None, kwargs=None):
        self._scheduler.enter(delay, 0, action,
                              argument=args or tuple(),
                              kwargs=kwargs or {})

    def run_every(self, seconds, action, args=None, kwargs=None):
        @functools.wraps(action)
        def _f(*args, **kwargs):
            try:
                action(*args, **kwargs)
            finally:
```

```
            self.run_after(seconds, _f, args=args, kwargs=kwargs)
        self.run_after(seconds, _f, args=args, kwargs=kwargs)

    def run(self):
        while self._running:
            delta = self._scheduler.run(blocking=False)
            if delta is None:
                delta = 0.5
            self._scheduler.delayfunc(min(delta, 0.5))

    def stop(self):
        self._running = False
```

BackgroundScheduler can be started and jobs can be added to it to start their execution at fixed times:

```
>>> import time
>>> s = BackgroundScheduler()
>>> s.run_every(2, lambda: print('Hello World'))
>>> time.sleep(5)
Hello World
Hello World
>>> s.stop()
>>> s.join()
```

How it works...

BackgroundScheduler subclasses threading.Thread so that it runs in the background while our application is doing something else. Registered tasks will fire and perform in a secondary thread without getting in the way of the primary code:

```
class BackgroundScheduler(threading.Thread):
    def __init__(self):
        self._scheduler = sched.scheduler()
        self._running = True
        super().__init__(daemon=True)
        self.start()
```

Whenever BackgroundScheduler is created, the thread for it is started too, so it becomes immediately available. The thread will run in daemon mode, which means that it won't block the program from exiting if it's still running at the time the program ends.

Usually Python waits for all threads when exiting the application, so setting a thread as a
`daemon` one makes it possible to quit without having to wait for them.

`threading.Thread` executes the `run` method as the thread code. In our case, it's a method
that runs the tasks registered in the scheduler over and over:

```
def run(self):
    while self._running:
        delta = self._scheduler.run(blocking=False)
        if delta is None:
            delta = 0.5
        self._scheduler.delayfunc(min(delta, 0.5))
```

`_scheduler.run(blocking=False)` means to pick one task to run from the scheduled
ones and run it. Then, it returns the time that it still has to be waited for before running the
next task. If no time is returned, it means there are no tasks to run.

Through `_scheduler.delayfunc(min(delta, 0.5))`, we wait for the time it takes
before the next task needs to run, which is most half a second at most.

We wait at most half a second, because while we are waiting, the scheduled tasks might
change. A new task might get registered and we want to ensure it won't have to wait more
than half a second for the scheduler to catch it.

If we waited exactly the time that was pending before the next task, we might do a run, get
back that the next task was in 60 seconds, and start waiting 60 seconds. But what if, while
we were waiting, the user registered a new task that had to run in 5 seconds? We would
run it in 60 seconds anyway, because we were already waiting. By waiting at most 0.5
seconds, we know that it will take half a second to pick up the next task and that it will run
properly in 5 seconds.

Waiting less than the time that is pending before the next task won't make the tasks run any
faster, because the scheduler won't run any tasks that don't already surpass its scheduled
time. So, if there are no tasks to run, the scheduler would continuously tell us, *you have to
wait*, and we would be waiting half a second for as many times as it was needed to reach
the scheduled time of the next scheduled task.

The `run_at`, `run_after`, and `run_every` methods are the ones actually involved in
registering functions for execution at specific times.

`run_at` and `run_after` simply wrap the `enterabs` and `enter` methods of the scheduler,
which allow us to register a task to run at a specific time or after *n* seconds.

The most interesting function is probably `run_every`, which runs a task over and over every *n* seconds:

```
def run_every(self, seconds, action, args=None, kwargs=None):
    @functools.wraps(action)
    def _f(*args, **kwargs):
        try:
            action(*args, **kwargs)
        finally:
            self.run_after(seconds, _f, args=args, kwargs=kwargs)
    self.run_after(seconds, _f, args=args, kwargs=kwargs)
```

The method takes the callable that has to be run and wraps it into a decorator that actually does run the function, but once it completes, it schedules the function back for re-execution. This way, it will run over and over until the scheduler is stopped, and whenever it completes, it's scheduled again.

Sharing data between processes

When working with threads or coroutines, data is shared across them by virtue of the fact that they share the same memory space. So, you can access any object from any thread, as long as attention is paid to avoiding race conditions and providing proper locking.

With processes, instead, things get far more complicated and no data is shared across them. So when using `ProcessPool` or `ProcessPoolExecutor`, we need to find a way to pass data across the processes and make them able to share a common state.

The Python standard library provides many tools to create a communication channel between processes: `multiprocessing.Queues`, `multiprocessing.Pipe`, `multiprocessing.Value`, and `multiprocessing.Array` can be used to create queues that one process can feed and the other consume, or simply values shared between multiple processes in a shared memory.

While all these are viable solutions, they have some limits: you must create all shared values before creating any process, so they are not viable if the amount of shared values is variable and they are limited in terms of types they can store.

`multiprocessing.Manager`, instead, allows us to store any number of shared values through a shared `Namespace`.

How to do it...

Here are the steps for this recipe:

1. `manager` should be created at the beginning of your application, then all processes will be able to set and read values from it:

```
import multiprocessing

manager = multiprocessing.Manager()
namespace = manager.Namespace()
```

2. Once we have our `namespace`, any process will be able to set values to it:

```
def set_first_variable():
    namespace.first = 42
p = multiprocessing.Process(target=set_first_variable)
p.start()
p.join()


def set_second_variable():
    namespace.second = dict(value=42)
p = multiprocessing.Process(target=set_second_variable)
p.start()
p.join()


import datetime
def set_custom_variable():
    namespace.last = datetime.datetime.utcnow()
p = multiprocessing.Process(target=set_custom_variable)
p.start()
p.join()
```

3. Any process will be able to access them all:

```
>>> def print_variables():
...     print(namespace.first, namespace.second, namespace.last)
...
>>> p = multiprocessing.Process(target=print_variables)
>>> p.start()
>>> p.join()
42 {'value': 42} 2018-05-26 21:39:17.433112
```

Without the need to create the variables early on or from the main process, all processes will be able to read or set any variable as far as they have access to Namespace.

How it works...

The multiprocessing.Manager class acts as a server that is able to store values accessible by any process that has a reference to Manager and to the values it wants to access.

Manager itself is accessible by knowing the address of the socket or pipe where it is listening, and each process that has a reference to the Manager instance knows those:

```
>>> manager = multiprocessing.Manager()
>>> print(manager.address)
/tmp/pymp-4133rgjq/listener-34vkfba3
```

Then, once you know how to contact the manager itself, you need to be able to tell the manager which object you want to access out of all that the manager is managing.

That can be done by having Token that represents and pinpoints that object:

```
>>> namespace = manager.Namespace()
>>> print(namespace._token)
Token(typeid='Namespace',
      address='/tmp/pymp-092482xr/listener-yreenkqo',
      id='7f78c7fd9630')
```

Particularly, Namespace is a kind of object that allows us to store any variable within it. So, it makes anything stored within Namespace accessible by using just the namespace token.

All processes, as they were copied from the same original process, that had the token of the namespace and the address of the manager are able to access namespace and thus set or read values from it.

There's more...

`multiprocessing.Manager` is not constrained to work with processes that originated from the same process.

It's possible to create a `Manager` that will listen on a network so that any process that is able to connect to it might be able to access its content:

```
>>> import multiprocessing.managers
>>> manager = multiprocessing.managers.SyncManager(
...     address=('localhost', 50000),
...     authkey=b'secret'
... )
>>> print(manager.address)
('localhost', 50000)
```

Then, once the server is started:

```
>>> manager.get_server().serve_forever()
```

The other processes will be able to connect to it by creating a `manager2` instance with the exact same arguments of the manager they want to connect to, and then explicitly connect:

```
>>> manager2 = multiprocessing.managers.SyncManager(
...     address=('localhost', 50000),
...     authkey=b'secret'
... )
>>> manager2.connect()
```

Let's create a `namespace` in manager and set a value into it:

```
>>> namespace = manager.Namespace()
>>> namespace.value = 5
```

Knowing the token value of `namespace`, it's possible to create a proxy object to access `namespace` from `manager2` through the network:

```
>>> from multiprocessing.managers import NamespaceProxy
>>> ns2 = NamespaceProxy(token, 'pickle',
...                      manager=manager2,
...                      authkey=b'secret')
>>> print(ns2.value)
5
```

10
Networking

In this chapter, we will cover following recipes:

- Sending emails—sending emails from your application
- Fetching emails—checking and reading newly-received emails in a folder
- FTP—uploading, listing, and downloading files from FTP
- Sockets—writing a chat system based on TCP/IP
- AsyncIO—an asynchronous HTTP server for static files based on coroutines
- Remote procedure calls—implementing RPC through XMLRPC

Introduction

Modern-day applications frequently need to interact with users or other software through networks. The more our society moves toward a connected world, the more users will expect software to be able to interact with remote services or across networks.

Networking-based applications rely on decades of stable and widely-tested tools and paradigms, and the Python standard library provides support for the most common technologies, from transport to application protocols.

Apart from providing support for the communication channels themselves, such as sockets, the standard library also provides the models to implement event-based applications that are typical of networking use cases as in most cases, the application will have to react to an input coming from the network and handle it accordingly.

In this chapter, we will see how to handle some of the most common application protocols, such as SMTP, IMAP, and FTP. But we will also see how to handle networking directly through sockets and how to implement our own protocol for RPC communication.

Sending emails

Emails are the most widespread communication tool nowadays, if you're on the internet, it's pretty much granted you have an email address and they are now highly integrated in smartphones too, so are accessible on the go.

For all those reasons, emails are the preferred tools for sending notifications to users, reports of completion, and results of long-running processes.

Sending emails requires some machinery and both the SMTP and MIME protocols are quite articulated if you want to support them by yourself.

Luckily, the Python standard library comes with built-in support for both and we can rely on the `smtplib` module to interact with the SMTP server to send our email and on `email` package to actually create the content of the email and tackle all the special formats and encoding required.

How to do it...

Sending an email is a three-step process:

1. Contact the SMTP server and authenticate to it
2. Prepare the email itself
3. Provide the email to the SMTP server

All three phases are covered in the Python standard library and we just need to wrap them up for convenience in an easier interface:

```
from email.header import Header
from email.mime.text import MIMEText
from email.utils import parseaddr, formataddr
from smtplib import SMTP


class EmailSender:
    def __init__(self, host="localhost", port=25, login="", password=""):
        self._host = host
        self._port = int(port)
```

```
        self._login = login
        self._password = password

    def send(self, sender, recipient, subject, body):
        header_charset = 'UTF-8'
        body_charset = 'UTF-8'

        sender_name, sender_addr = parseaddr(sender)
        recipient_name, recipient_addr = parseaddr(recipient)

        sender_name = str(Header(sender_name, header_charset))
        recipient_name = str(Header(recipient_name, header_charset))

        msg = MIMEText(body.encode(body_charset), 'plain', body_charset)
        msg['From'] = formataddr((sender_name, sender_addr))
        msg['To'] = formataddr((recipient_name, recipient_addr))
        msg['Subject'] = Header(subject, header_charset)

        smtp = SMTP(self._host, self._port)
        try:
            smtp.starttls()
        except:
            pass
        smtp.login(self._login, self._password)
        smtp.sendmail(sender, recipient, msg.as_string())
        smtp.quit()
```

Our `EmailSender` class can be used to easily send emails through our email provider:

```
es = EmailSender('mail.myserver.it',
                 login='amol@myserver.it',
                 password='mymailpassword')
es.send(sender='Sender <no-reply@senders.net>',
        recipient='amol@myserver.it',
        subject='Hello my friend!',
        body='''Here is a little email for you''')
```

How it works...

Sending an email requires connecting to an SMTP server, this requires data, such as the host on which the server is running, the port where it's exposed, and a username and password to authenticate against it.

All these details will be needed every time we want to send an email, as each email will require a separate connection. So, those are all details that our class in charge of sending email will always need to have available and thus are requested when the instance is created:

```
class EmailSender:
    def __init__(self, host="localhost", port=25, login="", password=""):
        self._host = host
        self._port = int(port)
        self._login = login
        self._password = password
```

Once all the details required to connect to the SMTP server are known, the only exposed method of our class is the one to actually send the emails:

```
def send(self, sender, recipient, subject, body):
```

Which requires the details needed to compose the email: the sender address, the address receiving the email, a subject, and the content of the email itself.

Our method has to parse the provided sender and recipient. The part with the name of the sender and recipient is separated from the part containing the address:

```
sender_name, sender_addr = parseaddr(sender)
recipient_name, recipient_addr = parseaddr(recipient)
```

If `sender` was something like `"Alessandro Molina <amol@myserver.it>"`, `sender_name` would be `"Alessandro Molina"` and `sender_addr` would be `"amol@myserver.it"`.

This is required because the name part will frequently contain names that are not constrained to plain ASCII, the mail might be delivered to China, or Korea, or any other place where you would have to properly support Unicode to handle recipient names.

So we have to properly encode those characters in a way that mail clients will understand when receiving the email, and that is done by using the `Header` class with the provided character set encoding, which in our case was `"UTF-8"`:

```
sender_name = str(Header(sender_name, header_charset))
recipient_name = str(Header(recipient_name, header_charset))
```

Once the sender and recipient names are encoded in the format expected by email headers, we can join them back with the address part to build back a full recipient and sender in the `"Name <address>"` form:

```
msg['From'] = formataddr((sender_name, sender_addr))
msg['To'] = formataddr((recipient_name, recipient_addr))
```

The same goes for `Subject`, which being a header field of the mail needs to be encoded too:

```
msg['Subject'] = Header(subject, header_charset)
```

The body of the message instead doesn't have to be encoded as a header and can be provided as its plain-bytes representation in any encoding as far as the encoding is specified.

In our case, the message was built with a body encoded to `UTF-8` too:

```
msg = MIMEText(body.encode(body_charset), 'plain', body_charset)
```

Then, once the message itself is ready and both the body and headers are properly encoded, the only part left is actually getting in touch with the SMTP server and sending the email.

This is done by creating an `SMTP` object for the known address and port:

```
smtp = SMTP(self._host, self._port)
```

Then, in case the SMTP server supports encryption through TLS, we start it. If it doesn't, we just ignore the error and proceed:

```
try:
    smtp.starttls()
except:
    pass
```

Once encryption is enabled, if available, we can finally authenticate against the SMTP server and send the mail itself to the involved recipient:

```
smtp.login(self._login, self._password)
smtp.sendmail(sender, recipient, msg.as_string())
smtp.quit()
```

To test that encoding is working as you would expect, you can try sending an email with characters that are out of the standard ASCII plane to see whether your client properly understands the email:

```
es.send(sender='Sender <no-reply@senders.net>',
        recipient='amol@myserver.it',
        subject='Have some japanese here: ã"ã,"ã«ã¡ã¯',
        body='''And some chinese here! ä½ å¥½''')
```

If everything worked as expected, you should be able to authenticate against your SMTP provider, send the email and see it in your inbox with the proper content.

Fetching emails

Frequently, applications need to react to some kind of event, they receive a message from a user or software and they need to act accordingly. The whole nature of networking-based applications lies in reacting to received messages, but a very specific and common case of this class of applications are applications that need to react to received emails.

The typical case is when a user needs to send some kind of document to your application (usually an ID card or signed contracts) and you want to react to that event, such as enabling the service once the user sent the signed contract.

This requires us to be able to access the received emails and scan through them to detect sender and content.

How to do it...

The steps for this recipe are as follows:

1. Using `imaplib` and `email` modules, it's possible to build a working IMAP client to fetch the most recent messages from a supported IMAP server:

```
import imaplib
import re
from email.parser import BytesParser


class IMAPReader:
    ENCODING = 'utf-8'
    LIST_PATTERN = re.compile(
        r'\((?P<flags>.*?)\) "(?P<delimiter>.*)" (?P<name>.*)'
    )
```

```python
    def __init__(self, host, username, password, ssl=True):
        if ssl:
            self._imap = imaplib.IMAP4_SSL(host)
        else:
            self._imap = imaplib.IMAP4(host)
        self._imap.login(username, password)

    def folders(self):
        """Retrieve list of IMAP folders"""
        resp, lines = self._imap.list()
        if resp != 'OK':
            raise Exception(resp)

        entries = []
        for line in lines:
            flags, _, name = self.LIST_PATTERN.match(
                line.decode(self.ENCODING)
            ).groups()
            entries.append(dict(
                flags=flags,
                name=name.strip('"')
            ))
        return entries

    def messages(self, folder, limit=10, peek=True):
        """Return ``limit`` messages from ``folder``

        peek=False will also fetch message body
        """
        resp, count = self._imap.select('"%s"' % folder,
readonly=True)
        if resp != 'OK':
            raise Exception(resp)

        last_message_id = int(count[0])
        msg_ids = range(last_message_id, last_message_id-limit, -1)

        mode = '(BODY.PEEK[HEADER])' if peek else '(RFC822)'

        messages = []
        for msg_id in msg_ids:
            resp, msg = self._imap.fetch(str(msg_id), mode)
            msg = msg[0][-1]

            messages.append(BytesParser().parsebytes(msg))
            if len(messages) >= limit:
                break
        return messages
```

```
        def get_message_body(self, message):
            """Given a message for which the body was fetched, returns
it"""
            body = []
            if message.is_multipart():
                for payload in message.get_payload():
                    body.append(payload.get_payload())
            else:
                body.append(message.get_payload())
            return body

        def close(self):
            """Close connection to IMAP server"""
            self._imap.close()
```

2. `IMAPReader` can then be used to access a compatible mail server to read the most recent emails:

```
mails = IMAPReader('imap.gmail.com',
                   YOUR_EMAIL, YOUR_PASSWORD,
                   ssl=True)

folders = mails.folders()
for msg in mails.messages('INBOX', limit=2, peek=True):
    print(msg['Date'], msg['Subject'])
```

3. This returns the title and timestamp of the last two received emails:

```
Fri, 8 Jun 2018 00:07:16 +0200 Hello Python CookBook!
Thu, 7 Jun 2018 08:21:11 -0400 SSL and turbogears.org
```

If we need the actual email content and attachments, we can retrieve them by using `peek=False` and then calling `IMAPReader.get_message_body` on the retrieved messages.

How it works...

Our class acts as a wrapper over the `imaplib` and `email` modules, providing an easier-to-use interface for the need of fetching mail from a folder.

There are actually two different objects that can be created from `imaplib` to connect to an IMAP server, one that uses SSL and one that doesn't. Depending on what's required by your server, you might have to turn it on or off (for example, Gmail requires SSL) and that's abstracted in `__init__`:

```
def __init__(self, host, username, password, ssl=True):
    if ssl:
        self._imap = imaplib.IMAP4_SSL(host)
    else:
        self._imap = imaplib.IMAP4(host)
    self._imap.login(username, password)
```

The __init__ method also takes care of logging you against the IMAP server, so that the once the reader is created, it's immediately usable.

Our reader then provides methods to list folders, so in case you want to read messages from all folders or you want to allow users to pick a folder, it's possible:

```
def folders(self):
    """Retrieve list of IMAP folders"""
```

The first thing our `folders` method does is grab the list of folders from the server. The `imaplib` methods already report exceptions themselves in case there is an error, but as a safety net, we also check that the response is OK:

```
resp, lines = self._imap.list()
if resp != 'OK':
    raise Exception(resp)
```

IMAP is a text-based protocol and the server is supposed to always respond OK <response> if it was able to understand your request and serve a response. Otherwise, a bunch of alternative response codes, such as NO or BAD, can be returned. In case any of those is returned, we consider our request failed.

Once we make sure we actually have the folders list, we need to parse it. The list is constituted by multiple lines of text. Each line contains details about exactly one folder, the details: flags and folder name. Those are separated by a separator, which is not standard. On some servers, it's a dot, while on others, it's a slash, so we need to be pretty flexible when parsing it. That's why we parse it with a regular expression that allows flags and a name separated by any separator:

```
LIST_PATTERN = re.compile(
    r'\((?P<flags>.*?)\) "(?P<delimiter>.*)" (?P<name>.*)'
)
```

Once we know how to parse those lines from the response, we can just build a list of dictionaries out of them that contain the name and the flags for those folders:

```
entries = []
for line in lines:
    flags, _, name = self.LIST_PATTERN.match(
```

```
        line.decode(self.ENCODING)
    ).groups()
    entries.append(dict(
        flags=flags,
        name=name.strip('"')
    ))
return entries
```

The flags themselves can then be parsed further using the `imaplib.ParseFlags` class.

Once we know the name of the folder we want to fetch messages for, we can retrieve the messages through the `messages` method:

```
def messages(self, folder, limit=10, peek=True):
    """Return ``limit`` messages from ``folder``

    peek=False will also fetch message body
    """
```

As IMAP is a stateful protocol, the first thing we need to do is select the folder for which we want to run subsequent commands:

```
resp, count = self._imap.select('"%s"' % folder, readonly=True)
if resp != 'OK':
    raise Exception(resp)
```

We provide a `readonly` option so we can't inadvertently destroy our emails, and we verify the response code as usual.

Then the content of the response of the `select` method is actually the ID of the last message that was uploaded to that folder.

As those IDs are incremental numbers, we can use it to generate the IDs of the last `limit` messages to fetch the most recent messages:

```
last_message_id = int(count[0])
msg_ids = range(last_message_id, last_message_id-limit, -1)
```

Then, based on the caller choice, we select what we want to download of those messages. If only the headers or the whole content:

```
mode = '(BODY.PEEK[HEADER])' if peek else '(RFC822)'
```

The mode will be provided to the `fetch` method to tell it what data we want to download:

```
resp, msg = self._imap.fetch(str(msg_id), mode)
```

The message itself is then composed as a list that contains a tuple of two elements. The first element contains the size and mode the message is returned in (as we provided the mode ourselves, we don't really care), and the last element of the tuple contains the message itself, so we just grab it:

```
msg = msg[0][-1]
```

Once we have the message available, we feed it to `BytesParser` so that we can get back a `Message` instance:

```
BytesParser().parsebytes(msg)
```

We loop over all the messages, parse them, and add to the list of messages that we will return. We stop as soon as we reach the desired amount of messages:

```
messages = []
for msg_id in msg_ids:
    resp, msg = self._imap.fetch(str(msg_id), mode)
    msg = msg[0][-1]

    messages.append(BytesParser().parsebytes(msg))
    if len(messages) >= limit:
        break
return messages
```

From the `messages` method, we get back a list of `Message` objects, for which we can easily access all data, apart from the body of the message itself. Because the body might actually be composed by multiple items (think of a message with attachments – it has text, images, PDF files, or whatever was attached).

For this reason, the reader provides a `get_message_body` method that retrieves all the parts of the message body in case it's a multipart message and returns them:

```
def get_message_body(self, message):
    """Given a message for which the body was fetched, returns it"""
    body = []
    if message.is_multipart():
        for payload in message.get_payload():
            body.append(payload.get_payload())
    else:
        body.append(message.get_payload())
    return body
```

Combining the `messages` and `get_message_body` methods, we are able to grab messages and their content from a mailbox, and then process them however we need.

There's more...

Writing a feature-complete and fully functioning IMAP client is a standalone project that is outside the scope of this book.

IMAP is a complex protocol that includes support for flags, searching, and many more features. Most of these commands are provided by `imaplib` and it's also possible to upload messages to the server or create tools to perform backups or copy messages from one mail account to another.

Also, when parsing complex emails, the `email` module will handle the various representation of data specified by the email-related RFCs, for example, our recipe returns dates as a string, but `email.utils.parsedate` can parse them to Python objects.

FTP

FTP is the most widely-used solution to save and retrieve files from a remote server. It has been around for decades and it's a fairly easy protocol to use that can deliver good performance as it provides minimal overhead over transferred content, while supporting powerful features, such as transfer recovery.

Often, software needs to receive files automatically uploaded by other software; FTP has been frequently used as a robust solution in these scenarios over the years. Whether your software is the one in need of uploading the content or the one that has to receive it, the Python standard library has support for FTP built-in so we can rely on `ftplib` to use the FTP protocol.

How to do it...

`ftplib` is a powerful foundation on which we can provider an easier API to interact with an FTP server, both to store and retrieve files:

```
import ftplib


class FTPCLient:
    def __init__(self, host, username='', password=''):
        self._client = ftplib.FTP_TLS(timeout=10)
        self._client.connect(host)

        # enable TLS
```

```
        try:
            self._client.auth()
        except ftplib.error_perm:
            # TLS authentication not supported
            # fallback to a plain FTP client
            self._client.close()
            self._client = ftplib.FTP(timeout=10)
            self._client.connect(host)

        self._client.login(username, password)

        if hasattr(self._client, 'prot_p'):
            self._client.prot_p()

    def cwd(self, directory):
        """Enter directory"""
        self._client.cwd(directory)

    def dir(self):
        """Returns list of files in current directory.

        Each entry is returned as a tuple of two elements,
        first element is the filename, the second are the
        properties of that file.
        """
        entries = []
        for idx, f in enumerate(self._client.mlsd()):
            if idx == 0:
                # First entry is current path
                continue
            if f[0] in ('..', '.'):
                continue
            entries.append(f)
        return entries

    def download(self, remotefile, localfile):
        """Download remotefile into localfile"""
        with open(localfile, 'wb') as f:
            self._client.retrbinary('RETR %s' % remotefile, f.write)

    def upload(self, localfile, remotefile):
        """Upload localfile to remotefile"""
        with open(localfile, 'rb') as f:
            self._client.storbinary('STOR %s' % remotefile, f)

    def close(self):
        self._client.close()
```

Then, we can test our class by uploading and fetching back a simple file:

```
with open('/tmp/hello.txt', 'w+') as f:
    f.write('Hello World!')

cli = FTPCLient('localhost', username=USERNAME, password=PASSWORD)
cli.upload('/tmp/hello.txt', 'hellofile.txt')
cli.download('hellofile.txt', '/tmp/hello2.txt')

with open('/tmp/hello2.txt') as f:
    print(f.read())
```

If everything worked as expected, the output should be `Hello World!`

How it works...

The `FTPClient` class provides an initializer that is in charge of setting up the correct connection to the server and a bunch of methods to actually do work against the connected server.

`__init__` does quite a lot of work to try setting up the proper connection to the remote server:

```
def __init__(self, host, username='', password=''):
    self._client = ftplib.FTP_TLS(timeout=10)
    self._client.connect(host)

    # enable TLS
    try:
        self._client.auth()
    except ftplib.error_perm:
        # TLS authentication not supported
        # fallback to a plain FTP client
        self._client.close()
        self._client = ftplib.FTP(timeout=10)
        self._client.connect(host)

    self._client.login(username, password)

    if hasattr(self._client, 'prot_p'):
        self._client.prot_p()
```

First it tries a TLS connection, which guarantees encrypting, because otherwise FTP is a plain-text protocol that would send all out data in a clear text way.

If our remote server supports TLS, it is enabled on the control connection by calling
.auth() and then on the data-transfer connection by calling prot_p().

FTP is based on two kinds of connections, the control connection where we send and
receive the commands for the server and their result, and a data connection where we send
the uploaded and downloaded data.

If possible, both of them should be encrypted. If our server doesn't support them, we fall
back to a plain FTP connection and proceed by just authenticating against it.

If your server doesn't require any authentication, providing anonymous as the username
with an empty password is usually enough to get in.

Once we are connected, we are free to move around the server, and that can be done with
the cwd command:

```
def cwd(self, directory):
    """Enter directory"""
    self._client.cwd(directory)
```

This method is just a proxy to the internal client one, as the internal one is already easy to
use and fully functional.

But once we get into a directory, we need to fetch its content and here's where the dir()
method comes into play:

```
def dir(self):
    """Returns list of files in current directory.

    Each entry is returned as a tuple of two elements,
    first element is the filename, the second are the
    properties of that file.
    """
    entries = []
    for idx, f in enumerate(self._client.mlsd()):
        if idx == 0:
            # First entry is current path
            continue
        if f[0] in ('..', '.'):
            continue
        entries.append(f)
    return entries
```

The dir() method calls the mlsd method of the internal client, which is in charge of
returning the list of files in the current directory.

This list is returned as a tuple of two elements:

```
('Desktop', {'perm': 'ceflmp',
            'unique': 'BAAAAT79CAAAAAAA',
            'modify': '20180522213143',
            'type': 'dir'})
```

The first entry of the tuple contains the filename, while the second contains its properties.

Our own method does just two additional steps, it skips the first returned entry—as that is always the current directory (the one we picked with `cwd()`)—and then skips any special entry for the parent or current directory. We are not really interested in them.

Once we are able to move around the structure of the directories, we can finally `upload` and `download` files into those directories:

```
def download(self, remotefile, localfile):
    """Download remotefile into localfile"""
    with open(localfile, 'wb') as f:
        self._client.retrbinary('RETR %s' % remotefile, f.write)

def upload(self, localfile, remotefile):
    """Upload localfile to remotefile"""
    with open(localfile, 'rb') as f:
        self._client.storbinary('STOR %s' % remotefile, f)
```

Those two methods are pretty straightforward, they just open local files for reading when we upload and for writing when we download, and send the FTP command required to retrieve or store a file.

When uploading a new `remotefile`, a file will be created with the same content that `localfile` had. When downloading, `localfile` is opened to write inside it the content that `remotefile` has.

There's more...

Not all FTP servers support the same commands. The protocol saw many extensions over the years, so some commands might be missing or have a different semantic.

For example, the `mlsd` function might be missing, but you might have `LIST` or `nlst`, which can perform a similar job.

You can refer to RFC 959 to know how the FTP protocol should work, but frequently experimenting explicitly with the FTP server you should be connecting to is the best way to assess which commands and which signature it's going to accept.

Frequently, FTP servers implement a HELP command you can use it to fetch the list of supported functions.

Sockets

Sockets are one of the lowest-level concepts that you can use to write networking applications. It means managing the whole connection ourselves, usually when relying on sockets directly, you would have to handle connection requests, accept them, and then start a thread or a loop to handle the subsequent commands or data that is sent through the newly created connection channel.

This is a flow that nearly all applications that rely on networking have to implement, everything you call a server usually has as a foundation in the aforementioned loop.

The Python standard library provides a great foundation to avoid having to manually rewrite that flow every time you have to work on a networking-based application. We can use the socketserver module and let it handle the connection loop for us, while we focus on just implementing the application layer protocol and handling messages.

How to do it...

You need to perform the following steps for this recipe:

1. Mixing the TCPServer and ThreadingMixIn classes, we can easily build a multithreaded server that will handle concurrent connections through TCP:

```
import socket
import threading
import socketserver


class EchoServer:
    def __init__(self, host='0.0.0.0', port=9800):
        self._host = host
        self._port = port
        self._server = ThreadedTCPServer((host, port),
EchoRequestHandler)
        self._thread =
```

```
            threading.Thread(target=self._server.serve_forever)
                self._thread.daemon = True

        def start(self):
            if self._thread.is_alive():
                # Already serving
                return

            print('Serving on %s:%s' % (self._host, self._port))
            self._thread.start()

        def stop(self):
            self._server.shutdown()
            self._server.server_close()


class ThreadedTCPServer(socketserver.ThreadingMixIn,
                        socketserver.TCPServer):
    allow_reuse_address = True


class EchoRequestHandler(socketserver.BaseRequestHandler):
    MAX_MESSAGE_SIZE = 2**16  # 65k
    MESSAGE_HEADER_LEN = len(str(MAX_MESSAGE_SIZE))

    @classmethod
    def recv_message(cls, socket):
        data_size = int(socket.recv(cls.MESSAGE_HEADER_LEN))
        data = socket.recv(data_size)
        return data

    @classmethod
    def prepare_message(cls, message):
        if len(message) > cls.MAX_MESSAGE_SIZE:
            raise ValueError('Message too big'

        message_size = str(len(message)).encode('ascii')
        message_size = message_size.zfill(cls.MESSAGE_HEADER_LEN)
        return message_size + message

    def handle(self):
        message = self.recv_message(self.request)
        self.request.sendall(self.prepare_message(b'ECHO: %s' %
message))
```

2. Once we have a working server, to test it, we need a client to send messages to it. For convenience, we will keep the client simple and just make it connect, send a message, and wait back for a short reply:

```
def send_message_to_server(ip, port, message):
    sock = socket.socket(socket.AF_INET, socket.SOCK_STREAM)
    sock.connect((ip, port))
    try:
        message = EchoRequestHandler.prepare_message(message)
        sock.sendall(message)
        response = EchoRequestHandler.recv_message(sock)
        print("ANSWER: {}".format(response))
    finally:
        sock.close()
```

3. Now that we have both the server and client, we can test that our server works as expected:

```
server = EchoServer()
server.start()

send_message_to_server('localhost', server._port, b"Hello World 1")
send_message_to_server('localhost', server._port, b"Hello World 2")
send_message_to_server('localhost', server._port, b"Hello World 3")

server.stop()
```

4. If everything worked properly, you should see:

```
Serving on 0.0.0.0:9800
ANSWER: b'ECHO: Hello World 1'
ANSWER: b'ECHO: Hello World 2'
ANSWER: b'ECHO: Hello World 3'
```

How it works...

The server part is composed of three different classes.

EchoServer, which orchestrates the server and provides the high-level API we can use. EchoRequestHandler, which manages the incoming messages and serves them. And ThreadedTCPServer, which is in charge of the whole networking part, opening sockets, listening on them, and spawning threads to handle connections.

EchoServer allows to start and stop our server:

```
class EchoServer:
    def __init__(self, host='0.0.0.0', port=9800):
        self._host = host
        self._port = port
        self._server = ThreadedTCPServer((host, port), EchoRequestHandler)
```

```
        self._thread = threading.Thread(target=self._server.serve_forever)
        self._thread.daemon = True

    def start(self):
        if self._thread.is_alive():
            # Already serving
            return

        print('Serving on %s:%s' % (self._host, self._port))
        self._thread.start()

    def stop(self):
        self._server.shutdown()
        self._server.server_close()
```

It creates a new thread where the server will be running and starts it if it's not already running. The thread will just run the `ThreadedTCPServer.serve_forever` method that loops over and over, serving one request after the other.

When we are done with our server, we can call the `stop()` method, which will shut down the server and wait for its completion (it will quit as soon as it is finished all currently-running requests).

`ThreadedTCPServer` is pretty much the standard one provided by the standard library, if not for the reason that we inherit from `ThreadingMixIn` too. `Mixin` is a set of additional features that you can inject in a class by inheriting from it, in this specific case, it provides threading features for the socket server. So instead of being able to serve a single request at a time, we can server multiple requests concurrently.

We also set the `allow_reuse_address = True` attribute of the server, so that in case it crashes or in case of timeouts, the socket can be instantly reused instead of having to wait for the system to close them.

Finally `EchoRequestHandler` is the one providing the whole message-handling and parsing. Whenever `ThreadedTCPServer` receives a new connection, it will call the `handle` method on the handler, and it's up to the handler to do the right thing.

In our case, we are just implementing a simple server that responds back whatever was sent to it, so the handler has to do two things:

- Parse the incoming message to understand its content
- Send back a message with the same content

One of the major complexities when working with sockets is that they are not really message-based. They are a continuous stream of data (well, UDP is message-based, but for what concerns us, the interface doesn't change much). This means that it is impossible to know when a new message begins and when a message ends.

The `handle` method just tells us that there is a new connection, but on that connection, multiple messages might be sent one after the other and unless we have a way of knowing where a message ends, we would read them as a single big message.

To solve this need, we use a very simple yet effective approach, that is, prefixing all messages with their own size. Thus, when a new message is received we always know that we just need to read the size of the message and then, once the size is known, we will read the remaining bytes specified by the size.

To read those messages, we rely on a utility method, `recv_message`, that will be able to read a message made this way from any provided socket:

```
@classmethod
def recv_message(cls, socket):
    data_size = int(socket.recv(cls.MESSAGE_HEADER_LEN))
    data = socket.recv(data_size)
    return data
```

The first thing that the function does is read from the socket exactly `MESSAGE_HEADER_LEN` bytes. Those will be the bytes that contain the size of the message. All sizes must be the same size. For this reason, sizes such as `10` will have to be represented as `00010`. The prefixed zeros will then be ignored. Then, this size is converted using `int`, and we will get back the right number. The sizes must be all the same, otherwise we wouldn't know how many bytes we need to read to fetch the size.

We decided to constrain our message size to 65,000, this leads to a `MESSAGE_HEADER_LEN` of five as five digits are necessary to represent numbers up to 65,536:

```
MAX_MESSAGE_SIZE = 2**16  # 65k
MESSAGE_HEADER_LEN = len(str(MAX_MESSAGE_SIZE))
```

The size doesn't really matter, and we just picked a fairly big value. The bigger the messages are that you allow, the more bytes you will need to represent their sizes.

The `recv_message` method is then used by `handle()` to read the sent message:

```
def handle(self):
    message = self.recv_message(self.request)
    self.request.sendall(self.prepare_message(b'ECHO: %s' % message))
```

Once the message is known, the `handle()` method also sends back a new message prepared the same way and to prepare the response, it relies on `prepare_message`, which is also used by the client to send the messages in the first place:

```
@classmethod
def prepare_message(cls, message):
    if len(message) > cls.MAX_MESSAGE_SIZE:
        raise ValueError('Message too big')

    message_size = str(len(message)).encode('ascii')
    message_size = message_size.zfill(cls.MESSAGE_HEADER_LEN)
    return message_size + message
```

What this function does is, given a message, it ensures it's not bigger than the maximum allowed size and then prefixes it with its size.

The size is computed by grabbing the length of the message as text and then encoding it as bytes using `ascii` encoding. As the size will only contain numbers, the `ascii` encoding is more than enough to represent them:

```
message_size = str(len(message)).encode('ascii')
```

As the resulting string can have any size (from one to five bytes), we always pad it with zeros until it reaches the expected size:

```
message_size = message_size.zfill(cls.MESSAGE_HEADER_LEN)
```

The resulting bytes are then prepended to the message and the prepared message is returned.

With those two functions, the server is able to receive and send back messages of arbitrary size.

The client function works nearly the same way, as it has to send a message and then receive the answer back:

```
def send_message_to_server(ip, port, message):
    sock = socket.socket(socket.AF_INET, socket.SOCK_STREAM)
    sock.connect((ip, port))
    try:
        message = EchoRequestHandler.prepare_message(message)
        sock.sendall(message)
        response = EchoRequestHandler.recv_message(sock)
        print("ANSWER: {}".format(response))
    finally:
        sock.close()
```

It still uses `EchoRequestHandler.prepare_message` to prepare the message to send to the server, and `EchoRequestHandler.recv_message` to read the server response.

The only additional parts are related to connecting to the server. To do this, we actually create a socket of type `AF_INET`, `SOCK_STREAM`, which actually means we want to use TCP/IP.

Then we connect to the `ip` and `port` where the server is running, and once we're connected, we just send the message through the resulting socket `sock` and read the answer back on the same socket.

When we are done, we have to remember to close the socket or we will be leaking them until the OS decides to kill them because they were inactive for too long.

AsyncIO

While asynchronous solutions have been around for years, they are getting more and more common these days. The primary reason is that having an application without thousands of concurrent users is not an uncommon scenario anymore; it's actually the norm for a small/medium-sized application and we can scale to millions with major services used worldwide.

Being able to serve such volumes doesn't scale well with approaches based on threads or processes. Especially when many of the connections that users are triggering might be sitting there doing nothing most of the time. Think of a service such as Facebook Messenger or WhatsApp. Whichever you use, you probably send a message once in a while and most of the time your connection to the server is sitting there doing nothing. Maybe you are a heavy chatter and you receive a message every second, but that still means that out of the millions of clocks per second your computer can do, most of them will be doing nothing. Most of the heavy lifting in this kind of application is done by the networking part, so there are a lot of resources that can be shared by undergoing multiple connections in a single process.

Asynchronous technologies allow exactly that, to write a networking application that instead of requiring multiple separate threads (that would be wasting memory and kernel efforts), we can have a single process and thread composed by multiple coroutines that do nothing until there is actually something to do.

As long as what the coroutines have to do is super-quick (such as grabbing a message and forwarding it to another contact of yours), most of the work will happen at the networking layer and thus can proceed in parallel.

How to do it...

The steps for this recipe are as follows:

1. We are going to replicate our echo server, but instead of using threads, it's going to use AsyncIO and coroutines to serve requests:

```python
import asyncio

class EchoServer:
    MAX_MESSAGE_SIZE = 2**16  # 65k
    MESSAGE_HEADER_LEN = len(str(MAX_MESSAGE_SIZE))

    def __init__(self, host='0.0.0.0', port=9800):
        self._host = host
        self._port = port
        self._server = None

    def serve(self, loop):
        coro = asyncio.start_server(self.handle, self._host,
self._port,
                                    loop=loop)
        self._server = loop.run_until_complete(coro)
        print('Serving on %s:%s' % (self._host, self._port))
        loop.run_until_complete(self._server.wait_closed())
        print('Done')

    @property
    def started(self):
        return self._server is not None and self._server.sockets

    def stop(self):
        print('Stopping...')
        self._server.close()

    async def handle(self, reader, writer):
        data = await self.recv_message(reader)
        await self.send_message(writer, b'ECHO: %s' % data)
        # Signal we finished handling this request
        # or the server will hang.
        writer.close()

    @classmethod
    async def recv_message(cls, socket):
        data_size = int(await socket.read(cls.MESSAGE_HEADER_LEN))
        data = await socket.read(data_size)
        return data
```

```
@classmethod
async def send_message(cls, socket, message):
    if len(message) > cls.MAX_MESSAGE_SIZE:
        raise ValueError('Message too big')

    message_size = str(len(message)).encode('ascii')
    message_size = message_size.zfill(cls.MESSAGE_HEADER_LEN)
    data = message_size + message

    socket.write(data)
    await socket.drain()
```

2. Now that we have the server implementation, we need a client to test it. As in practice the client does the same that we did for the previous recipe, we are just going to reuse the same client implementation. So the client won't be AsyncIO- and coroutines-based, but will be a normal function using socket:

```
import socket

def send_message_to_server(ip, port, message):
    def _recv_message(socket):
        data_size = int(socket.recv(EchoServer.MESSAGE_HEADER_LEN))
        data = socket.recv(data_size)
        return data

    def _prepare_message(message):
        if len(message) > EchoServer.MAX_MESSAGE_SIZE:
            raise ValueError('Message too big')

        message_size = str(len(message)).encode('ascii')
        message_size =
message_size.zfill(EchoServer.MESSAGE_HEADER_LEN)
        return message_size + message

    sock = socket.socket(socket.AF_INET, socket.SOCK_STREAM)
    sock.connect((ip, port))
    try:
        sock.sendall(_prepare_message(message))
        response = _recv_message(sock)
        print("ANSWER: {}".format(response))
    finally:
        sock.close()
```

3. Now we can put the pieces together. To run both client and server in the same process, we are going to run the `asyncio` loop in a separate thread. So, we can concurrently start clients against it. This is not in any way required to serve multiple clients, it's just a convenience to avoid having to start two different Python scripts to play server and client.

4. First of all, we create a thread for the server that will go on for 3 seconds. After 3 seconds, we will explicitly stop our server:

```
server = EchoServer()
def serve_for_3_seconds():
    loop = asyncio.new_event_loop()
    asyncio.set_event_loop(loop)
    loop.call_later(3, server.stop)
    server.serve(loop)
    loop.close()

import threading
server_thread = threading.Thread(target=serve_for_3_seconds)
server_thread.start()
```

5. Then, as soon as the server has started, we make the three clients and send three messages:

```
while not server.started:
    pass

send_message_to_server('localhost', server._port, b"Hello World 1")
send_message_to_server('localhost', server._port, b"Hello World 2")
send_message_to_server('localhost', server._port, b"Hello World 3")
```

6. Once finished, we wait for the server to quit, as after 3 seconds it should stop and quit:

```
server_thread.join()
```

7. If everything worked as expected, you should see the server start, serve three clients, and then quit:

```
Serving on 0.0.0.0:9800
ANSWER: b'ECHO: Hello World 1'
ANSWER: b'ECHO: Hello World 2'
ANSWER: b'ECHO: Hello World 3'
Stopping...
Done
```

How it works...

The client side of this recipe is mostly taken as is from the socket serve recipe. The difference lies in the server side, which is not threaded anymore; instead, it's based on coroutines.

Given an `asyncio` event loop (the one we created with `asyncio.new_event_loop()` within the `serve_for_3_seconds` thread) the `EchoServer.serve` method creates a new coroutine-based server and tells the loop to serve requests forever until the server itself is not closed:

```
def serve(self, loop):
    coro = asyncio.start_server(self.handle, self._host, self._port,
                                loop=loop)
    self._server = loop.run_until_complete(coro)
    print('Serving on %s:%s' % (self._host, self._port))
    loop.run_until_complete(self._server.wait_closed())
    print('Done')
```

`loop.run_until_complete` will block until the specified coroutine doesn't quit, and `self._server.wait_closed()` will quit only when the server itself is stopped.

To ensure that the server is stopped after a short time, when we created the loop, we issued the `loop.call_later(3, server.stop)` call. This means that after 3 seconds, the server will stop and thus the whole loop will quit.

Meanwhile, until the server is actually stopped, it will serve requests. Each request will spawn a coroutine that runs the `handle` function:

```
async def handle(self, reader, writer):
    data = await self.recv_message(reader)
    await self.send_message(writer, b'ECHO: %s' % data)
    # Signal we finished handling this request
    # or the server will hang.
    writer.close()
```

The handler will receive two streams as arguments. One for incoming data and the other for outgoing data.

Much like we did in the case of the threaded socket server, we read the incoming message from the `reader` stream. To do so, we reimplement the `recv_message` as a coroutine, so that we can read the data concurrently with other requests being served:

```
@classmethod
async def recv_message(cls, socket):
    data_size = int(await socket.read(cls.MESSAGE_HEADER_LEN))
    data = await socket.read(data_size)
    return data
```

When both the size of the message and the message itself are available, we just return the message so that the `send_message` function can echo it back to the client.

The only particular change from `socketserver` in this context is that we write to the stream writer, but then we have to drain it:

```
socket.write(data)
await socket.drain()
```

This is done because after we wrote into the socket, we needed to send back control to the `asyncio` loop so that it had a chance actually to flush this data.

After three seconds, the `server.stop` method is called and that will stop the server, wake up the `wait_closed()` function, and thus make the `EchoServer.serve` method quit as it is completed.

Remote procedure calls

There are hundreds of systems to perform RPC in Python, but because it has powerful networking tools and is a dynamic language, everything we need is already built into the standard library.

How to do it...

You need to perform the following steps for this recipe:

1. Using `xmlrpc.server`, we can easily create an XMLRPC-based server that exposes multiple services:

    ```
    import xmlrpc.server

    class XMLRPCServices:
    ```

```
    class ExposedServices:
        pass

    def __init__(self, **services):
        self.services = self.ExposedServices()
        for name, service in services.items():
            setattr(self.services, name, service)

    def serve(self, host='localhost', port=8000):
        print('Serving XML-RPC on {}:{}'.format(host, port))
        self.server = xmlrpc.server.SimpleXMLRPCServer((host,
port))
        self.server.register_introspection_functions()
        self.server.register_instance(self.services,
                                    allow_dotted_names=True)
        self.server.serve_forever()

    def stop(self):
        self.server.shutdown()
        self.server.server_close()
```

2. Particularly, we are going to expose two services: one to get back current time, and the other to multiply a number by 2:

```
class MathServices:
    def double(self, v):
        return v**2

class TimeServices:
    def currentTime(self):
        import datetime
        return datetime.datetime.utcnow()
```

3. Once we have our services, we can consume them using `xmlrpc.client.ServerProxy`, which provides a simple call interface against the XMLRPC server.

4. As usual, to start both client and server in the same process, we can use a thread for the server and let the server run within that thread while the client drives the main thread:

```
xmlrpcserver = XMLRPCServices(math=MathServices(),
                              time=TimeServices())

import threading
server_thread = threading.Thread(target=xmlrpcserver.serve)
server_thread.start()
```

```
from xmlrpc.client import ServerProxy
client = ServerProxy("http://localhost:8000")
print(
    client.time.currentTime()
)

xmlrpcserver.stop()
server_thread.join()
```

5. If everything worked properly, you should see the current time being printed on the terminal:

```
Serving XML-RPC on localhost:8000
127.0.0.1 - - [10/Jun/2018 23:41:25] "POST /RPC2 HTTP/1.1" 200 -
20180610T21:41:25
```

How it works...

The `XMLRPCServices` class takes all services that we want to expose as initialization arguments and exposes them:

```
xmlrpcserver = XMLRPCServices(math=MathServices(),
                              time=TimeServices())
```

This is done because we expose a local object (`ExposedServices`) that by default is empty, but we attach to its instance all the provided services as attributes:

```
def __init__(self, **services):
    self.services = self.ExposedServices()
    for name, service in services.items():
        setattr(self.services, name, service)
```

So, we end up exposing a `self.services` object that has two attributes: `math` and `time`, which refer to the `MathServices` and `TimeServices` classes.

Serving them is actually done by the `XMLRPCServices.serve` method:

```
def serve(self, host='localhost', port=8000):
    print('Serving XML-RPC on {}:{}'.format(host, port))
    self.server = xmlrpc.server.SimpleXMLRPCServer((host, port))
    self.server.register_introspection_functions()
    self.server.register_instance(self.services,
                                  allow_dotted_names=True)
    self.server.serve_forever()
```

This creates a `SimpleXMLRPCServer` instance, which is the HTTP server in charge of responding to the XMLRPC requests.

To that instance, we then attach the `self.services` object we created before and allow it to access subproperties so that the nested `math` and `time` attributes are exposed as services:

```
self.server.register_instance(self.services,
                              allow_dotted_names=True)
```

Before actually starting the server, we also enabled introspection functions. Those are all the functions that allow us to access the list of exposed services, and ask for their help and signature:

```
self.server.register_introspection_functions()
```

Then we actually start the server:

```
self.server.serve_forever()
```

This will block the `serve` method and loop forever serving requests until the `stop` method is called.

That's the reason why, in the example, we started the server in a separate thread; that is, so that it won't block the main thread that we could use for the client.

The `stop` method is in charge of stopping the server, so that the `serve` method can exit. This method asks the server to terminate as soon as it finishes the current request and then closes the associated network connection:

```
def stop(self):
    self.server.shutdown()
    self.server.server_close()
```

So, just creating `XMLRPCServices` and serving it is enough to have our RPC server up and running:

```
xmlrpcserver = XMLRPCServices(math=MathServices(),
                              time=TimeServices())
xmlrpcserver.serve()
```

On the client side, the code base is a lot easier; it's just a matter of creating a `ServerProxy` against the URL where the server is exposed:

```
client = ServerProxy("http://localhost:8000")
```

Then, all the methods of the services exposed by the server will be accessible through dot notation:

```
client.time.currentTime()
```

There's more...

`XMLRPCServices` has big security implications, and so you should never use `SimpleXMLRPCServer` on an open network.

The most obvious concern is that you are allowing remote-code execution to anyone as the XMLRPC server is unauthenticated. So, the server should only run on private networks where you can ensure that only trusted clients will be able to access the services.

But even if you provide proper authentication in front of the service (which is possible by using any HTTP proxy in front of it), you still want to ensure that you trust the data your clients are going to send because `XMLRPCServices` suffers from some security limitations.

The data being served is exchanged in clear text, so anyone able to sniff your network will be able to see it.

This can be worked around with some effort by subclassing the `SimpleXMLRPCServer` and replacing its `socket` instance with an SSL-wrapped one (the same should happen for the client to be able to connect).

But, even when a hardening of the communication channel is involved, you still need to trust the data that will be sent because the parser is naive and can be brought out of service by sending large amounts of recursive data. Imagine you have an entity that's expanded to dozens of entities that each expand to dozens of entities and so on for 10-20 levels. That will quickly require gigabytes and gigabytes of RAM to decode, but requires no more than a few kilobytes to build and send through the network.

Also, the fact that we are exposing subproperties means we are exposing far more than we expect.

You certainly expect to expose the `currentTime` method of the `time` service:

```
client.time.currentTime()
```

Note that you are exposing every single property or method declared in `TimeServices` whose name does not start with an _.

In older Python versions (such as 2.7), this actually meant exposing internal code too, as you could access all public variables by doing something such as:

```
client.time.currentTime.im_func.func_globals.keys()
```

You could then retrieve their values through:

```
client.time.currentTime.im_func.func_globals.get('varname')
```

This was a major security concern.

Luckily, the `im_func` attribute of functions was renamed to `__func__` and, thus, is no longer accessible. However, the concern still remains for any attribute you declared yourself.

11
Web Development

In this chapter, we will cover the following recipes:

- Treating JSON—how to parse and write JSON objects
- Parsing URLs—how to parse the path, query, and other parts of a URL
- Consuming HTTP—how to read data from an HTTP endpoint
- Submitting forms to HTTP—how to POST HTML forms to an HTTP endpoint
- Building HTML—how to generate HTML with proper escaping
- Serving HTTP—serving dynamic content over HTTP
- Serving static files—how to serve static files over HTTP
- Errors in web applications—how to report errors in web applications
- Handling forms and files—parsing data received from HTML forms and uploaded files
- REST API—serving a basic REST/JSON API
- Handling cookies—how to handle cookies to identify a returning user

Introduction

The HTTP protocol and, more generally, the web set of technologies, are being recognized as an effective and robust way to create distributed systems that can leverage a widespread and reliable way to implement inter-process communication with ready available technologies and paradigms for caching, error propagation, reiterable requests, and best practices for contexts where services might fail without impacting the overall system status.

Python has many very good and reliable web frameworks, from full stack solutions, such as Django and TurboGears, to more finely tweakable frameworks, such as Pyramid and Flask. However, for many cases, the standard library might already provide the tools you need to implement an HTTP-based software without the need to rely on external libraries and frameworks.

In this chapter, we will look at some some common recipes and tools provided by the standard library that can be convenient in the context of HTTP and web-based applications.

Treating JSON

One of the most frequent needs when working with web-based solutions is parsing and speaking JSON. Python has built-in support for XML and HTML, but also for JSON encoding and decoding.

The JSON encoder can also be specialized to handle non-standard types, such as dates.

How to do it...

For this recipe, the following steps are to be performed:

1. The JSONEncoder and JSONDecoder classes can be specialized to implement custom encoding and decoding behaviors:

```python
import json
import datetime
import decimal
import types


class CustomJSONEncoder(json.JSONEncoder):
    """JSON Encoder with support for additional types.

    Supports dates, times, decimals, generators and
    any custom class that implements __json__ method.
    """
    def default(self, obj):
        if hasattr(obj, '__json__') and callable(obj.__json__):
            return obj.__json__()
        elif isinstance(obj, (datetime.datetime, datetime.time)):
            return obj.replace(microsecond=0).isoformat()
        elif isinstance(obj, datetime.date):
            return obj.isoformat()
        elif isinstance(obj, decimal.Decimal):
            return float(obj)
        elif isinstance(obj, types.GeneratorType):
            return list(obj)
        else:
            return super().default(obj)
```

2. Our custom encoder can then be passed to `json.dumps` to encode the JSON output according to our rules:

```
jsonstr = json.dumps({'s': 'Hello World',
                      'dt': datetime.datetime.utcnow(),
                      't': datetime.datetime.utcnow().time(),
                      'g': (i for i in range(5)),
                      'd': datetime.date.today(),
                      'dct': {
                          's': 'SubDict',
                          'dt': datetime.datetime.utcnow()
                      }},
                      cls=CustomJSONEncoder)
```

```
>>> print(jsonstr)
{"t": "10:53:53",
 "s": "Hello World",
 "d": "2018-06-29",
 "dt": "2018-06-29T10:53:53",
 "dct": {"dt": "2018-06-29T10:53:53", "s": "SubDict"},
 "g": [0, 1, 2, 3, 4]}
```

3. We can also encode any custom class as far as it provides a `__json__` method:

```
class Person:
    def __init__(self, name, surname):
        self.name = name
        self.surname = surname

    def __json__(self):
        return {
            'name': self.name,
            'surname': self.surname
        }
```

4. The result will be a JSON object that contains the provided data:

```
>>> print(json.dumps({'person': Person('Simone', 'Marzola')},
                     cls=CustomJSONEncoder))
{"person": {"name": "Simone", "surname": "Marzola"}}
```

5. Loading back-encoded values will, by the way, lead to plain strings being decoded, because they are not JSON types:

```
>>> print(json.loads(jsonstr))
{'g': [0, 1, 2, 3, 4],
 'd': '2018-06-29',
 's': 'Hello World',
```

```
        'dct': {'s': 'SubDict', 'dt': '2018-06-29T10:56:30'},
        't': '10:56:30',
        'dt': '2018-06-29T10:56:30'}
```

6. If we want to also parse back dates, we can try to specialize a JSONDecoder to
   guess whether a string contains a date in ISO 8601 format and try to parse it back:

```python
class CustomJSONDecoder(json.JSONDecoder):
    """Custom JSON Decoder that tries to decode additional types.

    Decoder tries to guess dates, times and datetimes in ISO
format.
    """
    def __init__(self, *args, **kwargs):
        super().__init__(
            *args, **kwargs, object_hook=self.parse_object
        )

    def parse_object(self, values):
        for k, v in values.items():
            if not isinstance(v, str):
                continue

            if len(v) == 10 and v.count('-') == 2:
                # Probably contains a date
                try:
                    values[k] = datetime.datetime.strptime(v, '%Y-
                    %m-%d').date()
                except:
                    pass
            elif len(v) == 8 and v.count(':') == 2:
                # Probably contains a time
                try:
                    values[k] = datetime.datetime.strptime(v,
                    '%H:%M:%S').time()
                except:
                    pass
            elif (len(v) == 19 and v.count('-') == 2 and
                v.count('T') == 1 and v.count(':') == 2):
                # Probably contains a datetime
                try:
                    values[k] = datetime.datetime.strptime(v, '%Y-
                    %m-%dT%H:%M:%S')
                except:
                    pass
        return values
```

7. Loading back at previous data should lead to the expected types:

```
>>> jsondoc = json.loads(jsonstr, cls=CustomJSONDecoder)
>>> print(jsondoc)
{'g': [0, 1, 2, 3, 4],
 'd': datetime.date(2018, 6, 29),
 's': 'Hello World',
 'dct': {'s': 'SubDict', 'dt': datetime.datetime(2018, 6, 29, 10,
56, 30)},
 't': datetime.time(10, 56, 30),
 'dt': datetime.datetime(2018, 6, 29, 10, 56, 30)}
```

How it works...

To generate JSON representation of Python objects, the `json.dumps` method is used. This method accepts an additional argument, `cls`, where a custom encoder class can be provided:

```
json.dumps({'key': 'value'}, cls=CustomJSONEncoder)
```

The `default` method of the provided class will be called whenever it is required to encode an object that the encoder doesn't know how to encode.

Our `CustomJSONEncoder` class provides a `default` method that handles encoding dates, times, generators, decimals, and any custom class that provides a `__json__` method:

```
class CustomJSONEncoder(json.JSONEncoder):
    def default(self, obj):
        if hasattr(obj, '__json__') and callable(obj.__json__):
            return obj.__json__()
        elif isinstance(obj, (datetime.datetime, datetime.time)):
            return obj.replace(microsecond=0).isoformat()
        elif isinstance(obj, datetime.date):
            return obj.isoformat()
        elif isinstance(obj, decimal.Decimal):
            return float(obj)
        elif isinstance(obj, types.GeneratorType):
            return list(obj)
        else:
            return super().default(obj)
```

This is done by checking one after the other the properties of the encoded object. Remember that objects that the encoder knows how to encode won't be provided to the `default` method; only objects that the encoder doesn't know how to treat will be passed to the `default` method.

So we only have to check for the objects we want to support additionally to the standard ones.

Our first check is to verify if the provided object has a __json__ method:

```
if hasattr(obj, '__json__') and callable(obj.__json__):
    return obj.__json__()
```

For any object that has a __json__ attribute that is a callable, we will rely on calling it to retrieve a JSON representation of the object. All the __json__ method has to do is return any object that the JSON encoder knows how to encode, usually a `dict` where the properties of the object will be stored.

For the case of dates, we will encode them using a simplified form of the ISO 8601 format:

```
elif isinstance(obj, (datetime.datetime, datetime.time)):
    return obj.replace(microsecond=0).isoformat()
elif isinstance(obj, datetime.date):
    return obj.isoformat()
```

This usually allows easy parsing from clients, such as JavaScript interpreters that might have to build `date` objects back from the provided data.

`Decimal` is just converted to a floating point number for convenience. This will suffice in most cases and is fully compatible with any JSON decoder without any additional machinery required. Of course, nothing prevents us from returning a more complex object, such as a dictionary, to retain fixed precision:

```
elif isinstance(obj, decimal.Decimal):
    return float(obj)
```

Finally, generators are consumed and a list of the contained values is returned from them. This is usually what you would expect, and representing the generator logic itself would require an unreasonable effort to guarantee cross-languages compatibility:

```
elif isinstance(obj, types.GeneratorType):
    return list(obj)
```

For any object we don't know how to handle, we just let the parent implement the `default` method and proceed:

```
else:
    return super().default(obj)
```

This will just complain that the object is not JSON-serializable and will inform the developer that we don't know how to handle it.

The custom decoder support instead works slightly differently.

While the encoder will receive objects that it knows and objects that it doesn't know (as the Python objects are richer than the JSON objects), it's easy to see how it can only request additional guidance for the objects that it doesn't know and behave in a standard way for those that it knows how to handle.

The decoder instead receives only valid JSON objects; otherwise, the provided string wouldn't be valid JSON at all.

How can it know that the provided string must be decoded as a normal string or if it should ask for additional guidance?

It can't, and for this reason it asks for guidance on any single decoded object.

This is the reason why the decoder is based on an `object_hook` callable that will receive every single decoded JSON object and can check it to perform additional transformations or it can let it go if the normal decoding was the right one.

In our implementation, we subclassed the decoder and provided a default `object_hook` argument that is based on a local class method, `parse_object`:

```
class CustomJSONDecoder(json.JSONDecoder):
    def __init__(self, *args, **kwargs):
        super().__init__(
            *args, **kwargs, object_hook=self.parse_object
        )
```

The `parse_object` method will then receive any JSON object that was found decoding the JSON (top or nested ones); thus, it will receive a bunch of dictionaries that it can check in any way that is needed and edit their content to perform additional conversions on top of those performed by the JSON decoder itself:

```
def parse_object(self, values):
    for k, v in values.items():
        if not isinstance(v, str):
            continue

        if len(v) == 10 and v.count('-') == 2:
            # Probably contains a date
            try:
                values[k] = datetime.datetime.strptime(v, '%Y-%m-
                %d').date()
            except:
                pass
        elif len(v) == 8 and v.count(':') == 2:
```

```
                    # Probably contains a time
                    try:
                        values[k] = datetime.datetime.strptime(v,
                        '%H:%M:%S').time()
                    except:
                        pass
                elif (len(v) == 19 and v.count('-') == 2 and
                    v.count('T') == 1 and v.count(':') == 2):
                    # Probably contains a datetime
                    try:
                        values[k] = datetime.datetime.strptime(v,  '%Y-%m-
                        %dT%H:%M:%S')
                    except:
                        pass
        return values
```

The received argument is actually a full JSON object, so it will never be a single field alone; it will always be an object (so, a full Python dictionary with multiple key values).

Look at the following object:

```
{'g': [0, 1, 2, 3, 4],
 'd': '2018-06-29',
 's': 'Hello World',
```

You won't receive a g key but you will receive the whole Python dictionary. This means that if your JSON document has no nested JSON objects, your object_hook will be called exactly once with the whole document and nothing more.

So, our custom object_hook provided by the parse_object method iterates over all the properties of the decoded JSON object:

```
for k, v in values.items():
    if not isinstance(v, str):
        continue
```

And as dates and times in JSON are usually represented in strings in ISO 8601 format, it just ignores everything that is not a string.

We are perfectly fine with the way numbers, lists, and dictionaries were converted (you might have to jump into lists if you expect dates to be placed inside lists) so if the value is not a string, we just skip it.

When the value is a string instead, we check its properties and if we guess it might be a date, we try to parse it as a date.

We can consider a proper definition of a date: three values separated by two dashes, followed by three values separated by two colons with a `"T"` in the middle splitting the two:

```
elif (len(v) == 19 and v.count('-') == 2 and
        v.count('T') == 1 and v.count(':') == 2):
    # Probably contains a datetime
```

If that definition is matched, we actually try to decode it as a Python `datetime` object and replace the value in the decoded JSON object:

```
# Probably contains a datetime
try:
    values[k] = datetime.datetime.strptime(v, '%Y-%m-%dT%H:%M:%S')
except:
    pass
```

There's more...

You probably noticed that while encoding Python to JSON is fairly reasonable and robust, the trip back is full of issues.

JSON is not a very expressive language; it doesn't provide any machinery for custom types, so you have a standard way to give back hints to the decoder about the type that you would expect something to be decoded to.

While we can *guess* that something like `2017-01-01T13:21:17` is a date, we have no guarantee at all. Maybe, originally, it was actually some text that by chance contained something that can be decoded as a date, but was never meant to become a `datetime` object in Python.

For this reason, it's usually safe to implement custom decoding only in constrained environments. If you know and control the source you will be receiving data from, it's usually safe to provide custom decoding. And you might want to go for extending JSON with custom properties that might guide the decoder (like having a __type__ key that tells you whether it's a date or a string), but in the open web world, it is usually not a very good idea to try to guess what people are sending you, as the web is very diverse.

There are extended standard versions of JSON that try to solve exactly this ambiguity in decoding data, such as JSON-LD and JSON Schema, that allow you to express more complex entities in JSON.

If you feel the need, you should rely on those standards to avoid the risk of reinventing the wheel and facing limits of your solution that were already solved by existing standards.

Parsing URLs

When working with web-based software, it's frequently necessary to understand links, protocols, and paths.

You might be tempted to rely on regular expressions or strings splitting to parse URLs, but if you account for all the oddities a URL might include (things such as credentials or particular protocols), it might not be as easy as you expect.

Python provides utilities in the `urllib` and `cgi` modules that make life easier when you want to account for all the possible different formats a URL can have.

Relying on them can make life easier and your software more robust.

How to do it...

The `urllib.parse` module has multiple tools to parse URLs. The most commonly used solution is to rely on `urllib.parse.urlparse`, which can handle the most widespread kinds of URLs:

```python
import urllib.parse


def parse_url(url):
    """Parses an URL of the most widespread format.

    This takes for granted there is a single set of parameters
    for the whole path.
    """
    parts = urllib.parse.urlparse(url)
    parsed = vars(parts)
    parsed['query'] = urllib.parse.parse_qs(parts.query)
    return parsed
```

The preceding code snippet can be called on the command line, as follows:

```
>>> url =
'http://user:pwd@host.com:80/path/subpath?arg1=val1&arg2=val2#fragment'
>>> result = parse_url(url)
>>> print(result)
OrderedDict([('scheme', 'http'),
```

```
             ('netloc', 'user:pwd@host.com:80'),
             ('path', '/path/subpath'),
             ('params', ''),
             ('query', {'arg1': ['val1'], 'arg2': ['val2']}),
             ('fragment', 'fragment')])
```

The returned `OrderedDict` contains all the parts that compose our URL and also, for the query arguments, it provides them already parsed.

There's more...

Nowadays, the URIs also support parameters to be provided at each path segment. Those are very rarely used in practice, but if your code is expected to receive those kind of URIs, then you should not rely on `urllib.parse.urlparse` because it tries to parse the parameters from the URL, which is not properly supported for those URIs:

```
>>> url =
'http://user:pwd@host.com:80/root;para1/subpath;para2?arg1=val1#fragment'
>>> result = urllib.parse.urlparse(url)
>>> print(result)
ParseResult(scheme='http', netloc='user:pwd@host.com:80',
            path='/root;para1/subpath',
            params='para2',
            query='arg1=val1',
            fragment='fragment')
```

You might have noticed that parameters for the last part of the path were properly parsed in `params`, but the parameters for the first part were left in `path`.

In such case, you might want to rely on `urllib.parse.urlsplit`, which won't parse the parameters and will leave them as they are for you to parse. So you can split the URL segments from the parameters on your own:

```
>>> parsed = urllib.parse.urlsplit(url)
>>> print(parsed)
SplitResult(scheme='http', netloc='user:pwd@host.com:80',
            path='/root;para1/subpath;para2',
            query='arg1=val1',
            fragment='fragment')
```

See that, in this case, all parameters were left in place in `path` and you can then split them yourself.

Consuming HTTP

You might be interacting with a third-party service based on HTTP REST APIs, or you might be fetching content from a third party or just downloading a file that your software needs as the input. It doesn't really matter. Nowadays, it's virtually impossible to write an application and ignore HTTP; you will have to face it sooner or later. People expect HTTP support from all kind of applications. If you are writing an image viewer, they probably expect to be able to throw a URL that leads to an image to it and see it appear.

While they have never been really user friendly and obvious, the Python standard library has always had ways to interact with HTTP, and they are available out of the box.

How to do it...

The steps for this recipe are as follows:

1. The `urllib.request` module provides the machinery required to submit an HTTP request. A light wrapper around it can solve most needs in terms of using HTTP:

```python
import urllib.request
import urllib.parse
import json


def http_request(url, query=None, method=None, headers={},
data=None):
    """Perform an HTTP request and return the associated
response."""
    parts = vars(urllib.parse.urlparse(url))
    if query:
        parts['query'] = urllib.parse.urlencode(query)

    url = urllib.parse.ParseResult(**parts).geturl()
    r = urllib.request.Request(url=url, method=method,
                               headers=headers,
                               data=data)
    with urllib.request.urlopen(r) as resp:
        msg, resp = resp.info(), resp.read()

        if msg.get_content_type() == 'application/json':
            resp = json.loads(resp.decode('utf-8'))

        return msg, resp
```

2. We can use our `http_request` function to perform requests to fetch files:

```
>>> msg, resp = http_request('https://httpbin.org/bytes/16')
>>> print(msg.get_content_type(), resp)
application/octet-stream
b'k\xe3\x05\x06=\x17\x1a9%#\xd0\xae\xd8\xdc\xf9>'
```

3. We can also use it to interact with JSON-based APIs:

```
>>> msg, resp = http_request('https://httpbin.org/get', query={
...     'a': 'Hello',
...     'b': 'World'
... })
>>> print(msg.get_content_type(), resp)
application/json
{'url': 'https://httpbin.org/get?a=Hello&b=World',
 'headers': {'Accept-Encoding': 'identity',
             'User-Agent': 'Python-urllib/3.5',
             'Connection': 'close',
             'Host': 'httpbin.org'},
 'args': {'a': 'Hello', 'b': 'World'},
 'origin': '127.19.102.123'}
```

4. Also, it can be used to submit or upload data to endpoints:

```
>>> msg, resp = http_request('https://httpbin.org/post',
method='POST',
...                          data='This is my posted
data!'.encode('ascii'),
...                          headers={'Content-Type':
'text/plain'})
>>> print(msg.get_content_type(), resp)
application/json
{'data': 'This is my posted data!',
 'json': None,
 'form': {},
 'args': {},
 'files': {},
 'headers': {'User-Agent': 'Python-urllib/3.5',
             'Connection': 'close',
             'Content-Type': 'text/plain',
             'Host': 'httpbin.org',
             'Accept-Encoding': 'identity',
             'Content-Length': '23'},
 'url': 'https://httpbin.org/post',
 'origin': '127.19.102.123'}
```

How it works...

The `http_request` method takes care of creating a `urllib.request.Request` instance, sending it through the network and fetching back the response.

A request is sent to the specified URL to which query arguments are appended.

The first thing the function does is parse the URL, so that it can replace parts of it. This is done to be able to replace/append the query arguments with the one provided:

```
parts = vars(urllib.parse.urlparse(url))
if query:
    parts['query'] = urllib.parse.urlencode(query)
```

`urllib.parse.urlencode` will accept a dictionary of arguments, such as `{'a': 5, 'b': 7}`, and will give you back the string with the `urlencode` arguments: `'b=7&a=5'`.

The resulting query string is then placed into the parsed parts of the `url` to replace the currently existing query arguments.

Then the `url` is built back from all the parts that now include the right query arguments:

```
url = urllib.parse.ParseResult(**parts).geturl()
```

Once the `url` with the encoded query is ready, it builds a request out of it, proxying the specified method, headers, and body of the request:

```
r = urllib.request.Request(url=url, method=method, headers=headers,
                           data=data)
```

When doing a plain GET request, those will be the default ones, but being able to specify them allows us to perform also more advanced kinds of requests, such as POST, or provide special headers into our requests.

The request is then opened and the response is read back:

```
with urllib.request.urlopen(r) as resp:
    msg, resp = resp.info(), resp.read()
```

The response comes back as a `urllib.response.addinfourl` object, with two relevant parts: the body of the response and an `http.client.HTTPMessage`, from which we can get all the response info, such as headers, URL, and so on.

The body is retrieved by reading the response like a file, while the `HTTPMessage` is retrieve through the `info()` method.

Through the retrieved info, we can check whether the response is a JSON response, and in this case, we decode it back to a dictionary so we can navigate the response instead of just receiving plain bytes:

```
if msg.get_content_type() == 'application/json':
    resp = json.loads(resp.decode('utf-8'))
```

For all responses, we return the message and the body. The caller can just ignore the message if it's not needed:

```
return msg, resp
```

There's more...

Making HTTP requests can be very simple for simple cases and very complicated for more complex cases. Perfectly handling the HTTP protocol can be a long and complex job, especially since the protocol specifications themselves are not always clear in enforcing how things should work and a lot comes from experience of how real existing web servers and clients work.

For this reason, if you have needs that go further than just fetching simple endpoints, you might want to rely on a third-party library for performing HTTP requests, such as the requests library that is available for nearly all Python environments.

Submitting forms to HTTP

Sometimes you have to interact with HTML forms or upload files. This usually requires handling the `multipart/form-data` encoding.

Forms can mix files and text data, and there can be multiple different fields within a form. Thus, it requires a way to express multiple fields in the same request and some of those fields can be binary files.

That's why encoding data in multipart can get tricky, but it's possible to roll out a basic recipe using only standard library tools that will work in most cases.

How to do it...

Here are the steps for this recipe:

1. `multipart` itself requires tracking all the fields and files we want to encode and then performing the encoding itself.

2. We will rely on `io.BytesIO` to store all the resulting bytes:

```python
import io
import mimetypes
import uuid


class MultiPartForm:
    def __init__(self):
        self.fields = {}
        self.files = []

    def __setitem__(self, name, value):
        self.fields[name] = value

    def add_file(self, field, filename, data, mimetype=None):
        if mimetype is None:
            mimetype = (mimetypes.guess_type(filename)[0] or
                        'application/octet-stream')
        self.files.append((field, filename, mimetype, data))

    def _generate_bytes(self, boundary):
        buffer = io.BytesIO()
        for field, value in self.fields.items():
            buffer.write(b'--' + boundary + b'\r\n')
            buffer.write('Content-Disposition: form-data; '
'name="{}"\r\n'.format(field).encode('utf-8'))
            buffer.write(b'\r\n')
            buffer.write(value.encode('utf-8'))
            buffer.write(b'\r\n')
        for field, filename, f_content_type, body in self.files:
            buffer.write(b'--' + boundary + b'\r\n')
            buffer.write('Content-Disposition: file; '
                        'name="{}"; filename="{}"\r\n'.format(
                            field, filename
                        ).encode('utf-8'))
            buffer.write('Content-Type: {}\r\n'.format(
                f_content_type
            ).encode('utf-8'))
            buffer.write(b'\r\n')
            buffer.write(body)
```

```
            buffer.write(b'\r\n')
        buffer.write(b'--' + boundary + b'--\r\n')
        return buffer.getvalue()

    def encode(self):
        boundary = uuid.uuid4().hex.encode('ascii')
        while boundary in
self._generate_bytes(boundary=b'NOBOUNDARY'):
            boundary = uuid.uuid4().hex.encode('ascii')

        content_type = 'multipart/form-data; boundary={}'.format(
            boundary.decode('ascii')
        )
        return content_type, self._generate_bytes(boundary)
```

3. We can then provide and encode our `form` data:

```
>>> form = MultiPartForm()
>>> form['name'] = 'value'
>>> form.add_file('file1', 'somefile.txt', b'Some Content',
'text/plain')
>>> content_type, form_body = form.encode()
>>> print(content_type, '\n\n', form_body.decode('ascii'))
multipart/form-data; boundary=6c5109dfa19a450695013d4eecac2b0b

--6c5109dfa19a450695013d4eecac2b0b
Content-Disposition: form-data; name="name"

value
--6c5109dfa19a450695013d4eecac2b0b
Content-Disposition: file; name="file1"; filename="somefile.txt"
Content-Type: text/plain

Some Content
--6c5109dfa19a450695013d4eecac2b0b--
```

4. Using this with our `http_request` method from previous recipe, we can submit any `form` through HTTP:

```
>>> _, resp = http_request('https://httpbin.org/post',
method='POST',
                            data=form_body,
                            headers={'Content-Type': content_type})
>>> print(resp)
{'headers': {
    'Accept-Encoding': 'identity',
    'Content-Type': 'multipart/form-data;
boundary=6c5109dfa19a450695013d4eecac2b0b',
```

```
        'User-Agent': 'Python-urllib/3.5',
        'Content-Length': '272',
        'Connection': 'close',
        'Host': 'httpbin.org'
    },
    'json': None,
    'url': 'https://httpbin.org/post',
    'data': '',
    'args': {},
    'form': {'name': 'value'},
    'origin': '127.69.102.121',
    'files': {'file1': 'Some Content'}}
```

As you can see, `httpbin` properly received our `file1` and and our `name` field and processed both.

How it works...

`multipart` is practically based on encoding multiple requests within a single body. Each part is separated by a **boundary** and within the boundary lies the data of that part.

Each part can provide both data and metadata, such as the content type of the provided data.

This way the receiver can know whether the contained data is binary, text, or whatever. For example, the part specifying the value for the `surname` field of a `form` would look like this:

```
Content-Disposition: form-data; name="surname"

MySurname
```

And the part providing data for an uploaded file would look like this:

```
Content-Disposition: file; name="file1"; filename="somefile.txt"
Content-Type: text/plain

Some Content
```

Our `MultiPartForm` allows us to store aside both plain `form` fields by setting them with dictionary syntax:

```
def __setitem__(self, name, value):
    self.fields[name] = value
```

We can call it on a command line, as follows:

```
>>> form['name'] = 'value'
```

And to provide files by adding them with the add_file method:

```
def add_file(self, field, filename, data, mimetype=None):
    if mimetype is None:
        mimetype = (mimetypes.guess_type(filename)[0] or
                    'application/octet-stream')
    self.files.append((field, filename, mimetype, data))
```

We can call this method on a command line, as follows:

```
>>> form.add_file('file1', 'somefile.txt', b'Some Content', 'text/plain')
```

Those just record the wanted fields and files in a dictionary and a list that are only used later on when _generate_bytes is called to actually generate the full multipart content.

All the hard work is done by _generate_bytes that goes through all those fields and files and creates a part for each one of them:

```
for field, value in self.fields.items():
    buffer.write(b'--' + boundary + b'\r\n')
    buffer.write('Content-Disposition: form-data; '
                 'name="{}"\r\n'.format(field).encode('utf-8'))
    buffer.write(b'\r\n')
    buffer.write(value.encode('utf-8'))
    buffer.write(b'\r\n')
```

As the boundary must separate every part, it's very important to verify that the boundary is not contained within the data itself, or the receiver might wrongly consider a part ended when it encounters it.

That's why our MultiPartForm class generates a boundary, checks whether it's contained within the multipart response, and if it is, it generates a new one, until it can find a boundary that is not contained within the data:

```
boundary = uuid.uuid4().hex.encode('ascii')
while boundary in self._generate_bytes(boundary=b'NOBOUNDARY'):
    boundary = uuid.uuid4().hex.encode('ascii')
```

Once we have found a valid `boundary`, we can use it to generate the multipart content and return it to the caller with the content type that must be used (as the content type provides a hint to the receiver about which `boundary` to check):

```
content_type = 'multipart/form-data; boundary={}'.format(
    boundary.decode('ascii')
)
return content_type, self._generate_bytes(boundary)
```

There's more...

Multipart encoding is not an easy subject; for example, encoding of names within the multipart body is not an easy topic.

Over the years, it was changed and discussed multiple times about what's the proper encoding for the name of fields and name of files within the multipart content.

Historically, it's safe to only rely on plain ASCII names in those fields, so if you want to make sure the server you are submitting data to is able to properly receive your data, you might want to stick to simple filenames and fields that don't involve Unicode characters.

Over the years, multiple other ways to encode those fields and filenames were suggested. UTF-8 is one of the officially supported fallback for HTML5. The suggested recipe relies on UTF-8 to encode filenames and fields, so that it's backward compatible with cases where plain ASCII names are used but it's still possible to rely on Unicode characters when the server supports them.

Building HTML

Whenever you are building a web page, an email, or a report, you are probably going to rely on replacing placeholders in an HTML template with actual values that you need to show to your users.

We already saw in `Chapter 2`, *Text Management*, how a minimal, simple template engine can be implemented, but it wasn't specific to HTML in any way.

When working with HTML, it's particularly important to pay attention to escaping the values provided by users, as that might lead to broken pages or even XSS attacks.

You clearly don't want your users to get mad at you just because you registered yourself on your website with the surname "`<script>alert('You are hacked!')</script>`".

For this reason, the Python standard library provides escaping tools that can be used to properly prepare content for insertion into HTML.

How to do it...

Combining the `string.Formatter` and `cgi` modules, it is possible to create a formatter that takes care of escaping for us:

```python
import string
import cgi

class HTMLFormatter(string.Formatter):
    def get_field(self, field_name, args, kwargs):
        val, key = super().get_field(field_name, args, kwargs)
        if hasattr(val, '__html__'):
            val = val.__html__()
        elif isinstance(val, str):
            val = cgi.escape(val)
        return val, key


class Markup:
    def __init__(self, v):
        self.v = v
    def __str__(self):
        return self.v
    def __html__(self):
        return str(self)
```

Then we can use the `HTMLFormatter` and the `Markup` classes while also retaining the ability to inject raw `html` when needed:

```python
>>> html = HTMLFormatter().format('Hello {name}, you are {title}',
                                  name='<strong>Name</strong>',
                                  title=Markup('<em>a developer</em>'))
>>> print(html)
Hello &lt;strong&gt;Name&lt;/strong&gt;, you are <em>a developer</em>
```

We can also easily combine this recipe with the one regarding text template engines to implement a minimalistic HTML template engine with escaping.

How it works...

Whenever the `HTMLFormatter` has to replace a value in the format string, it will check whether the retrieved value has a __html__ method:

```
if hasattr(val, '__html__'):
    val = val.__html__()
```

If that method exists, it's expected to return the HTML representation of the value. And that's expected to be a perfectly valid and escaped HTML.

Otherwise, the value is expected to be a string that needs escaping:

```
elif isinstance(val, str):
    val = cgi.escape(val)
```

This makes it so that any value we provide to the `HTMLFormatter` gets escaped by default:

```
>>> html = HTMLFormatter().format('Hello {name}',
                                  name='<strong>Name</strong>')
>>> print(html)
Hello &lt;strong&gt;Name&lt;/strong&gt;
```

If we want to avoid escaping, we can rely on the `Markup` object, which can wrap out a string to make it pass as is without any escaping:

```
>>> html = HTMLFormatter().format('Hello {name}',
                                  name=Markup('<strong>Name</strong>'))
>>> print(html)
Hello <strong>Name</strong>
```

This works because our `Markup` object implements an __html__ method that returns the string as is. As our `HTMLFormatter` ignores any value that has an __html__ method, our string will get through without any form of escaping.

While `Markup` permits us to disable escaping on demand, when we know that we actually want HTML in there, we can apply the HTML method to any other object. Any object that needs to be represented in a web page can provide an __html__ method and will automatically get converted to HTML according to it.

For example, you can add __html__ to your `User` class and any time you want to put your user in a web page, you just need to provide the `User` instance itself.

Serving HTTP

Interacting through HTTP is one of the most frequent means of communication between distributed applications or even totally separated software and it's also the foundation of all existing web applications and web-based tools.

While Python has tens of great web frameworks that can satisfy most different needs, the standard library itself has all the foundations that you might need to implement a basic web application.

How to do it...

Python has a convenient protocol named WSGI to implement HTTP-based applications. While for more advanced needs, a web framework might be required; for very simple needs, the `wsgiref` implementation built into Python itself can meet our needs:

```python
import re
import inspect
from wsgiref.headers import Headers
from wsgiref.simple_server import make_server
from wsgiref.util import request_uri
from urllib.parse import parse_qs


class WSGIApplication:
    def __init__(self):
        self.routes = []

    def route(self, path):
        def _route_decorator(f):
            self.routes.append((re.compile(path), f))
            return f
        return _route_decorator

    def serve(self):
        httpd = make_server('', 8000, self)
        print("Serving on port 8000...")
        httpd.serve_forever()

    def _not_found(self, environ, resp):
        resp.status = '404 Not Found'
        return b"""<h1>Not Found</h1>"""

    def __call__(self, environ, start_response):
        request = Request(environ)
```

```
            routed_action = self._not_found
            for regex, action in self.routes:
                match = regex.fullmatch(request.path)
                if match:
                    routed_action = action
                    request.urlargs = match.groupdict()
                    break

            resp = Response()

            if inspect.isclass(routed_action):
                routed_action = routed_action()
            body = routed_action(request, resp)

            resp.send(start_response)
            return [body]


    class Response:
        def __init__(self):
            self.status = '200 OK'
            self.headers = Headers([
                ('Content-Type', 'text/html; charset=utf-8')
            ])

        def send(self, start_response):
            start_response(self.status, self.headers.items())


    class Request:
        def __init__(self, environ):
            self.environ = environ
            self.urlargs = {}

        @property
        def path(self):
            return self.environ['PATH_INFO']

        @property
        def query(self):
            return parse_qs(self.environ['QUERY_STRING'])
```

Then we can create a WSGIApplication and register any number of routes with it:

```
app = WSGIApplication()

@app.route('/')
def index(request, resp):
```

```
        return b'Hello World, <a href="/link">Click here</a>'

@app.route('/link')
def link(request, resp):
    return (b'You clicked the link! '
            b'Try <a href="/args?a=1&b=2">Some arguments</a>')

@app.route('/args')
def args(request, resp):
    return (b'You provided %b<br/>'
            b'Try <a href="/name/HelloWorld">URL Arguments</a>' %
            repr(request.query).encode('utf-8'))

@app.route('/name/(?P<first_name>\\w+)')
def name(request, resp):
    return (b'Your name: %b' %
request.urlargs['first_name'].encode('utf-8'))
```

Once we are ready, we just need to serve the application:

```
app.serve()
```

If everything worked properly, by pointing your browser to `http://localhost:8000`, you should see an **Hello World** text and a link leading you to further pages providing query arguments, URL arguments, and being served on various URLs.

How it works...

The `WSGIApplication` creates a WSGI server that is in charge of serving the web application itself (`self`):

```
def serve(self):
    httpd = make_server('', 8000, self)
    print("Serving on port 8000...")
    httpd.serve_forever()
```

On every request, `WSGIApplication.__call__` is called by the server to retrieve a response for that request.

`WSGIApplication.__call__` scans through all the registered routes (each route can be registered with `app.route(path)`, where `path` is a regular expression). When a regular expression matches the current URL path, the registered function is called to produce a response of that route:

```python
def __call__(self, environ, start_response):
    request = Request(environ)

    routed_action = self._not_found
    for regex, action in self.routes:
        match = regex.fullmatch(request.path)
        if match:
            routed_action = action
            request.urlargs = match.groupdict()
            break
```

Once a function matching the path is found, that function is called to get a response body and then the resulting body is returned to the server:

```python
resp = Response()
body = routed_action(request, resp)

resp.send(start_response)
return [body]
```

Right before returning the body, `Response.send` is called to send the response HTTP headers and status through the `start_response` callable.

The `Response` and `Request` objects are instead used to keep around the environment of the current request (and any additional argument parsed from the URL), the headers, and status of the response. This is so that the actions called to handle the request can receive them and inspect the request or add/remove headers from the response before it's sent.

There's more...

While basic HTTP-based applications can be served using the provided implementation of `WSGIApplication`, there is a lot that is missing or incomplete for a full featured application.

Parts such as caching, sessions, authentication, authorization, managing database connections, transactions, and administration are usually required when more complex web applications are involved, and they are easily provided for you by most Python web frameworks.

Implementing a complete web framework is out of the scope of this book and you should probably try to avoid reinventing the wheel when there are many great web frameworks available in the Python environment.

Python has a wide range of web frameworks covering everything from full-stack frameworks for rapid development, such as Django; API-oriented micro frameworks, such as Flask; to flexible solutions, such as Pyramid and TurboGears, where the required pieces can be enabled, disabled, or replaced on demand, ranging from full-stack solutions to microframeworks.

Serving static files

Sometimes when working on JavaScript-based applications or static websites, it's necessary to be able to serve the content of a directory directly from disk.

The Python standard library has a ready-made HTTP server that handles requests, mapping them to files in a directory, so we can quickly roll our own HTTP server to write websites without the need to install any other tool.

How to do it...

The `http.server` module provides most of what is needed to implement an HTTP server in charge of serving content of a directory:

```
import os.path
import socketserver
from http.server import SimpleHTTPRequestHandler, HTTPServer

def serve_directory(path, port=8000):
    class ConfiguredHandler(HTTPDirectoryRequestHandler):
        SERVED_DIRECTORY = path
    httpd = ThreadingHTTPServer(("", port), ConfiguredHandler)
    print("serving on port", port)
    try:
        httpd.serve_forever()
    except KeyboardInterrupt:
        httpd.server_close()
```

```
class ThreadingHTTPServer(socketserver.ThreadingMixIn, HTTPServer):
    pass


class HTTPDirectoryRequestHandler(SimpleHTTPRequestHandler):
    SERVED_DIRECTORY = '.'

    def translate_path(self, path):
        path = super().translate_path(path)
        relpath = os.path.relpath(path)
        return os.path.join(self.SERVED_DIRECTORY, relpath)
```

Then `serve_directory` can be started against any path, to serve the content of that path on `http://localhost:8000`:

```
serve_directory('/tmp')
```

Pointing your browser to `http://localhost:8000` should list the content of the `/tmp` directory and allow you to navigate it and see content of any file.

How it works...

`ThreadingHTTPServer` joins `HTTPServer` with `ThreadingMixin`, which allows you to serve more than a single request at a time.

This is especially important when serving static websites because browsers frequently keep connections open longer than needed, and when serving a single request at a time, you might be unable to fetch your CSS or JavaScript files until the browser closes the previous connection.

For each request, the `HTTPServer` forwards it for processing to a specified handler. The `SimpleHTTPRequestHandler` is able to serve the requests, mapping them to local files on disk, but on most Python versions, it is only able to serve them from the current directory.

To be able to serve requests from any directory, we provided a custom `translate_path` method, which replaces the path resulting from the standard implementation that is relative to the `SERVED_DIRECTORY` class variable.

`serve_directory` then puts everything together and joins `HTTPServer` with the customized request handler to create a server able to handle requests for the provided path.

There's more...

A lot has changed in more recent Python versions regarding the `http.server` module. The newest version, Python 3.7, already provides the `ThreadingHTTPServer` class out of the box and it's now possible to configure a specific directory to be served by `SimpleHTTPRequestHandler`, thus removing the need to customize the `translate_path` method to serve a specific directory.

Errors in web applications

Usually, when a Python WSGI web application crashes, you get a traceback in the Terminal and an empty path in your browser.

That doesn't make it very easy to debug what's going on and unless you explicitly check your Terminal, it might be easy to miss that your page is not showing up because it actually crashed.

Luckily, the Python standard library provides some basic debugging tools for web applications that make it possible to report crashes into the browser so you can see them and fix them without having to jump away from your browser.

How to do it...

The `cgitb` module provides tools to format an exception and its traceback as HTML, so we can leverage it to implement a WSGI middleware that can wrap any web application to provide better error reporting in the browser:

```python
import cgitb
import sys

class ErrorMiddleware:
    """Wrap a WSGI application to display errors in the browser"""
    def __init__(self, app):
        self.app = app

    def __call__(self, environ, start_response):
        app_iter = None
        try:
            app_iter = self.app(environ, start_response)
            for item in app_iter:
                yield item
        except:
```

```
            try:
                start_response('500 INTERNAL SERVER ERROR', [
                    ('Content-Type', 'text/html; charset=utf-8'),
                    ('X-XSS-Protection', '0'),
                ])
            except Exception:
                # There has been output but an error occurred later on.
                # In that situation we can do nothing fancy anymore,
                # better log something into the error log and fallback.
                environ['wsgi.errors'].write(
                    'Debugging middleware caught exception in streamed '
                    'response after response headers were already sent.\n'
                )
            else:
                yield cgitb.html(sys.exc_info()).encode('utf-8')
        finally:
            if hasattr(app_iter, 'close'):
                app_iter.close()
```

`ErrorMiddleware` can be used to wrap any WSGI application, so that in case of errors, it will display the error into the web browser.

We can, for example, grab back our `WSGIApplication` from the previous recipe, add a route that will cause a crash, and serve the wrapped application to see how errors are reported into the web browser:

```
from web_06 import WSGIApplication
from wsgiref.simple_server import make_server

app = WSGIApplication()

@app.route('/crash')
def crash(req, resp):
    raise RuntimeError('This is a crash!')

app = ErrorMiddleware(app)

httpd = make_server('', 8000, app)
print("Serving on port 8000...")
httpd.serve_forever()
```

Once you point your browser to `http://localhost:8000/crash`, you should see a nicely formatted traceback of the triggered exception.

How it works...

`ErrorMiddleware` receives the original application and replaces it in the request handling.

All HTTP requests will be received by `ErrorMiddleware`, which will then proxy them to the application, returning the resulting response provided by the application.

If an exception arises while the application response was being consumed, it will stop the standard flow, and instead of consuming the response of the application any further, it will format the exception and send it back as the response to the browser.

This is done because `ErrorMiddleware.__call__` in fact calls the wrapped application and iterates over any provided result:

```
def __call__(self, environ, start_response):
    app_iter = None
    try:
        app_iter = self.app(environ, start_response)
        for item in app_iter:
            yield item
    ...
```

This approach works with both applications that return a normal response and applications that return a generator as the response.

If an error arises when calling the application or while consuming the response, the error is trapped and a new `start_response` is attempted to notify the server error to the browser:

```
except:
    try:
        start_response('500 INTERNAL SERVER ERROR', [
            ('Content-Type', 'text/html; charset=utf-8'),
            ('X-XSS-Protection', '0'),
        ])
```

If `start_response` fails, it means that the wrapped application already called `start_response` and thus it's not possible to change the response status code or headers anymore.

In this case, as we can't provide the nicely formatted response anymore, we just fall back to providing an error on the Terminal:

```
except Exception:
    # There has been output but an error occurred later on.
    # In that situation we can do nothing fancy anymore,
    # better log something into the error log and fallback.
```

```
environ['wsgi.errors'].write(
    'Debugging middleware caught exception in streamed '
    'response after response headers were already sent.\n'
)
```

If `start_response` succeeded, instead, we stop returning the content of the application response and, instead, we return the error and traceback, nicely formatted by `cgitb`:

```
else:
    yield cgitb.html(sys.exc_info()).encode('utf-8')
```

In both cases, then, if it provided a `close` method, we close the application response. This way, if it was a file or any source that needs to be closed, we avoid leaking it:

```
finally:
    if hasattr(app_iter, 'close'):
        app_iter.close()
```

There's more...

More complete solutions for error reporting in web applications in Python are available out of the standard library. If you have further needs or want to get the errors notified by email or through cloud error reporting solutions, such as Sentry, you might want to provide an error reporting WSGI library.

The `Werkzeug` debugger from Flask, the `WebError` library from the Pylons project, and the `Backlash` library from the TurboGears project are probably the most common solutions for this purpose.

You might also want to check whether your web framework provides some advanced error reporting configuration, as many of them provide it out of the box, relying on those libraries or other tools.

Handling forms and files

When submitting forms and uploading files, they are usually sent with the `multipart/form-data` encoding.

We already saw how to create data encoded in `multipart/form-data`, and submit it to an endpoint, but how can we handle incoming data in such a format?

How to do it...

The `cgi.FieldStorage` class in the standard library already provides all the machinery required to parse multipart data and send it back to you in a way that is easy to handle.

We will create a simple web application (based on `WSGIApplication`) to show how `cgi.FieldStorage` can be used to parse the uploaded file and show it back to the user:

```
import cgi

from web_06 import WSGIApplication
import base64

app = WSGIApplication()

@app.route('/')
def index(req, resp):
    return (
        b'<form action="/upload" method="post" enctype="multipart/form-
            data">'
        b'    <input type="file" name="uploadedfile"/>'
        b'    <input type="submit" value="Upload">'
        b'</form>'
    )

@app.route('/upload')
def upload(req, resp):
    form = cgi.FieldStorage(fp=req.environ['wsgi.input'],
                            environ=req.environ)
    if 'uploadedfile' not in form:
        return b'Nothing uploaded'

    uploadedfile = form['uploadedfile']
    if uploadedfile.type.startswith('image'):
        # User uploaded an image, show it
        return b'<img src="data:%b;base64,%b"/>' % (
            uploadedfile.type.encode('ascii'),
            base64.b64encode(uploadedfile.file.read())
        )
    elif uploadedfile.type.startswith('text'):
        return uploadedfile.file.read()
    else:
        return b'You uploaded %b' % uploadedfile.filename.encode('utf-8')

app.serve()
```

How it works...

The application exposes two web pages. One is on the root of the website (through the `index` function) that only shows a simple form with an upload field.

The other, the `upload` function, instead receives the uploaded file and shows it back if it's an image or a text file. In all other cases, it will just show the name of the uploaded file.

All that is required to handle the upload in multipart format is to create a `cgi.FieldStorage` out of it:

```
form = cgi.FieldStorage(fp=req.environ['wsgi.input'],
                        environ=req.environ)
```

The whole body of the POST request is always available in the `environ` request with the `wsgi.input` key.

This provides a file-like object that can be read to consume the posted data. Make sure you save aside the `FieldStorage` after it has been created if you need to use it multiple times, because once the data is consumed from `wsgi.input`, it becomes inaccessible.

`cgi.FieldStorage` provides a dictionary-like interface, so we can check whether a file was uploaded just by checking whether the `uploadedfile` entry exists:

```
if 'uploadedfile' not in form:
    return b'Nothing uploaded'
```

That's because in our form, we provided `uploadedfile` as the name of the field:

```
b'   <input type="file" name="uploadedfile"/>'
```

That specific field will be accessible with `form['uploadedfile']`.

As it's a file, it will return an object that provides the `type`, `filename`, and `file` attributes through which we can check the MIME type of uploaded file to see whether it's an image:

```
if uploadedfile.type.startswith('image'):
```

And if it's an image, we can read its content to encode it in `base64` so that it can be displayed by the `img` tag:

```
base64.b64encode(uploadedfile.file.read())
```

The `filename` attribute is instead only used if the uploaded file is of an unrecognized format, so that we can at least print back the name of the uploaded file:

```
return b'You uploaded %b' % uploadedfile.filename.encode('utf-8')
```

REST API

REST with JSON has become the de facto standard in cross-application communication technologies for web-based applications.

It's a very effective protocol, and the fact that the definition can be understood by everyone made it popular pretty quickly.

Also, a rapid REST implementation can be rolled out pretty quickly compared to other more complex communication protocols.

As the Python standard library provides the foundations we needed to build WSGI-based applications, it's not hard to extend our existing recipe to support REST-based dispatch of requests.

How to do it...

We are going to use `WSGIApplication` from our previous recipe, but instead of registering a function for a root, we are going to register a particular class able to dispatch based on the request method.

1. All the REST classes we want to implement must inherit from a single `RestController` implementation:

```
class RestController:
    def __call__(self, req, resp):
        method = req.environ['REQUEST_METHOD']
        action = getattr(self, method, self._not_found)
        return action(req, resp)

    def _not_found(self, environ, resp):
        resp.status = '404 Not Found'
        return b'{}'  # Provide an empty JSON document
```

2. Then we can subclass `RestController` to implement all the specific GET, POST, DELETE, and PUT methods and register the resources on a specific route:

```python
import json
from web_06 import WSGIApplication

app = WSGIApplication()

@app.route('/resources/?(?P<id>\\w*)')
class ResourcesRestController(RestController):
    RESOURCES = {}

    def GET(self, req, resp):
        resource_id = req.urlargs['id']
        if not resource_id:
            # Whole catalog requested
            return json.dumps(self.RESOURCES).encode('utf-8')

        if resource_id not in self.RESOURCES:
            return self._not_found(req, resp)

        return
json.dumps(self.RESOURCES[resource_id]).encode('utf-8')

    def POST(self, req, resp):
        content_length = int(req.environ['CONTENT_LENGTH'])
        data =
req.environ['wsgi.input'].read(content_length).decode('utf-8')

        resource = json.loads(data)
        resource['id'] = str(len(self.RESOURCES)+1)
        self.RESOURCES[resource['id']] = resource
        return json.dumps(resource).encode('utf-8')

    def DELETE(self, req, resp):
        resource_id = req.urlargs['id']
        if not resource_id:
            return self._not_found(req, resp)
        self.RESOURCES.pop(resource_id, None)

        req.status = '204 No Content'
        return b''
```

This already provides basic functionalities that allow us to add, remove and list resources from an in-memory catalog.

3. To test this, we can start a server in a background thread and use the
`http_request` function from our previous recipe:

```
import threading
threading.Thread(target=app.serve, daemon=True).start()

from web_03 import http_request
```

4. We can then create a new resource:

```
>>> _, resp = http_request('http://localhost:8000/resources',
method='POST',
                                    data=json.dumps({'name': 'Mario',
                                                      'surname':
'Mario'}).encode('utf-8'))
>>> print('NEW RESOURCE: ', resp)
NEW RESOURCE:  b'{"surname": "Mario", "id": "1", "name": "Mario"}'
```

5. Here we list them all:

```
>>> _, resp = http_request('http://localhost:8000/resources')
>>> print('ALL RESOURCES: ', resp)
ALL RESOURCES:  b'{"1": {"surname": "Mario", "id": "1", "name":
"Mario"}}'
```

6. Add a second one:

```
>>> http_request('http://localhost:8000/resources', method='POST',
                 data=json.dumps({'name': 'Luigi',
                                    'surname':
'Mario'}).encode('utf-8'))
```

7. Next, we see that now both resources are listed:

```
>>> _, resp = http_request('http://localhost:8000/resources')
>>> print('ALL RESOURCES: ', resp)
ALL RESOURCES:  b'{"1": {"surname": "Mario", "id": "1", "name":
"Mario"},
                  "2": {"surname": "Mario", "id": "2", "name":
"Luigi"}}'
```

8. Then we can ask for a specific resource out of the catalog:

```
>>> _, resp = http_request('http://localhost:8000/resources/1')
>>> print('RESOURCES #1: ', resp)
RESOURCES #1:  b'{"surname": "Mario", "id": "1", "name": "Mario"}'
```

9. We can also delete a specific resource:

```
>>> http_request('http://localhost:8000/resources/2',
method='DELETE')
```

10. Then see that it was actually deleted:

```
>>> _, resp = http_request('http://localhost:8000/resources')
>>> print('ALL RESOURCES', resp)
ALL RESOURCES b'{"1": {"surname": "Mario", "id": "1", "name":
"Mario"}}'
```

This should allow us to provide a REST interface for most simple cases relying on what is already available in the Python standard library itself.

How it works...

Most of the magic is done by RestController.__call__:

```
class RestController:
    def __call__(self, req, resp):
        method = req.environ['REQUEST_METHOD']
        action = getattr(self, method, self._not_found)
        return action(req, resp)
```

Whenever a subclass of RestController is called, it will look at the HTTP request method and look for an instance method named like the HTTP method.

If there is one, the method is called and the response provided by the method itself returned. If there is none, then self._not_found is called, which will just respond a 404 error.

This relies on the WSGIApplication.__call__ support for classes instead of functions.

When WSGIApplication.__call__ finds an object associated to a route through app.route that is a class, it will always create an instance of it, and then it will call the instance:

```
if inspect.isclass(routed_action):
    routed_action = routed_action()
body = routed_action(request, resp)
```

If `routed_action` is a `RestController` subclass, what will happen is that `routed_action = routed_action()` will replace the class with an instance of it, and then `routed_action(request, resp)` will call the `RestController.__call__` method to actually serve the request.

The `RestController.__call__` method can then forward the request to the right instance method based on the HTTP method.

Note that as REST resources are identified by providing the resource identifier in the URL, the route assigned to `RestController` must have an `id` argument and an optional `/`:

```
@app.route('/resources/?(?P<id>\\w*)')
```

Otherwise you won't be able to distinguish between a request for the whole GET resources catalog, `/resources`, and a request for a specific GET resource, `/resources/3`.

The lack of an `id` argument is exactly the way our GET method decided when to return the content for the whole catalog or not:

```python
def GET(self, req, resp):
    resource_id = req.urlargs['id']
    if not resource_id:
        # Whole catalog requested
        return json.dumps(self.RESOURCES).encode('utf-8')
```

For methods that receive the data in the request body, such as POST, PUT, and PATCH, you will have to read the request body from `req.environ['wsgi.input']`.

In this case, it's important to provide exactly how many bytes to read, as the connection might never be closed, and the read might otherwise block forever.

The `Content-Length` header can be used to know the length of the input:

```python
def POST(self, req, resp):
    content_length = int(req.environ['CONTENT_LENGTH'])
    data = req.environ['wsgi.input'].read(content_length).decode('utf-8')
```

Handling cookies

Cookies are frequently used in web applications to store data in browsers. The most frequent use case is user identification.

We are going to implement a very simple and insecure identification system based on cookies to show how to use them.

How to do it...

The `http.cookies.SimpleCookie` class provides all the facilities required to parse and generate cookies.

1. We can rely on it to create a web application endpoint that will set a cookie:

```
from web_06 import WSGIApplication

app = WSGIApplication()

import time
from http.cookies import SimpleCookie

@app.route('/identity')
def identity(req, resp):
    identity = int(time.time())

    cookie = SimpleCookie()
    cookie['identity'] = 'USER: {}'.format(identity)

    for set_cookie in cookie.values():
        resp.headers.add_header('Set-Cookie',
set_cookie.OutputString())
    return b'Go back to <a href="/">index</a> to check your
identity'
```

2. We can use it to create one that will parse the cookie and tell us who the current user is:

```
@app.route('/')
def index(req, resp):
    if 'HTTP_COOKIE' in req.environ:
        cookies = SimpleCookie(req.environ['HTTP_COOKIE'])
        if 'identity' in cookies:
            return b'Welcome back, %b' %
cookies['identity'].value.encode('utf-8')
    return b'Visit <a href="/identity">/identity</a> to get an
identity'
```

3. Once you start the application you can point your browser to `http://localhost:8000` and you should see the web application complaining that you are lacking an identity:

```
app.serve()
```

Once you click on the suggested link, you should get one and, going back to the index page, it should recognize you through the cookie.

How it works...

The `SimpleCookie` class represents a cookie, as a set of one or more values.

Each value can be set into the cookie as if it was a dictionary:

```
cookie = SimpleCookie()
cookie['identity'] = 'USER: {}'.format(identity)
```

If the cookie `morsel` has to accept more options, those can be set with dictionary syntax too:

```
cookie['identity']['Path'] = '/'
```

Each cookie can contain multiple values and each one of them should be set with a `Set-Cookie` HTTP header.

Iterating over the cookie will retrieve all the key/value pairs that constitute the cookie, and then calling `OutputString()` on them will return the cookie value encoded as expected by the `Set-Cookie` header, with all the additional attributes:

```
for set_cookie in cookie.values():
    resp.headers.add_header('Set-Cookie', set_cookie.OutputString())
```

Practically, once the cookie is set, calling `OutputString()` will send you back the string you need to send to the browser:

```
>>> cookie = SimpleCookie()
>>> cookie['somevalue'] = 42
>>> cookie['somevalue']['Path'] = '/'
>>> cookie['somevalue'].OutputString()
'somevalue=42; Path=/'
```

Reading back a cookie is as simple as building it from the `environ['HTTP_COOKIE']` value if it's available:

```
cookies = SimpleCookie(req.environ['HTTP_COOKIE'])
```

Once the cookie has parsed, the values stored within it can be accessed with dictionary syntax:

```
cookies['identity']
```

There's more...

When working with cookies, one particular condition you should pay attention to is their life cycle.

Cookies can have an `Expires` attribute, which will state on which date they should die (the browser will discard them), and actually, that's the way you delete a cookie. Setting a cookie again with an `Expires` date in the past will delete it.

But cookies can also have a `Max-Age` attribute, which states how long they should stick around or can be created as session cookies that will disappear when the browser window is closed.

So, if you face problems with your cookies randomly disappearing or not being loaded back correctly, always check those properties as the cookie might just have been deleted by the browser.

12
Multimedia

In this chapter, we will cover following recipes:

- Determining the type of a file—how to guess the type of a file
- Detecting an image type—inspecting an image to understand what type of image it is
- Detecting an image size—inspecting an image to retrieve its size
- Playing audio/video/images—playing audio, video, or showing images on desktop systems

Introduction

Multimedia applications, such as videos, sounds, and games usually need to rely on very specific libraries to manage the formats used to store the data and the hardware needed to play their content.

Due to the variety of formats for data storage, the continuous improvements in the field of video and audio storage that lead to new formats, and the heavy integration with native operating system functions and specific hardware programming languages, multimedia-related features are rarely integrated in the standard library.

Having to maintain support for all the image formats that exist, when a new one is created every few months, requires a full-time effort that a dedicated library can tackle far better than the team maintaining the programming language itself.

For this reason, Python has relatively few multimedia-related functions, but some core ones are available and they can be very helpful in applications where multimedia is not the main focus, but maybe they need to handle multimedia files to properly work; for example, a web application that might need to check that the user-uploaded file is in a valid format supported by browsers.

Determining the type of a file

When we receive a file from our users, it's frequently necessary to detect its type. Doing so through the filename without the need to actually read the data can be achieved through the `mimetypes` module.

How to do it...

For this recipe, the following steps are to be performed:

1. While the `mimetypes` module is not bullet proof, as it relies on the name of the file to detect the expected type, it's frequently enough to handle most common cases.

2. Users will usually assign proper names to their files for their own benefit (especially Windows users, where the extension is vital for the proper working of the file), guessing the type with `mimetypes.guess_type` is often enough:

```python
import mimetypes

def guess_file_type(filename):
    if not getattr(guess_file_type, 'initialised', False):
        mimetypes.init()
        guess_file_type.initialised = True
    file_type, encoding = mimetypes.guess_type(filename)
    return file_type
```

3. We can call `guess_file_type` against any file to get back its type:

```python
>>> print(guess_file_type('~/Pictures/5565_1680x1050.jpg'))
'image/jpeg'
>>> print(guess_file_type('~/Pictures/5565_1680x1050.jpeg'))
'image/jpeg'
>>> print(guess_file_type('~/Pictures/avatar.png'))
'image/png'
```

4. If the type it's unknown, `None` will be returned:

```
>>> print(guess_file_type('/tmp/unable_to_guess.blob'))
None
```

5. Also, note that the file itself doesn't have to really exist. All you care about is it's filename:

```
>>> print(guess_file_type('/this/does/not/exists.txt'))
'text/plain'
```

How it works...

The `mimetypes` module keeps a list of MIME types associated to each file extension.

When a filename is provided, only the extension is analyzed.

If the extension is in a list of known MIME types, the associated type is returned. Otherwise `None` is returned.

Calling `mimetypes.init()` also loads any MIME type registered in your system configuration, usually from `/etc/mime.types` on Linux systems and from the registry on Windows systems.

This allows us to cover far more extensions that might not be known by Python itself and to also easily support custom extensions if your system is configured to support them.

Detecting image types

When you know you are working with image files, it's frequently necessary to verify their type to ensure they are in a format your software is able to handle.

One possible use case is to ensure they are images in a format that a browser might be able to show back when they are uploaded to a website.

The type of a multimedia file can usually be detected by inspecting the file header, the initial part of a file that stores details about the content of the file.

The header usually contains details about the kind of file, the size of the contained image, the number of bits per color, and so on. All these details are required to reproduce the content stored within the file itself.

By inspecting the header, it's possible to confirm the format of the stored data. This requires supporting the specific header format and the Python standard library has support for most common image formats.

How to do it...

The `imghdr` module can help us understand what kind of image file we are facing:

```
import imghdr


def detect_image_format(filename):
    return imghdr.what(filename)
```

This allows us to detect the format of any image on disk or of a stream of bytes provided:

```
>>> print(detect_image_format('~/Pictures/avatar.jpg'))
'jpeg'
>>> with open('~/Pictures/avatar.png', 'rb') as f:
...        print(detect_image_format(f))
'png'
```

How it works...

When the provided filename is a string containing the path of a file, `imghdr.what` is called directly on it.

This just returns the type of the file or `None` if it's not supported.

If, instead, a file-like object is provided (a file itself or a `io.BytesIO`, for example) then it will peak the first 32 bytes of it and detect the header based on those.

Given that most image types have a header with a size in the order of little more than 10 bytes, reading 32 bytes ensures that we should have more than enough to detect any image.

After reading the bytes, it will go back to the beginning of the file, so that any subsequent call is still able to read the file (otherwise, the first 32 bytes would be consumed and lost forever).

There's more...

The Python standard library also provides a sndhdr module that behaves much like imghdr for audio files.

The formats recognized by sndhdr are usually very basic formats and thus it's usually mostly helpful when wave or aiff files are involved.

Detecting image sizes

If we know what kind of image we are facing, detecting the resolution is usually a matter of reading it from the image header.

For most image types, this is relatively simple, and as we can use imghdr to guess the right image type, we can then read the right part of the header, according to the detected type, to extract the size portion.

How to do it...

Once imghdr detects the image type, we can read the content of the header with the struct module:

```python
import imghdr
import struct
import os
from pathlib import Path


class ImageReader:
    @classmethod
    def get_size(cls, f):
        requires_close = False
        if isinstance(f, (str, getattr(os, 'PathLike', str))):
            f = open(f, 'rb')
            requires_close = True
        elif isinstance(f, Path):
            f = f.expanduser().open('rb')
            requires_close = True

        try:
            image_type = imghdr.what(f)
            if image_type not in ('jpeg', 'png', 'gif'):
```

```
                    raise ValueError('Unsupported image format')

            f.seek(0)
            size_reader = getattr(cls, '_size_{}'.format(image_type))
            return size_reader(f)
        finally:
            if requires_close: f.close()

    @classmethod
    def _size_gif(cls, f):
        f.read(6)  # Skip the Magick Numbers
        w, h = struct.unpack('<HH', f.read(4))
        return w, h

    @classmethod
    def _size_png(cls, f):
        f.read(8)  # Skip Magic Number
        clen, ctype = struct.unpack('>I4s', f.read(8))
        if ctype != b'IHDR':
            raise ValueError('Unsupported PNG format')
        w, h = struct.unpack('>II', f.read(8))
        return w, h

    @classmethod
    def _size_jpeg(cls, f):
        start_of_image = f.read(2)
        if start_of_image != b'\xff\xd8':
            raise ValueError('Unsupported JPEG format')
        while True:
            marker, segment_size = struct.unpack('>2sH', f.read(4))
            if marker[0] != 0xff:
                raise ValueError('Unsupported JPEG format')
            data = f.read(segment_size - 2)
            if not 0xc0 <= marker[1] <= 0xcf:
                continue
            _, h, w = struct.unpack('>cHH', data[:5])
            break
        return w, h
```

Then we can use the `ImageReader.get_size` class method to detect the size of any supported image:

```
>>> print(ImageReader.get_size('~/Pictures/avatar.png'))
(300, 300)
>>> print(ImageReader.get_size('~/Pictures/avatar.jpg'))
(300, 300)
```

How it works...

There are four core parts of the `ImageReader` class that work together to provide support for reading image sizes.

The first, the `ImageReader.get_size` method itself, is in charge of opening the image file and detecting the image type.

The first part is all related to opening the file in case it's provided as a path in a string, as a `Path` object, or if it's already a file object:

```
requires_close = False
if isinstance(f, (str, getattr(os, 'PathLike', str))):
    f = open(f, 'rb')
    requires_close = True
elif isinstance(f, Path):
    f = f.expanduser().open('rb')
    requires_close = True
```

If it's a string or a pathlike object (`os.PathLike` is only supported on Python 3.6+), the file is opened and the `requires_close` variable is set to `True`, so that once we are finished, we will close the file.

If it's a `Path` object and we are on a Python version that doesn't support `os.PathLike`, then the file is opened through the path itself.

If, instead, the provided object was already an open file, we do nothing and `requires_close` remains `False`, so that we don't close the provided file.

Once the file is opened, it gets passed to `imghdr.what` to guess the file type, and if it's not one of the supported types, it gets rejected:

```
image_type = imghdr.what(f)
if image_type not in ('jpeg', 'png', 'gif'):
    raise ValueError('Unsupported image format')
```

Finally, we head back to the beginning of the file, so we can read the header and we call the relevant `cls._size_png`, `cls._size_jpeg` or `cls._size_gif` method:

```
f.seek(0)
size_reader = getattr(cls, '_size_{}'.format(image_type))
return size_reader(f)
```

Each method is specialized in understanding the size of a specific file format, from the easiest one (GIF) to the most complex one (JPEG).

For the GIF itself, all we have to do is skip the magic number (which only `imghdr.what` cared about; we already know it's a GIF) and read the subsequent four bytes as unsigned shorts (16 bits number) in a little-endian byte ordering:

```
@classmethod
def _size_gif(cls, f):
    f.read(6)  # Skip the Magick Numbers
    w, h = struct.unpack('<HH', f.read(4))
    return w, h
```

`png` is nearly as complex. We skip the magic number and read the subsequent bytes as an `unsigned int` (32 bits number) in a big-endian order, followed by a four-bytes string:

```
@classmethod
def _size_png(cls, f):
    f.read(8)  # Skip Magic Number
    clen, ctype = struct.unpack('>I4s', f.read(8))
```

That gives us back the size of the image header followed by the image section name, which must be `IHDR`, to confirm we are reading an image header:

```
if ctype != b'IHDR':
    raise ValueError('Unsupported PNG format')
```

Once we know we are within the image header, we can just read the first two `unsigned int` numbers (still in big-endian) to extract the width and height of the image:

```
w, h = struct.unpack('>II', f.read(8))
return w, h
```

The last method is the most complex one, as JPEG has a far more complex structure than GIF or PNG. The JPEG header is composed of multiple sections. Each section is identified by `0xff` followed by an identifier of the section and by the section length.

At the beginning, we just read the first two bytes and confirm that we face the **start of image (SOI)** section:

```
@classmethod
def _size_jpeg(cls, f):
    start_of_image = f.read(2)
    if start_of_image != b'\xff\xd8':
        raise ValueError('Unsupported JPEG format')
```

Then we look for a section that declares the JPEG as a baseline DCT, progressive DCT, or lossless frame.

That is done by reading the first two bytes of each section and its size:

```
while True:
    marker, segment_size = struct.unpack('>2sH', f.read(4))
```

As we know that each section starts with `0xff`, if we face a section that starts with a different byte, it means that the image is invalid:

```
if marker[0] != 0xff:
    raise ValueError('Unsupported JPEG format')
```

If the section is valid, we can read its content. We know the size because it was specified as a two bytes unsigned short in a big-endian notation right after the two bytes marker:

```
data = f.read(segment_size - 2)
```

Now, before being able to read the width and height from the data we just read, we need to check that the section that we are looking at is actually a start of frame one, for baseline, progressive, or lossless. This means it must be one of the sections from `0xc0` to `0xcf`.

Otherwise, we just skip this section and move to the next one:

```
if not 0xc0 <= marker[1] <= 0xcf:
    continue
```

Once we find one of the valid sections (depending on the kind of encoding the image has), we can read the size by looking at the first five bytes.

The first byte is the sample precision. We really don't care about it so we can ignore it. Then the remaining four bytes are the height and the width of the image as two unsigned shorts in a big-endian notation:

```
_, h, w = struct.unpack('>cHH', data[:5])
```

Playing audio/video/images

The Python standard library provides no utilities to open images, and has limited support for playing audio files.

While it's possible to somehow play audio files in some formats by combining the `wave` and `ossaudiodev` or `winsound` modules, the OSS audio system has long been deprecated on Linux systems and neither of those is available on Mac systems.

For images, it would be possible to show an image using the `tkinter` module, but we would be constrained to very simple image formats as decoding the images would be on our own.

But there is one little trick we can use to actually display most image files and play most audio files.

On most systems, trying to open a file with the default web browser will by the way play the file, and we can rely on this trick and the `webbrowser` module to play most file types through Python.

How to do it...

The steps for this recipe are as follows:

1. Given a path that points to a supported file, we can build a `file://` url out of it and then use the `webbrowser` module to open it:

```
import pathlib
import webbrowser

def playfile(fpath):
    fpath = pathlib.Path(fpath).expanduser().resolve()
    webbrowser.open('file://{}'.format(fpath))
```

2. Opening an image should display it:

```
>>> playfile('~/Pictures/avatar.jpg')
```

3. Also, opening an audio file should play it:

```
>>> playfile('~/Music/FLY_ME_TO_THE_MOON.mp3')
```

So, we can use this method on most systems to show the content of a file to the user.

How it works...

The `webbrowser.open` function does actually start the browser on Linux systems, but on macOS and Windows systems it does a fairly different job.

On Windows and macOS systems, it will ask the system to open the specified path with the most suitable application.

If the path is an HTTP URL, the most suitable application is, of course, `webbrowser`, but if the path is a local `file://` URL, the system will look for a software able to handle that file type and will open the file with that software.

That is achieved by using an `os.startfile` on Windows systems and by running a small Apple script snippet through the `osascript` command on a macOS.

This allows us to open image and audio files, and as most image and audio file formats are also supported by browsers, it will also work on Linux systems.

13
Graphical User Interfaces

In this chapter, we will cover the following recipes:

- Alerts—showing alert dialogs on graphical systems
- Dialog boxes—how to ask simple questions with a dialog box
- ProgressBar dialog—how to provide a graphical progress dialog
- Lists—how to implement a scrollable list of elements to pick from
- Menus—how to create menus in a GUI application to allow multiple actions

Introduction

Python comes with a feature that is rarely shipped with a programming language: a built-in **graphical user interface (GUI)** library.

Python ships with a working version of the `Tk` widgets toolkit, which can be controlled through the `tkinter` module provided by the standard library.

The `Tk` toolkit actually is used through a simple language called `Tcl`. All `Tk` widgets can be controlled through the `Tcl` commands.

Most of these commands are very simple, and take the following form:

```
classname widgetid options
```

For example, something such as the following would lead to a button (identified as `mybutton`) with a red "`click here`" text:

```
button .mybutton -fg red  -text "click here"
```

As those commands are usually relatively simple, Python ships with a built-in `Tcl` interpreter and uses it to drive the `Tk` widgets.

Nowadays, nearly everyone, even the more hardcore computer users, are used to relying on GUIs for many of their tasks, especially for simple applications that require basic interactions, such as picking a choice, confirming an entry, or showing some progress. The usage of a GUI can therefore be pretty convenient.

With graphical applications, the user frequently has no need to go through the help page of the application, read the documentation, and get through the options provided by the application to learn their specific syntax. GUIs have been providing a consistent interaction language for decades and are a good way to keep the entry barrier to your software low, if used properly.

As Python ships with what you need to create powerful console applications and also good GUIs, the next time you need to create a new tool it might be a good idea to stop thinking for a moment about what your users will find more convenient and head to `tkinter` if your choice is for a graphical application.

While `tkinter` can be limited compared to powerful toolkits, such as Qt or GTK, it surely is a fully platform-independent solution that is good enough for most applications.

Alerts

The most simple type of GUI is the alert. Just print something to inform the user of a result or event in a graphical box:

How to do it...

Alerts in `tkinter` are managed by the `messagebox` object and we can create one simply by asking `messagebox` to show one for us:

```
from tkinter import messagebox


def alert(title, message, kind='info', hidemain=True):
    if kind not in ('error', 'warning', 'info'):
        raise ValueError('Unsupported alert kind.')

    show_method = getattr(messagebox, 'show{}'.format(kind))
    show_method(title, message)
```

Once we have our `alert` helper in place, we can initialize a `Tk` interpreter and show as many alerts as we want:

```
from tkinter import Tk

Tk().withdraw()
alert('Hello', 'Hello World')
alert('Hello Again', 'Hello World 2', kind='warning')
```

If everything worked as expected, we should see a pop-up dialog and, once dismissed, a new one should come up with `Hello Again`.

How it works...

The `alert` function itself is just a thin wrapper over what `tkinter.messagebox` provides.

There are three types of message boxes we can show: `error`, `warning`, and `info`. If an unsupported kind of dialog box is requested, we just reject it:

```
if kind not in ('error', 'warning', 'info'):
    raise ValueError('Unsupported alert kind.')
```

Each kind of dialog box is shown by relying on a different method of the `messagebox`. The information boxes are shown using `messagebox.showinfo`, while errors are shown using `messagebox.showerror`, and so on.

So, we grab the relevant method of `messagebox`:

```
show_method = getattr(messagebox, 'show{}'.format(kind))
```

Then, we call it to display our box:

```
show_method(title, message)
```

The `alert` function is very simple, but there is one more thing that we need to keep in mind.

The `tkinter` library works by interacting with `Tk` through its own interpreter and environment, and this has to be created and started.

If we don't start one ourselves, `tkinter` will start one for us as soon as it needs to send some commands. But, this leads to an empty main window always being created.

So, if you use `alert` as it is, you will get your alert, but you will also get empty windows in the corner of your screen.

To avoid this, we need to initialize the `Tk` environment ourselves and disable the main window, as we don't have any use for it:

```
from tkinter import Tk
Tk().withdraw()
```

Then we can show as many alerts as we want, without the risk of leaking empty unwanted windows around the screen.

Dialog boxes

Dialog boxes are the most simple and common interaction a user interface can provide. Asking for one simple input, such as a number, text, or yes/no, handles many needs of interaction with a user in simple applications.

`tkinter` comes with dialogs for most cases, but it might be hard to spot them all if you don't already know the library. As a pointer, all dialog boxes provided by `tkinter` share a very similar signature, so it's easy to make a `dialog` function that allows us to show them all:

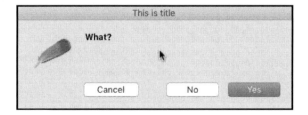

The dialog box will look as shown:

The window to open a file appears as shown in the following screenshot:

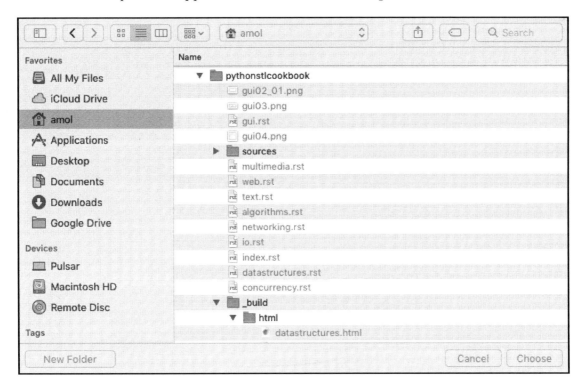

How to do it...

We can create a `dialog` function to hide the minor differences between dialog types and call the appropriate dialog depending on the kind of request:

```
from tkinter import messagebox
from tkinter import simpledialog
from tkinter import filedialog

def dialog(ask, title, message=None, **kwargs):
    for widget in (messagebox, simpledialog, filedialog):
        show = getattr(widget, 'ask{}'.format(ask), None)
        if show:
            break
    else:
        raise ValueError('Unsupported type of dialog: {}'.format(ask))

    options = dict(kwargs, title=title)
    for arg, replacement in dialog._argsmap.get(widget, {}).items():
        options[replacement] = locals()[arg]
    return show(**options)
dialog._argsmap = {
    messagebox: {'message': 'message'},
    simpledialog: {'message': 'prompt'}
}
```

We can then test our `dialog` method to show all the possible dialog types, and show back the user choice:

```
>>> from tkinter import Tk

>>> Tk().withdraw()
>>> for ask in ('okcancel', 'retrycancel', 'yesno', 'yesnocancel',
...             'string', 'integer', 'float', 'directory', 'openfilename'):
...     choice = dialog(ask, 'This is title', 'What?')
...     print('{}: {}'.format(ask, choice))
okcancel: True
retrycancel: False
yesno: True
yesnocancel: None
string: Hello World
integer: 5
float: 1.3
directory: /Users/amol/Documents
openfilename: /Users/amol/Documents/FileZilla_3.27.1_macosx-x86.app.tar.bz2
```

How it works...

The kinds of dialog provided by `tkinter` are divided between the `messagebox`, `simpledialog`, and `filedialog` modules (you might consider `colorchooser` too, but it's rarely needed).

So, depending on the kind of dialog that the user wants, we need to pick the right module and call the function required to show it:

```
from tkinter import messagebox
from tkinter import simpledialog
from tkinter import filedialog

def dialog(ask, title, message=None, **kwargs):
    for widget in (messagebox, simpledialog, filedialog):
        show = getattr(widget, 'ask{}'.format(ask), None)
        if show:
            break
    else:
        raise ValueError('Unsupported type of dialog: {}'.format(ask))
```

If none of the modules expose a function to show the requested kind of dialog (all the functions are named `ask*`), the loop will finish without ever breaking and thus will enter the `else` clause, raising an exception to notify the caller that the requested type is unavailable.

If the loop instead exited with `break`, the `widget` variable will point to the module that is able to show the requested dialog and the `show` variable will lead to the function actually being able to show it.

Once we have the right function in place, we need to account for the minor differences between the various dialog functions.

The major one is related to `messagebox` dialogs that have a `message` argument, while the `simpledialog` dialog has a prompt argument to show the message for the user. The `filedialog` doesn't require any message at all.

This is done by creating a basic dictionary of options with the custom-provided options and the `title` option, as it is always available in all kinds of dialog:

```
options = dict(kwargs, title=title)
```

Then the `message` option is replaced with the right name (or skipped) by looking up in the `dialog._argsmap` dictionary the mapping from the name of the `dialog` argument to the expected one.

For example, in the case of `simpledialog`, the `{'message': 'prompt'}` mapping is used. The `message` variable is looked up in function local variables (`locals()[arg]`) and it's then assigned to the options dictionary with the `prompt` name as specified by `replacement`. Then, the function assigned to `show` is finally called to display the dialog:

```
for arg, replacement in dialog._argsmap.get(widget, {}).items():
    options[replacement] = locals()[arg]
return show(**options)

dialog._argsmap = {
    messagebox: {'message': 'message'},
    simpledialog: {'message': 'prompt'}
}
```

ProgressBar dialog

When doing a long-running operation, the most frequent way to inform a user of progress is through a progress bar.

While running an operation in a thread, we can update a progress bar to show that the operation is moving forward and give the user a hint about the time it might take to complete the work:

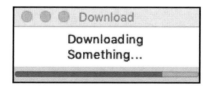

How to do it...

The `simpledialog.SimpleDialog` widget is used to create simple dialogs with some text and buttons. We are going to leverage it to display a progress bar instead of the buttons:

```
import tkinter
from tkinter import simpledialog
from tkinter import ttk
```

```
from queue import Queue

class ProgressDialog(simpledialog.SimpleDialog):
    def __init__(self, master, text='', title=None, class_=None):
        super().__init__(master=master, text=text, title=title,
                         class_=class_)
        self.default = None
        self.cancel = None

        self._bar = ttk.Progressbar(self.root, orient="horizontal",
                                    length=200, mode="determinate")
        self._bar.pack(expand=True, fill=tkinter.X, side=tkinter.BOTTOM)
        self.root.attributes("-topmost", True)

        self._queue = Queue()
        self.root.after(200, self._update)

    def set_progress(self, value):
        self._queue.put(value)

    def _update(self):
        while self._queue.qsize():
            try:
                self._bar['value'] = self._queue.get(0)
            except Queue.Empty:
                pass
        self.root.after(200, self._update)
```

Then `ProgressDialog` can be created and we can use a background thread to let the operation progress (like a download), and then update the progress bar whenever our operation moves forward:

```
if __name__ == '__main__':
    root = tkinter.Tk()
    root.withdraw()

    # Prepare the progress dialog
    p = ProgressDialog(master=root, text='Downloading Something...',
                       title='Download')

    # Simulate a download running for 5 seconds in background
    import threading
    def _do_progress():
        import time
        for i in range(1, 11):
            time.sleep(0.5)
            p.set_progress(i*10)
        p.done(0)
```

```
t = threading.Thread(target=_do_progress)
t.start()

# Display the dialog and wait for the download to finish.
p.go()
print('Download Completed!')
```

How it works...

Our dialog itself is mostly based on the `simpledialog.SimpleDialog` widget. We create it and then set `self.default = None` to prevent the user from being able to close the dialog by pressing the <Return> key, and we also set `self.default = None` to prevent the user from closing the dialog by pressing the button on the window. We want the dialog to stay open until it has been completed:

```
class ProgressDialog(simpledialog.SimpleDialog):
    def __init__(self, master, text='', title=None, class_=None):
        super().__init__(master=master, text=text, title=title,
class_=class_)
        self.default = None
        self.cancel = None
```

Then we actually need the progress bar itself, which will be shown below the text message, and we also move the dialog in front, because we want the user to be aware that something is happening:

```
self._bar = ttk.Progressbar(self.root, orient="horizontal",
                            length=200, mode="determinate")
self._bar.pack(expand=True, fill=tkinter.X, side=tkinter.BOTTOM)
self.root.attributes("-topmost", True)
```

In the last part, we need to schedule `self._update`, which will continue to loop until the dialog quits updating the progress bar if there is a new progress value available. The progress value can be provided through `self._queue`, where we will insert new progress values whenever they are provided through the `set_progress` method:

```
self._queue = Queue()
self.root.after(200, self._update)
```

We need to go through `Queue` because the dialog with the progress bar update would block the whole program.

While the `Tkinter mainloop` function is running (which is called by `simpledialog.SimpleDialog.go()`), nothing else can move forward.

So the UI and the download must proceed in two different threads, and as we can't update the UI from a different thread, we must send the progress values from the thread that produces them to the UI thread that will consume them to update the progress bar.

The thread performing the operation and producing the progress updates can then send those progress updates to the UI thread through the `set_progress` method:

```
def set_progress(self, value):
    self._queue.put(value)
```

On the other side, the UI thread will be calling the `self._update` method continuously (every 200 ms), to check if there is an update request in `self._queue`, and then applying it:

```
def _update(self):
    while self._queue.qsize():
        try:
            self._bar['value'] = self._queue.get(0)
        except Queue.Empty:
            pass
    self.root.after(200, self._update)
```

At the end of the update, the method will reschedule itself:

```
self.root.after(200, self._update)
```

This way, we will go on forever checking if there is an update for the progress bar every 200 ms until `self.root mainloop` is quit.

To use `ProgressDialog`, we simulated a download taking 5 seconds. This was done by creating the dialog itself:

```
if __name__ == '__main__':
    root = tkinter.Tk()
    root.withdraw()

    # Prepare the progress dialog
    p = ProgressDialog(master=root, text='Downloading Something...',
                       title='Download')
```

And then we started a background thread that goes on for 5 seconds, updating the progress every half a second:

```
# Simulate a download running for 5 seconds in background
import threading

def _do_progress():
    import time
```

```
        for i in range(1, 11):
            time.sleep(0.5)
            p.set_progress(i*10)
        p.done(0)

    t = threading.Thread(target=_do_progress)
    t.start()
```

The update happens because the thread calls p.set_progress, which will set a new progress value in the queue, signaling to the UI thread that there is a new progress value to set.

Once the download is completed, the progress dialog will be exited through p.done(0).

Once we have our download thread in place, we can actually display the progress dialog and wait for it to quit:

```
# Display the dialog and wait for the download to finish.
p.go()
print('Download Completed!')
```

Lists

When more than two choices are available to the user, the best way to list them is through lists. The tkinter module provides a ListBox, which allows us to show a set of entries in a scrollable widget for the user to pick from.

We can use this to implement a dialog where the user can pick one of many options and grab the chosen one:

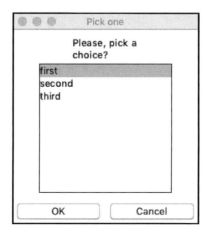

How to do it...

The `simpledialog.Dialog` class can be used to implement simple OK/cancel dialogs, and allows us to provide any body of the dialog with custom content.

We can use it to add a message and a list to a dialog and let the user make a selection:

```python
import tkinter
from tkinter import simpledialog


class ChoiceDialog(simpledialog.Dialog):
    def __init__(self, parent, title, text, items):
        self.selection = None
        self._items = items
        self._text = text
        super().__init__(parent, title=title)

    def body(self, parent):
        self._message = tkinter.Message(parent, text=self._text,
aspect=400)
        self._message.pack(expand=1, fill=tkinter.BOTH)
        self._list = tkinter.Listbox(parent)
        self._list.pack(expand=1, fill=tkinter.BOTH, side=tkinter.TOP)
        for item in self._items:
            self._list.insert(tkinter.END, item)
        return self._list

    def validate(self):
        if not self._list.curselection():
            return 0
        return 1

    def apply(self):
        self.selection = self._items[self._list.curselection()[0]]
```

Once we have `ChoiceDialog`, we can display it with a list of items and have the user pick one or cancel the dialog:

```python
if __name__ == '__main__':
    tk = tkinter.Tk()
    tk.withdraw()

    dialog = ChoiceDialog(tk, 'Pick one',
                          text='Please, pick a choice?',
                          items=['first', 'second', 'third'])
    print('Selected "{}"'.format(dialog.selection))
```

The `ChoiceDialog.selection` attribute will always contain the selected item, or `None` if the dialog was canceled.

How it works...

`simpledialog.Dialog` creates a dialog with `Ok` and `Cancel` buttons by default and only provides a title.

In our case, apart from creating the dialog itself, we also want to keep the message of the dialog and the items available for selection, so that we can show them to the user. Also, by default, we want to set that no item was selected yet. Finally, we can call `simpledialog.Dialog.__init__`, as once it's called, the main thread will block and we can't do anything else until the dialog is dismissed:

```
import tkinter
from tkinter import simpledialog

class ChoiceDialog(simpledialog.Dialog):
    def __init__(self, parent, title, text, items):
        self.selection = None
        self._items = items
        self._text = text
        super().__init__(parent, title=title)
```

We can add any additional content by overriding the `simpledialog.Dialog.body` method. This method can add more widgets as children of the dialog main body and can return a specific widget that should have focus:

```
def body(self, parent):
    self._message = tkinter.Message(parent, text=self._text, aspect=400)
    self._message.pack(expand=1, fill=tkinter.BOTH)
    self._list = tkinter.Listbox(parent)
    self._list.pack(expand=1, fill=tkinter.BOTH, side=tkinter.TOP)
    for item in self._items:
        self._list.insert(tkinter.END, item)
    return self._list
```

The `body` method is created within `simpledialog.Dialog.__init__`, so it's called before blocking the main thread.

After the content of the dialog is in place, the dialog will block waiting for a button to be clicked by the user.

If the `cancel` button is clicked, the dialog is dismissed automatically and the `ChoiceDialog.selection` will remain `None`.

If `Ok` is clicked, instead, the `ChoiceDialog.validate` method is called to check that the choice is valid. Our `validate` implementation will check if the user actually selected an entry before clicking `Ok` or not, and will only let the user dismiss the dialog if there was a selected item:

```
def validate(self):
    if not self._list.curselection():
        return 0
    return 1
```

If the validation passes, the `ChoiceDialog.apply` method is called to confirm the choice and we just set in `self.selection` the name of the selected item, so that it's accessible for the caller once the dialog is not visible anymore:

```
def apply(self):
    self.selection = self._items[self._list.curselection()[0]]
```

This makes it possible to show the dialog and read back the selected value from the `selection` attribute once it's dismissed:

```
dialog = ChoiceDialog(tk, 'Pick one',
                      text='Please, pick a choice?',
                      items=['first', 'second', 'third'])
print('Selected "{}"'.format(dialog.selection))
```

Menus

When your application allows you to perform more than one action, a menu is frequently the most common way to allow access to those actions:

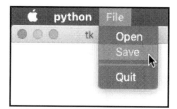

How to do it...

The `tkinter.Menu` class allows us to create menus, submenus, actions, and separators. So, it provides everything we might need to create basic menus in our GUI-based application:

```python
import tkinter


def set_menu(window, choices):
    menubar = tkinter.Menu(root)
    window.config(menu=menubar)

    def _set_choices(menu, choices):
        for label, command in choices.items():
            if isinstance(command, dict):
                # Submenu
                submenu = tkinter.Menu(menu)
                menu.add_cascade(label=label, menu=submenu)
                _set_choices(submenu, command)
            elif label == '-' and command == '-':
                # Separator
                menu.add_separator()
            else:
                # Simple choice
                menu.add_command(label=label, command=command)

    _set_choices(menubar, choices)
```

The `set_menu` function allows us to create whole menu hierarchies easily out of nested dictionaries of actions and submenus:

```python
import sys
root = tkinter.Tk()

from collections import OrderedDict
set_menu(root, {
    'File': OrderedDict([
        ('Open', lambda: print('Open!')),
        ('Save', lambda: print('Save')),
        ('-', '-'),
        ('Quit', lambda: sys.exit(0))
    ])
})
root.mainloop()
```

If you are using Python 3.6+, you can also avoid OrderedDict and use a plain dictionary, as the dictionary will already be ordered.

How it works...

Provided a window, the set_menu function creates a Menu object and sets it as the window menu:

```
def set_menu(window, choices):
    menubar = tkinter.Menu(root)
    window.config(menu=menubar)
```

Then it populates the menu with the choices provided through the choices argument. That is expected to be a dictionary where the key is the name of the menu entry and the value is the callable that should be called when the choice is selected, or another dictionary if the choice should lead to a submenu. Finally, it supports separators when both the label and the choice are set to -.

The menu is populated by traversing the tree of options through a recursive function that calls Menu.add_command, Menu.add_cascade, and Menu.add_separator, depending on the encountered entry:

```
def _set_choices(menu, choices):
    for label, command in choices.items():
        if isinstance(command, dict):
            # Submenu
            submenu = tkinter.Menu(menu)
            menu.add_cascade(label=label, menu=submenu)
            _set_choices(submenu, command)
        elif label == '-' and command == '-':
            # Separator
            menu.add_separator()
        else:
            # Simple choice
            menu.add_command(label=label, command=command)

_set_choices(menubar, choices)
```

14
Development Tools

In this chapter, we will cover the following recipes:

- Debugging—how to leverage the Python built-in debugger
- Testing—writing test suites with the Python standard library test framework
- Mocking—patching objects to simulate fake behaviors in tests
- Reporting errors in production—getting crashes reported by email
- Benchmarking—how to benchmark functions with the standard library
- Inspection—inspecting the type, attributes, and methods provided by an object
- Code evaluation—running Python code within Python code
- Tracing—how to trace which lines of code were executed
- Profiling—how to trace bottlenecks in code

Introduction

When writing software, you need tools that make achieving your goal easier and tools that help you to manage the complexity of the code base, which can get millions of line of code and can involve other people's code that you are not experienced with.

Even for small projects, if you are involving third-party libraries, frameworks, and tools, you are, in fact, bringing other people's code into yours and you will need a set of tools to understand what's going on when you rely on this code and to keep your own code under control and free from bugs.

Here is where techniques such as testing, debugging, profiling, and tracing can come in handy to verify the code base, understand what's going on, spot bottlenecks, and see what was executed and when.

The Python standard library comes with many of the tools you will need during daily development to implement most best practices and techniques in software development.

Debugging

While developing, you might face an unexpected behavior of your code or a crash, and you will want to dive into it, see the state of the variables, and check what's going on to understand how to handle the unexpected situation so that the software behaves properly.

This is typically part of debugging and usually requires dedicated tools, debuggers, to make your life easier (ever found yourself throwing `print` statements everywhere around the code just to see value of some variable?).

The Python standard library comes with a very powerful debugger, and while other third-party solutions exist, the internal `pdb` debugger is very powerful and is able to help you in nearly all situations.

How to do it...

If you want to stop code execution at a specific point and interactively move it forward while checking how your variables change and what flow the execution takes, you just want to set a tracing point where you want to stop, so that you will enter an interactive session in the shell where your code is running:

```python
def divide(x, y):
    print('Going to divide {} / {}'.format(x, y))

    # Stop execution here and enter the debugger
    import pdb; pdb.set_trace()

    return x / y
```

Now, if we call the `divide` function, we will enter an interactive debugger that lets us see the value of x and y and move forward with the execution:

```
>>> print(divide(3, 2))
Going to divide 3 / 2
> ../sources/devtools/devtools_01.py(4)divide()
-> return x / y
(Pdb) x
3
(Pdb) y
2
(Pdb) continue
1.5
```

How it works...

The `pdb` module exposes a `set_trace` function which, when called, stops execution and enters the interactive debugger.

From here on, your prompt will change (to `Pdb`) and you can send commands to the debugger or print variable values just by writing their name.

The `pdb` debugger has many commands; the most useful ones are the following:

- `next`: To continue execution of code one line at a time
- `continue`: To continue execution of code until the next breakpoint is reached
- `list`: To print the code that is currently being executed

To see a complete list of commands, you can use the `help` command, which will list all the available commands. And you can use the `help` command to get help on a specific command.

There's more...

Since version 3.7 of Python, it is no longer required to do the odd `import pdb; pdb.set_trace()` dance. You can just write `breakpoint()` and you will enter `pdb`.

Even better, if you have more advanced debuggers configured on your system, you will rely on those as `breakpoint()` uses the currently configured debugger instead of only relying on `pdb`.

Testing

To ensure that your code is correct and doesn't break on future changes, writing tests is usually one of the best things you can do.

In Python, there are a few frameworks to implement test suites that can automatically verify code reliability, implement different patterns such as **behavior-driver development (BDD)**, or even automatically find corner cases for you.

But simple automatic tests can be written just by relying on the standard library itself, so that you will need third-party testing frameworks only if you need specific plugins or patterns.

The standard library has the `unittest` module, which allows us to write tests for our software, run them, and report the state of the test suite.

How to do it...

For this recipe, the following steps are to be performed:

1. Say we have a `divide` function we want to write tests for:

    ```
    def divide(x, y):
        return x / y
    ```

2. We need to create a file named `test_divide.py` (it's important that files containing tests are named `test_*.py` or the tests won't run). Within the `test_divide.py` file, we can put all our tests:

    ```
    from divide import divide
    import unittest

    class TestDivision(unittest.TestCase):
        def setUp(self):
            self.num = 6

        def test_int_division(self):
            res = divide(self.num, 3)
            self.assertEqual(res, 2)

        def test_float_division(self):
            res = divide(self.num, 4)
            self.assertEqual(res, 1.5)

        def test_divide_zero(self):
            with self.assertRaises(ZeroDivisionError) as err:
                res = divide(self.num, 0)
            self.assertEqual(str(err.exception), 'division by zero')
    ```

3. Then, given that the `test_divide.py` module is within the same directory, we can run our tests with `python -m unittest`:

    ```
    $ python -m unittest
    ...
    ----------------------------------------------------------------------
    Ran 3 tests in 0.000s

    OK
    ```

4. If we want to also see which tests are running, we can also provide the −v option:

```
$ python -m unittest -v
test_divide_zero (test_devtools_02.TestDivision) ... ok
test_float_division (test_devtools_02.TestDivision) ... ok
test_int_division (test_devtools_02.TestDivision) ... ok


----------------------------------------------------------------
---
Ran 3 tests in 0.000s

OK
```

How it works...

The unittest module provides two major features:

- The unittest.TestCase class, which provides foundations to write tests and fixtures
- The unittest.TestLoader class, which provides the foundation for finding and running multiple tests from multiple sources, in a single run; the result can then be provided to a runner to run them all and report their progress

By creating a unittest.TestCase class, we can gather multiple tests under the same set of fixtures, which are provided by the class as the setUp and setUpClass methods. The setUpClass method is performed once for the whole class, while the setUp method is performed once for every test. Tests are all the class methods whose name starts with test*.

Once the tests have been completed, the tearDown and tearDownClass methods can be used to clean up the state.

So our TestDivision class will provide a self.num attribute for each test declared within it:

```
class TestDivision(unittest.TestCase):
    def setUp(self):
        self.num = 6
```

And then will have three tests, two of which (test_int_division and test_float_division) assert that the result of the division is the expected one (through self.assertEqual):

```
def test_int_division(self):
```

```
        res = divide(self.num, 3)
        self.assertEqual(res, 2)

    def test_float_division(self):
        res = divide(self.num, 4)
        self.assertEqual(res, 1.5)
```

Then, the third test (`test_divide_zero`) checks that our `divide` function actually raises the expected exception when a `0` is provided as the divisor:

```
    def test_divide_zero(self):
        with self.assertRaises(ZeroDivisionError) as err:
            res = divide(self.num, 0)
        self.assertEqual(str(err.exception), 'division by zero')
```

And then checks that the exception message is also the expected one.

Those tests are then saved in a file named `test_divide.py`, so that `TestLoader` is able to find them.

When `python -m unittest` is executed, what actually happens is that `TestLoader.discover` is called. This looks for all modules and packages named `test*` in the local directory and runs all the tests declared in those modules.

There's more...

The standard library `unittest` module provides nearly all you need to write tests for your libraries or applications.

But if you find you need more features, such as retrying flaky tests, reporting in more formats, and support for driving browsers, you might want to try a testing framework such as `pytest`. Those usually provide a plugin infrastructure that permits you to expand their behavior with additional features.

Mocking

When testing your code, you might face the need to replace the behavior of an existing function or class and to track whether a function was called or not with the proper arguments.

For example, say you have a function such as the following:

```
def print_division(x, y):
    print(x / y)
```

To test it, we don't want to go to the screen and check the output, but we still want to know whether the printed value was the expected one.

So a possible approach might be to replace `print` with something that doesn't print anything, but allows us to track the provided argument (which is the value that would be printed).

This is exactly the meaning of mocking: replacing an object or function in the code base with one that does nothing but allows us to inspect the call.

How it works...

You need to perform the following steps for this recipe:

1. The `unittest` package provides a `mock` module that allows us to create `Mock` objects and to `patch` existing objects, so we can rely on it to replace the behavior of `print`:

    ```
    from unittest import mock

    with mock.patch('builtins.print') as mprint:
        print_division(4, 2)

    mprint.assert_called_with(2)
    ```

2. Once we know that the mocked `print` was actually called with 2, which is the value we expected, we can go even further and print all the arguments that it received:

    ```
    mock_args, mock_kwargs = mprint.call_args
    >>> print(mock_args)
    (2, )
    ```

    In this case, it's not very helpful as there was a single argument, but in cases where you only want to check some arguments instead of the whole call, it might be convenient to be able to access some of the arguments.

How it works...

`mock.patch` replaces, within the context, the specified object or class with a `Mock` instance.

`Mock` will do nothing when called, but will track their arguments and will allow you to check that they were called as expected.

So with `mock.patch`, we replace `print` with `Mock` and we keep a reference to `Mock` as `mprint`:

```
with mock.patch('builtins.print') as mprint:
    print_division(4, 2)
```

This allows us to check that `print` was called with the expected arguments, through `Mock`, later on:

```
mprint.assert_called_with(2)
```

There's more...

The `Mock` objects are actually not constrained to doing nothing.

By providing the `side_effect` argument to `mock.patch`, you can have them raise exceptions when called. This is helpful in simulating failures in your code.

Or you can even replace their behavior with a totally different object by providing `new` to `mock.patch`, which is great to inject fake objects in place of the real implementation.

So, generally, `unittest.mock` can be used to replace the behavior of existing classes and objects with anything else, from mock objects, to fake objects, to different implementations.

But pay attention when using them, because if the caller had a reference to the original object saved aside, `mock.patch` might be unable to replace the function for it, as it's still constrained to the fact that Python is a reference-based language and if you have a reference to an object, there is no easy way for third-party code to hijack that reference.

So always make sure you apply `mock.patch` before using the things you are patching, to reduce the risk of references to the original object to be around.

Reporting errors in production

One of the most important aspects of production software is being notified in case of errors. As we are not the user of the software itself, we can only know that something is wrong if the software notifies us (or when it's too late and users are complaining).

Based on the Python standard library, we can easily build a solution that notifies developers in case of a crash by email.

How to do it...

The `logging` module has a way to report exceptions by email, so we can set up a logger and trap the exceptions to log them by email:

```python
import logging
import logging.handlers
import functools

crashlogger = logging.getLogger('__crashes__')

def configure_crashreport(mailhost, fromaddr, toaddrs, subject,
                          credentials, tls=False):
    if configure_crashreport._configured:
        return

    crashlogger.addHandler(
        logging.handlers.SMTPHandler(
            mailhost=mailhost,
            fromaddr=fromaddr,
            toaddrs=toaddrs,
            subject=subject,
            credentials=credentials,
            secure=tuple() if tls else None
        )
    )
    configure_crashreport._configured = True
configure_crashreport._configured = False


def crashreport(f):
    @functools.wraps(f)
    def _crashreport(*args, **kwargs):
        try:
            return f(*args, **kwargs)
        except Exception as e:
```

```
                crashlogger.exception(
                    '{} crashed\n'.format(f.__name__)
                )
                raise
        return _crashreport
```

Once the two functions are in place, we can configure `logging` and then decorate our main code base entry point so that all exceptions in our code base are reported by email:

```
@crashreport
def main():
    3 / 0

configure_crashreport(
    'your-smtp-host.com',
    'no-reply@your-smtp-host.com',
    'crashes_receiver@another-smtp-host.com',
    'Automatic Crash Report from TestApp',
    ('smtpserver_username', 'smtpserver_password'),
    tls=True
)

main()
```

How it works...

The `logging` module is able to send messages to any handler attached to logger, and has a feature to explicitly log crashes by logging an exception and its traceback through `.exception`.

So the root of our solution to send exceptions by email is to wrap the main function of our code base with a decorator that traps all exceptions and invokes the logger:

```
def crashreport(f):
    @functools.wraps(f)
    def _crashreport(*args, **kwargs):
        try:
            return f(*args, **kwargs)
        except Exception as e:
            crashlogger.exception(
                '{} crashed\n'.format(f.__name__)
            )
            raise
    return _crashreport
```

The `crashlogger.exception` method will build a message that contains our custom text (which reports the name of the decorated function) plus the traceback for the crash, and will send it to the associated handler.

Through the `configure_crashreport` method, we provided a custom handler for `crashlogger`. A handler then sends the messages by email:

```
def configure_crashreport(mailhost, fromaddr, toaddrs, subject,
                          credentials, tls=False):
    if configure_crashreport._configured:
        return

    crashlogger.addHandler(
        logging.handlers.SMTPHandler(
            mailhost=mailhost,
            fromaddr=fromaddr,
            toaddrs=toaddrs,
            subject=subject,
            credentials=credentials,
            secure=tuple() if tls else None
        )
    )
    configure_crashreport._configured = True
configure_crashreport._configured = False
```

The additional `_configured` flag is used as a guard to prevent the handler from being added twice.

Then we just have to invoke `configure_crashreport` to provide the credentials for the email service:

```
configure_crashreport(
    'your-smtp-host.com',
    'no-reply@your-smtp-host.com',
    'crashes_receiver@another-smtp-host.com',
    'Automatic Crash Report from TestApp',
    ('smtpserver_username', 'smtpserver_password'),
    tls=True
)
```

And all exceptions in the function will be logged in `crashlogger` and thus sent by email through the associated handler.

Benchmarking

When writing software, it's frequently important to ensure that some performance constraints are guaranteed. The standard library has most of the tools needed to ensure the timing and resource consumption of the functions we write.

Say we have two functions and we want to know which one is faster:

```
def function1():
    l = []
    for i in range(100):
        l.append(i)
    return l


def function2():
    return [i for i in range(100)]
```

How to do it...

The `timeit` module provides a bunch of utilities to time a function or whole script:

```
>>> import timeit

>>> print(
...     timeit.timeit(function1)
... )
10.132873182068579

>>> print(
...     timeit.timeit(function2)
... )
5.13165780401323
```

From the reported timing, we know that `function2` is twice as fast as `function1`.

There's more...

Normally, such a function would run in a few milliseconds, but the reported timings are in the order of seconds.

That's because, by default, `timeit.timeit` will run the benchmarked code 1 million times to provide a result where any temporary change in speed of the execution won't impact the final result much.

Inspection

Being a powerful dynamic language, Python allows us to change its runtime behavior based on the state of objects it's working with.

Inspecting the state of objects is the foundation of every dynamic language, and the standard library `inspect` module has most of the features needed for such a case.

How to do it...

For this recipe, the following steps are to be performed:

1. Based on the `inspect` module, we can quickly create a helper function that will tell us major object properties and type for most objects:

```
import inspect

def inspect_object(o):
    if inspect.isfunction(o) or inspect.ismethod(o):
        print('FUNCTION, arguments:', inspect.signature(o))
    elif inspect.isclass(o):
        print('CLASS, methods:',
            inspect.getmembers(o, inspect.isfunction))
    else:
        print('OBJECT ({}): {}'.format(
            o.__class__,
            [(n, v) for n, v in inspect.getmembers(o)
                if not n.startswith('__')]
        ))
```

2. Then, if we apply it to any object, we will get the details about its type, attributes, methods, and, if it's a function, its arguments. We can even make a custom type:

```
class MyClass:
    def __init__(self):
        self.value = 5

    def sum_to_value(self, other):
        return self.value + other
```

3. We inspect its methods:

```
>>> inspect_object(MyClass.sum_to_value)
FUNCTION, arguments: (self, other)
```

An instance of that type:

```
>>> o = MyClass()
>>> inspect_object(o)
OBJECT (<class '__main__.MyClass'>): [
    ('sum_to_value', <bound method MyClass.sum_to_value of ...>),
    ('value', 5)
]
```

Or the class itself:

```
>>> inspect_object(MyClass)
CLASS, methods: [
    ('__init__', <function MyClass.__init__ at 0x107bd0400>),
    ('sum_to_value', <function MyClass.sum_to_value at
0x107bd0488>)
]
```

How it works...

`inspect_object` relies on `inspect.isfunction`, `inspect.ismethod`, and `inspect.isclass` to decide the kind of argument that was provided.

Once it's clear that the object provided fits into one of those types, it provides the more reasonable information for that kind of object.

For functions and methods, it looks at the signature of the function:

```
if inspect.isfunction(o) or inspect.ismethod(o):
    print('FUNCTION, arguments:', inspect.signature(o))
```

The `inspect.signature` function returns a `Signature` object that contains all the details about arguments accepted by the given method.

When printed, those arguments are listed on screen, which is what we expected:

```
FUNCTION, arguments: (self, other)
```

In case of a class, we are mostly interested in the methods that the class exposes. So we are going to use `inspect.getmembers` to grab all attributes of the class, and then `inspect.isfunction` to filter those only for functions:

```
elif inspect.isclass(o):
    print('CLASS, methods:', inspect.getmembers(o, inspect.isfunction))
```

The second argument of `inspect.getmembers` can be any predicate that will be used to filter the members.

In the case of objects, we want to show the attributes and methods of the object.

Objects usually have tens of methods that are provided by default in Python to support the standard operators and behaviors. Those are the so-called magic methods, which we usually don't care about. So we have to only list the public methods and attributes:

```
else:
    print('OBJECT ({}): {}'.format(
        o.__class__,
        [(n, v) for n, v in inspect.getmembers(o)
            if not n.startswith('__')]
    ))
```

As we know, `inspect.getmembers` accepts a predicate to filter which members to return. But the predicate can only act on the member itself; it has no way to know its name. So we have to filter the result of `inspect.getmembers` ourselves with a list comprehension that removes any attribute whose name starts with a dunder (__).

The results are the public attributes and methods of the provided object:

```
OBJECT (<class '__main__.MyClass'>): [
    ('sum_to_value', <bound method MyClass.sum_to_value of ...>),
    ('value', 5)
]
```

We also printed the __class__ of the object itself to provide a hint about what kind of object we are looking at.

There's more...

The `inspect` module has tens of functions that can be used to dive deep into Python objects.

It can be a really powerful tool when investigating third-party code or when implementing heavily dynamic code that has to cope with objects of unknown shape and type.

Code evaluation

Python is an interpreted language, and the interpreter features are exposed in the standard library too.

This means that we can evaluate expressions and statements coming from files or text sources and have them run as Python code within Python code itself.

It's also possible to evaluate code in a fairly safe way that allows us to create objects from expressions but prevents the execution of any function.

How to do it...

The steps for this recipe are as follows:

1. The `eval`, `exec`, and `ast` functions and modules provide most of the machinery needed for execution of code from strings:

```
import ast

def run_python(code, mode='evalsafe'):
    if mode == 'evalsafe':
        return ast.literal_eval(code)
    elif mode == 'eval':
        return eval(compile(code, '', mode='eval'))
    elif mode == 'exec':
        return exec(compile(code, '', mode='exec'))
    else:
        raise ValueError('Unsupported execution model
                         {}'.format(mode))
```

2. The `run_python` function in `evalsafe` mode allows us to run basic Python expressions in a safe way. This means that we can create Python objects from their literal representation:

```
>>> print(run_python('[1, 2, 3]'))
[1, 2, 3]
```

3. We can't run functions or perform more advanced commands such as indexing:

```
>>> print(run_python('[1, 2, 3][0]'))
[ ... ]
malformed node or string: <_ast.Subscript object at 0x10ee57ba8>
```

4. If we want to run those, we need to `eval` in a non-safe manner:

```
>>> print(run_python('[1, 2, 3][0]', 'eval'))
1
```

5. This is discouraged, because it allows execution of malicious code in the current interpreter session. But even if it allows more widespread execution, it still doesn't allow more complex statements such as definition of functions:

```
>>> print(run_python('''
... def x():
...      print("printing hello")
... x()
... ''', 'eval'))
[ ... ]
invalid syntax (, line 2)
```

6. To allow full Python support, we need to use the `exec` mode, which will allow execution of all Python code, but won't give us back the result of the expression anymore (as the provided code might not be an expression at all):

```
>>> print(run_python('''
... def x():
...      print("printing hello")
... x()
... ''', 'exec'))
printing hello
None
```

Tracing code

The `trace` module provides a powerful and easy tool to trace which lines of code were executed during a run.

Tracing can be used both to ensure testing coverage and to see the behavior of our software or third-party function.

How to do it...

You need to perform the following steps for this recipe:

1. We can implement a function that traces the execution of a provided function and returns the modules that were executed and the lines for each module:

```
import trace
import collections

def report_tracing(func, *args, **kwargs):
    outputs = collections.defaultdict(list)

    tracing = trace.Trace(trace=False)
    tracing.runfunc(func, *args, **kwargs)

    traced = collections.defaultdict(set)
    for filename, line in tracing.results().counts:
        traced[filename].add(line)

    for filename, tracedlines in traced.items():
        with open(filename) as f:
            for idx, fileline in enumerate(f, start=1):
                outputs[filename].append(
                    (idx, idx in tracedlines, fileline))
                )
    return outputs
```

2. Then, once we have the tracing, we need to actually print it so that it's human-readable. To do that, we are going to read the source code for each traced module and print it with a + marker that is going to signal whether a line was executed or not:

```
def print_traced_execution(tracings):
    for filename, tracing in tracings.items():
        print(filename)
        for idx, executed, content in tracing:
            print('{:04d}{}  {}'.format(idx,
                                        '+' if executed else ' ',
                                        content),
                  end='')
        print()
```

3. Given any function, we can see which lines of code are being executed in various conditions:

```
def function(should_print=False):
```

```
                a = 1
                b = 2
                if should_print:
                    print('Usually does not execute!')
                return a + b
```

4. First, we can print the tracing for the function with `should_print=False`:

```
>>> print_traced_execution(
...         report_tracing(function)
... )
devtools_08.py
0001    def function(should_print=False):
0002+       a = 1
0003+       b = 2
0004+       if should_print:
0005            print('Usually does not execute!')
0006+       return a + b
```

5. Then we can check what happens with `should_print=True`:

```
>>> print_traced_execution(
...         report_tracing(function, True)
... )
Usually does not execute!
devtools_08.py
0001    def function(should_print=False):
0002+       a = 1
0003+       b = 2
0004+       if should_print:
0005+           print('Usually does not execute!')
0006+       return a + b
```

You can see that line `0005` is now marked with the + sign as it was executed.

How it works...

The `report_tracing` function is the one actually in charge of tracing the execution of another function.

First of all, as the execution is per module, it creates `defaultdict`, where the tracing can be stored. The key will be the module, and the value will be a list containing information for each line of that module:

```
def report_tracing(func, *args, **kwargs):
    outputs = collections.defaultdict(list)
```

Then, it creates the actual tracing machinery. The `trace=False` option is especially important to avoid the tracing being printed on screen. Right now, we want to save it aside, not print it:

```
tracing = trace.Trace(trace=False)
```

Once the tracer is available, we can use it to run the provided function with any given argument:

```
tracing.runfunc(func, *args, **kwargs)
```

The result of the tracing is saved into the tracer itself, so we can access it with `tracing.results()`. What we are interested in is whether a line of code was executed at least once, so we are going to look for the counts, and add each line of code that was executed to the set of executed lines of code for the given module:

```
traced = collections.defaultdict(set)
for filename, line in tracing.results().counts:
    traced[filename].add(line)
```

The resultant `traced` dictionary contains all the lines of code that were actually executed for a given module. It doesn't, by the way, contain any detail about those that were not executed.

So far, we only have the line number, and no other detail about the executed lines of code. We, of course, also want the line of code itself, and we want to have all lines of code, not just the executed ones, so we can print back the source code with no gaps.

That's why `report_tracing` then opens the source code for each executed module and reads its content. For each line, it checks whether it's in the set of the executed ones for that module and stores aside a tuple containing the line number, a Boolean value that states whether it was executed or not, and the line content itself:

```
for filename, tracedlines in traced.items():
    with open(filename) as f:
        for idx, fileline in enumerate(f, start=1):
            outputs[filename].append((idx, idx in tracedlines, fileline))
```

Finally, the resultant dictionary contains all modules that were executed, with their source code, annotated with details about the line number and whether it was executed or not:

```
return outputs
```

`print_traced_execution` is then far easier: its only purpose is to take the data we gathered and print it on screen, so that a human being can see the source code and what was executed.

The function iterates on every traced module and prints the `filename` module:

```
def print_traced_execution(tracings):
    for filename, tracing in tracings.items():
        print(filename)
```

Then, for each module, it iterates over the tracing details and prints the line number (as a four-digit number, so that code is indented properly for any line number up to 9999), a + sign if the line was executed, and the line content itself:

```
for idx, executed, content in tracing:
    print('{:04d}{}  {}'.format(idx,
                                '+' if executed else ' ',
                                content),
          end='')
print()
```

There's more...

Using tracing, you can easily check whether the code you wrote was executed or not by your tests. You just have to limit the tracing to the modules you wrote and you are interested in.

There are third-party modules that specialize in coverage reporting of tests; the most widespread one is probably the `coverage` module twhich has support for the most common testing frameworks, such as `pytest` and `nose`.

Profiling

When you need to speed up your code or understand where a bottleneck is, profiling is one of the most effective techniques.

The Python standard library provides a built-in profiler that traces the execution and timing for each function and allows you to spot the functions that are more expensive or that run too many times, consuming most of the execution time.

How to do it...

For this recipe, the following steps are to be performed:

1. We can take any function we want to profile (which can even be the main entry point of the program):

```
import time

def slowfunc(goslow=False):
    l = []
    for i in range(100):
        l.append(i)
        if goslow:
            time.sleep(0.01)
    return l
```

2. We can profile it using the `cProfile` module:

```
from cProfile import Profile

profiler = Profile()
profiler.runcall(slowfunc, True)
profiler.print_stats()
```

3. That will print the timing for the function and the slowest functions called by the profiled one:

```
202 function calls in 1.183 seconds

Ordered by: standard name

ncalls  tottime  percall  cumtime  percall
filename:lineno(function)
    1    0.002    0.002    1.183    1.183
devtools_09.py:3(slowfunc)
  100    1.181    0.012    1.181    0.012 {built-in method
time.sleep}
  100    0.000    0.000    0.000    0.000 {method 'append' of
'list' objects}
```

How it works...

The `cProfile.Profile` object is able to run any function with provided arguments and gather execution statistics with a minor overload.

The `runcall` function is the one that actually runs the function providing the passed arguments (in this case, `True` is provided as the first function argument, which means `goslow=True`):

```
profiler = Profile()
profiler.runcall(slowfunc, True)
```

Once the profiling data is gathered, we can print it on screen to provide details about what was executed:

```
profiler.print_stats()
```

The printed output includes the list of functions executed during the call, the total time it took for each of those functions, the time each function took on each call, and the total number of calls:

```
ncalls  tottime  percall  cumtime  percall filename:lineno(function)
     1    0.002    0.002    1.183    1.183 devtools_09.py:3(slowfunc)
   100    1.181    0.012    1.181    0.012 {built-in method time.sleep}
   ...
```

We can see that the major bottleneck of `slowfunc` was the `time.sleep` call: it took `1.181` out of the total `1.183` time it took to run whole `slowfunc`.

We can try to call `slowfunc` with `goslow=False` and see how the timing changes:

```
profiler.runcall(slowfunc, False)
profiler.print_stats()
```

And, in this case, we see that the whole function runs in `0.000` instead of `1.183` and there is no more reference to `time.sleep`:

```
102 function calls in 0.000 seconds

Ordered by: standard name

ncalls  tottime  percall  cumtime  percall filename:lineno(function)
     1    0.000    0.000    0.000    0.000 devtools_09.py:3(slowfunc)
   100    0.000    0.000    0.000    0.000 {method 'append' of 'list'
objects}
```

Other Books You May Enjoy

If you enjoyed this book, you may be interested in these other books by Packt:

Python Programming Blueprints
Daniel Furtado, Marcus Pennington

ISBN: 978-1-78646-816-1

- Learn object-oriented and functional programming concepts while developing projects
- The dos and don'ts of storing passwords in a database
- Develop a fully functional website using the popular Django framework
- Use the Beautiful Soup library to perform web scrapping
- Get started with cloud computing by building microservice and serverless applications in AWS
- Develop scalable and cohesive microservices using the Nameko framework
- Create service dependencies for Redis and PostgreSQL

Secret Recipes of the Python Ninja

Cody Jackson

ISBN: 978-1-78829-487-4

- Know the differences between .py and .pyc files
- Explore the different ways to install and upgrade Python packages
- Understand the working of the PyPI module that enhances built-in decorators
- See how coroutines are different from generators and how they can simulate multithreading
- Grasp how the decimal module improves floating point numbers and their operations
- Standardize sub interpreters to improve concurrency
- Discover Python's built-in docstring analyzer

Leave a review - let other readers know what you think

Please share your thoughts on this book with others by leaving a review on the site that you bought it from. If you purchased the book from Amazon, please leave us an honest review on this book's Amazon page. This is vital so that other potential readers can see and use your unbiased opinion to make purchasing decisions, we can understand what our customers think about our products, and our authors can see your feedback on the title that they have worked with Packt to create. It will only take a few minutes of your time, but is valuable to other potential customers, our authors, and Packt. Thank you!

Index